TWELFTH-CENTURY EUROPE AND THE FOUNDATIONS OF MODERN SOCIETY

Edited by
Marshall Clagett
Gaines Post
Robert Reynolds

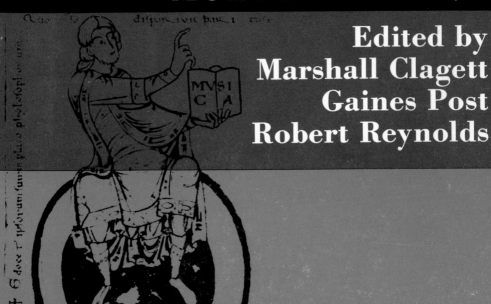

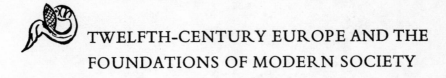

TWELFTH-CENTURY EUROPE AND THE FOUNDATIONS OF MODERN SOCIETY

INTRODUCTION

The studies now published are the final version of papers read by the authors in a symposium held at the University of Wisconsin, 12–14 November 1957. The editors were appointed by the Executive Committee of the Division of the Humanities as a planning committee for the symposium. They chose the twelfth century, in their minds an age extending from the eleventh to the thirteenth century, as the principal theme. For the twelfth century was indeed a great age, "one of the great constructive ages in European history" (Geoffrey Barraclough, *History in a Changing World* [Oxford, 1955], p. 78). It was more than another "renaissance." If the men of the period rested on the shoulders of giants, they did at times as "moderns" see farther and look towards our own "modern" civilization.

There was, to be sure, a revival, a renaissance of importance—Charles Homer Haskins was right. In the monastic and cathedral schools of France and England men of learning, in secular as well as religious ways that belong to medieval humanism, read and cherished the Latin classics. Ancient philosophy in Augustinian and Neoplatonic terms found a new home and interpretation in the school of Chartres. At Paris the study of Aristotle's logic resulted in a methodology that became fruitful in all fields of learning. In Sicily and Spain, Western Christian scholars found, in Arabic and Greek versions which were rapidly translated into Latin, the main body not only of Islamic but also of ancient Greek learning in Aristotelian and Neoplatonic philosophy, and in medicine, mathematics, astronomy, and the natural sciences. Finally, the classical Roman law, in the *Corpus Juris Civilis*, was fully revived at Bologna and became the basis of our modern legal science. Of the classical tradition, only the belles-lettres of Greece, except Plato's *Meno* and *Phaedo*, and portions of the *Timaeus*, remained unknown in the West in the twelfth century. But if the direct knowledge of Greek literature had to wait for the fifteenth century, the twelfth century was the real beginning of the later Renaissance, and can be directly associated with the term because of the revival of interest in and extensive recovery of ancient learning.

More important, however, is the fact that the twelfth century was a great period of creative, even revolutionary, activity in all aspects of civilization—and Haskins would agree. This was particularly true in Latin western Europe, but partly true also in central and eastern Europe—less true in the Greek, Byzantine Empire, and in the world of Islam, for by the twelfth century the Greek and Islamic contributions were declining, yielding to the dynamic vigor of the West, as Professor von Grunebaum's paper at least partly reveals. The decline in the West that accompanied the end of the Roman Empire, the barbarian invasions, the Arabic-Moorish conquest of Spain, the failure of the Carolingian Empire, and the anarchy of feudalism, was reversed by the appearance of a greater political stability in the rise of feudal monarchies, in the revival of the ideal of the Roman Empire in Germany and Italy, in the organization of the spiritual monarchy of the papacy over the Roman Church, and in the growth of communes which in Italy were becoming powerful city-states. If these states and the Church were often in conflict, partly as a result of their increasing strength and consciousness of their rights, and the Empire itself was to fail to become a state precisely because emperors like Frederick Barbarossa went beyond their resources in trying to recreate the Roman Empire as a universal state, nonetheless the gain in the direction of developing modern national states was greater than the loss. In England and France, and in Castile and Aragon, the monarchy was gradually able, with the aid of feudal custom and principles of public law deriving from ideas in the *Corpus Juris Civilis* and the legists of Bologna, to centralize their governments and territorial states as the basis for modern nations. The papers of Professors Kantorowicz and Strayer are of interest for theoretical and practical aspects of this centralization. Despite the traditional Christian ideal of the subordination of the state to moral ends and to God, the state was becoming a natural end in itself, and lawyers and kings were well aware of the necessity and "reason of State" as a justification for the growth of the central public authority.

This political development accompanied, in part drew aid from, a significant revival of economic activities. For a new activity in trade and industry created a money economy which furnished able kings with the means for enforcing law and order, organizing an army, persuading feudal lords to respect the public interest, and increasing the royal domain. At the same time the merchants and artisans in their guilds, with an ever larger population made possible by the new economic life and social and political order, became the bourgeoisie, the middle class, and organized town governments. Here was the beginning of our modern city institutions and civic life. With the growth of cities and the need of educated men for business, law and justice, and government, learning itself moved from monasteries to cathedral schools and universities, as Professor Holmes has shown in his paper, and naturally the new wealth and urban environment stimulated the revival of art and architecture, as they did the establishment of more parishes and church buildings to take care of the spiritual welfare of the people. Religion and culture alike found a home in the city. A new "civilization," in the literal sense of all that relates to the city and civil life, was at hand. Thus if in these studies Professor Krueger devotes his attention to northern economic growth, his paper is closely related to the other important aspects of the century.

The consequences of all these movements were tremendous for the Holy Roman Church. In our period the Church was a successful continuation of the ancient Roman tradition of unity and universalism in the Christian faith and in the body of the faithful. It was successful because a strong, centralized papal monarchy, from Gregory VII to Innocent III and beyond, staunchly defended and maintained the ideal of the supremacy of Church over State, of the spiritual realm over the secular, of the eternal welfare of the soul over the temporal, and temporary, welfare of the body. This supremacy extended likewise into the realm of culture: all learning and all schools were ultimately subject to the jurisdiction of the pope, whose duty it was, according to the divine command, to superintend all learning lest ideas contrary to the faith be taught. The pope, indeed, in the later twelfth and early thirteenth centuries, encouraged the rise and organization of the first universities, and protected their autonomy in relation to local ecclesiastical and secular authorities. As a result, if under the Church no complete academic freedom could be permitted, the papacy did protect, to a surprising degree, the right of the professors to study and teach pagan and Islamic thought and to discuss problems of philosophy and revelation in rational terms; and the popes encouraged the study and teaching of all fields of learning—there was no hostility to the sciences, medicine, and Roman law.

The centralization of the state of the Church, however, was not complete; nor was it aimed at the destruction of local customs and traditions. In fact, local popular religion, often stimulated by learned saints like Bernard of Clairvaux, might be more creative than papal leadership in the spiritual realm. The cult of the Virgin Mary reached a great climax in our century. It came in part from the people, in part from St. Bernard. It was expressed in popular devotion, in learned mysticism, in Latin hymns, and in the building of magnificent Romanesque and Gothic cathedrals dedicated to Our Lady. At the same time masters of theology in the cathedral school of Paris and elsewhere were actively debating problems relating to the sacraments. They prepared the way for the decrees of the Fourth Lateran Council, 1215, which established the number of sacraments at seven and promulgated the doctrine of transubstantiation. Because of crusades and the closer relations with the Greek Church and Constantinople, Western Latin theologians revived the old Christological debate about the divine and human natures in Christ. Such discussions, which Professor Anastos recounts, reflected both an important intellectual activity at Paris and the renewed unity of Mediterranean-European culture amid the diversity of opinions.

Great as the twelfth-century church was, however, as an institution embodying the ideal of unity in the faith and in culture under the leadership of popes like Gregory VII, Alexander III, and Innocent III, it contributed to the breakdown of medieval universalism in the Holy Roman Empire—or at least it recognized the inevitable in the new economic and social life, the communes, and the rising independent states. While opposing the German emperors who hoped to create a great state including Germany and Italy in the Empire, the papacy recognized kingdoms to the east and west of Germany as independent states, and in Italy supported the rise of the communes as city-states that in fact recognized no superior in the emperor. If the canonists and popes felt that unity was the more victorious as a Christian unity in the one Church and under a pope-emperor, or a pope who had the ultimate supreme authority over emperors and kings alike, in fact their policy helped create those national states which by 1300 were refusing obedience to Boniface VIII.

Despite these tendencies inherent in the circumstances of the age, despite all localism and diversities in learning, a remarkable unity prevailed in learning and culture and civilization. Christian ideals pervaded political, economic, social, and cultural developments. Latin was the universal, living language of government, law, business, religion, and education. Trade was free of national tariffs. Within this kind of universalism scholars, men of letters and artists and architects, using the subject matter and ideas inherited from Greece and Rome, and from Islam, laid the cultural foundations of modern European-American civilization.

To repeat, and to elaborate what has been said above, they created a new kind of institution of higher education, the university, which is still the most characteristic center of learning in the modern world. At the University of Bologna professors of law began to develop a new legal science in adapting the revived Roman law to the medieval environment. The English common law, which was itself a great medieval achievement, profited from the Roman influences spreading from Bologna. While the English law contained the ideal of fair trial (as in Magna Carta), the Roman law contributed a clear statement of the ideal in terms of the presumption of innocence and the right of all accused parties to be properly summoned and to enjoy a more adequate defense through a better system of court procedure. The public law of Rome greatly aided kings in "systematizing" feudalism and organizing a central government. The idea of the state, already becoming a national state, reappeared. Indeed, both "reason of state" and nationalism found early expression by 1200. But if the head of the new state, the king, was as a result more powerful, not only the old Christian-Augustinian ideal of law and justice, of the fundamental law of God, but also the Roman and feudal emphasis on equity, fair trial, and the legal rights of subjects, limited his power and prevented the early appearance of statism and absolutism.

Philosophy enjoyed a new period of creative activity in the University of Paris. The debates of realists and nominalists, the brilliance of Abelard, and the recovery of Aristotelian philosophy culminated in the great medieval synthesis achieved by Thomas Aquinas. But it must be remembered that Aristotle did not completely triumph at the expense of Plato and Christian Neoplatonism. From Chartres, as Professor Klibansky shows, came a deeper appreciation of nature which played an important role in art and architecture as well as literature and political and legal thought. For while God and divine reason and measure and number remained in nature, there was a stronger emphasis on studying nature and imitating nature, and on the naturalness of society and the state. The very stress on natural objects as symbols of God's plan in the creation of the world led to the study of physical light by means of mathematics and optics. Here medieval symbolism and the Neoplatonic and Augustinian doctrine of divine illumination made use of the newly received Greco-Islamic science, and in part contributed to the rise of modern science.

In the twelfth century we find the foundation laid for the first creative activity of European mathematics, medicine, and the natural sciences. The immature, practical geometry of the early Middle Ages was replaced in the course of the century by complete versions of Euclid's *Elements* introduced into the Latin educational community in some five different translations. Even the relatively complex geometry of Archimedes that was to be a crucial tool of the new science came to the attention of scholars for the first time in the twelfth century. At the same time, Latin mathematicians came into intimate contact in Arabic guise with the Indian system of numerals and calculation. With it came also Arabic algebra and trigonometry. In addition, the twelfth century saw the introduction of the best examples of the Greek efforts to use mathematics in the description of the physical world. Ptolemy's great *Mathematical Syntaxis* or *Almagest*—the final mature product of Greek astronomy—was translated and began to be followed by Western astronomers. It must be remembered that the later efforts of Copernicus toward reorienting astronomy are inconceivable without a prior mastery of Ptolemaic astronomy. Similar Greek treatises of a crucial nature for the development of the sciences of mechanics and optics passed into the Latin schools in this century. Finally, the Arabic-Greek medicine was absorbed in the school of Salerno to make Salerno the fountainhead of European medicine. It is thus evident in all areas of scientific activity that a virtual revolution took place in the twelfth century—a revolution marked by the transformation of the early medieval descriptive, compendious, and nonmathematical science into a more mature mathematical and experiential science on the lines of the Greek model. The extraordinary development of modern science came about, at least in part, as the result of the introduction of, and reaction to, the twin traditions of Greek philosophy and science that were transmitted to Europe in the twelfth century.

Outside the schools and universities, creative activities were perhaps equally important. But it must be remembered that frequently new technological developments as well as literature and art and architecture profited from the learning in the schools. Whether the ideas, however, came to artisans from contacts with the East in the crusades, from masters who acquired the elements of physics and geometry in cathedral school or university, or from innate European inventiveness, the fact is that new machines, new technical processes like the refining of sugar, and new engineering skills, for example, in the building of castles and Gothic churches, made their appearance. Above all, Gothic architecture, scorned by men of the Italian Renaissance as barbarous, was a great and original contribution to the world. The Gothic church at its best was both a mighty symbol of religion and the divine plan, and a synthesis of academic learning and engineering technology. Further, it provided a stone framework for the stained glass windows which at Chartres are still incomparably beautiful; and it provided the background for the stone-carvers to create great sculpture, symbolic and naturalistic at the same time. Professor Katzenellenbogen's paper throws light on the artistic developments at Chartres.

Outside the schools too, although resulting in part from literacy in the Latin classics in the schools, the vernacular languages and literatures attained a surprising maturity. Inspired by local interests and stories of heroes, by pilgrimage and crusade, and by the desire to understand human nature, poets wrote feudal epics, Arthurian romances, sagas, lyrics, and fabliaux, and created French, Spanish, Italian, and German and Scandinavian literature. To be sure, some of the vernacular appeared earlier, particularly the Anglo-Saxon literature. But the twelfth century was the period of the real beginning of the modern national literatures, leading to Dante and Chaucer. It is interesting that the Jews were contributing to Italian literature in this period, as Professor Spitzer shows in analyzing an anonymous Judeo-Italian elegy.

Of all these creative movements, only a few aspects could be treated in the symposium. The papers presented here, however, offer the reader penetrating interpretations which cannot but increase his appreciation of a great period in the history of mankind, the twelfth century.

Madison, Wisconsin   THE EDITORS

THE CONTRIBUTORS

MILTON V. ANASTOS, Professor of Byzantine Theology, Harvard University Dumbarton Oaks Research Library.

GUSTAVE E. VON GRUNEBAUM, Professor of History and Director of Near Eastern Center, University of California.

URBAN T. HOLMES, JR., Professor of Romance Philology, University of North Carolina.

ERNST H. KANTOROWICZ, Professor of History, The Institute for Advanced Study, Princeton.

ADOLF KATZENELLENBOGEN, Professor of Art, The Johns Hopkins University.

RAYMOND KLIBANSKY, Professor of Philosophy, McGill University.

HILMAR C. KRUEGER, Professor of History, University of Cincinnati.

LEO SPITZER, Professor of Romance Philology, The Johns Hopkins University.

JOSEPH R. STRAYER, Professor and Chairman of the Department of History, Princeton University.

CONTENTS

PART III   EASTERN INFLUENCES ON
            EUROPEAN CULTURE

LIST OF ILLUSTRATIONS

Part I THOUGHT IN EUROPEAN
SOCIETY

Raymond Klibansky

The School of Chartres

The myth of the Dark Ages no longer determines the consideration of the epoch with which we are here concerned, the period between 1100 and 1150. It has, on the contrary, become the custom to speak of a "Renaissance of the twelfth century": the darkness has receded to more remote periods. In due course of time, however, it will appear that the attribute of darkness refers rather to the modern historian's lack of knowledge than to any lack of thought in those centuries. To call one age lighter or darker than another is justifiable only if technical progress is used as the standard of measurement, a very questionable criterion, which takes no account at all of man's spiritual aspirations and heroic endeavor; these we find in all ages, in the tenth century no less than in the twentieth. The conception of a rebirth, moreover, may convey a fundamentally wrong impression if it severs the connection of an age with those times which preceded it. It must be the aim of the historian not to let metaphors like birth, decline, waning, and rebirth dim his vision of the continuity of Occidental thought.

This continuity becomes evident if we reflect on the basic problem which dominated European philosophy from the moment when Greek *logos* and Latin *ratio* clashed, and merged, with the religious creeds of the Orient. It is the task of solving the conflict between knowledge and faith, between a truth attained by human reason and a truth derived from divine revelation, which stirs and inspires philosophical thought from late antiquity. By a surprising coincidence, this task receives its strict formulation in the ninth century, in Baghdad, in Sura, and in northern France: in Arabic, in Jewish, and in Christian philosophy.

In the Latin world, the decisive answer to the problem is given by the Irish philosopher, Johannes Scotus Eriugena, in his claim that the true philosophy is the true religion, and the true religion the true philosophy. This identification of religion and philosophy implies the conviction that all the main tenets of faith may in some way, and at least to some extent, be established by human reason. It follows therefrom that the authority of the Fathers can no longer remain the highest court of appeal, and that authority must always prove its claims before the bar of reason. The problem once defined with such precision, we can trace in the centuries following Eriugena a continuous succession of thinkers maintaining that authority must be tested by rational thought.

This results, on the one hand, in the fact that those upholding the right of a rational search for truth did not hesitate to submit even the teaching of the Church in matters of faith to their dialectical analysis. Such presumption of the human intellect provoked, on the other hand, a violent reaction from the defenders of an unquestioning acceptance of ecclesiastical dogma, a reaction which threatened the very foundations of learning and philosophy. Such was roughly the situation at the beginning of the twelfth century when the School of Chartres reached its full development.

A few words about the outward organization of this school. Of the three main types of schools in the early Middle Ages, preceding the rise of the universities—the monastic schools of the Benedictines, the court schools of the great princes, and the episcopal or chapter schools connected with the cathedrals—Chartres belonged to the third. As in other episcopal schools (some of which go back to late Roman times) originally the bishop himself gave instruction. At a later date, as the bishop's power increased and temporal affairs took more of his time, he arranged for an assistant to help him instruct the young clerks, and in most cases this assistant was the chancellor of the chapter. Such were the conditions at Chartres throughout the eleventh century, and miniatures of the early twelfth century show that the bishop still fulfilled the duty of chief teacher. But in 1115 a change in the organization came about; the chancellor whose function it had been previously to deputize for, and assist, the bishop, now took complete charge of the teaching, while the bishop withdrew altogether from taking any immediate part in the life of the school and confined himself to being its patron. Those functions which the chancellor had formerly fulfilled were now handed over in turn to the so-called *magister scholae*, the schoolmaster.

This change of organization in the teaching hierarchy is associated with Bernard of Chartres, whose principles and methods gave to the school its particular stamp.

What were the particular features that most impressed his contemporaries? First, his taking account of the individual gifts of his pupils, his care that their receptive powers should not be overtaxed, and his endeavor to combine intellectual and moral education. But most important in our context is his practice of basing instruction in the sciences on the reading of the pagan authors, and his thorough knowledge of the works of classical and late antiquity, which led contemporaries to call him "the most abounding spring of letters in Gaul." And yet, this close relation with antiquity which distinguishes his teaching from that of other masters of the twelfth century cannot be considered as a mere revival of the classics. He himself describes in an impressive image the relation of his own age to antiquity: "We are like dwarfs that sit on the shoulders of giants; hence we can see more and further than they, yet not by reason of the keenness of our vision nor the outstanding stature of our bodies, but because we have been raised aloft and are being carried by those men of giant dimensions." Bernard's image of the dwarfs sitting on the shoulders of giants is borrowed again and again in later centuries to the time of Newton and Bentley, to express the relation between modern achievement and the wisdom of the ancients.[1] Nowhere can there be found a truer symbol of the consciousness which Bernard's age had of itself— wondering admiration for the sublime heritage of antiquity, but, at the same time, the firm conviction of being superior to it since these inherited possessions had been assimilated and enlarged.

In the compass of this lecture I cannot treat of the particular way in which the philosophical heritage of antiquity was enriched by the attempt to reconcile Plato and Aristotle, and to fit this synthesis into the framework of Christian doctrine. I shall dwell rather on one special aspect, namely the function which is assigned to science in the work of Bernard's younger brother Thierry who eventually succeeded him as chancellor of the school.

Of Thierry's writings and of his activity as a teacher much still remains unknown. In his lectures he certainly covered most of the *auctores*. To the writings generally recognized as his we can add his Commentary on Boethius' *De arithmetica* which we have found, as well as traces of his lectures on Martianus Capella. His Commentary on Boethius' *De Trinitate* exercised a particularly strong influence and was extensively used by many later commentators.

Though he himself complains of having been subjected to bitter attacks from hostile critics, many documents bear witness to the high reputation Thierry enjoyed, both when he taught at Paris and afterwards when he had returned to Chartres. There can be no doubt that his fame was based on his comprehensive grasp of all the liberal arts; he was, in John of Salisbury's words, *artium studiosissimus investigator*. Indeed, he was the first master of his time to conceive the idea of combining the most important texts representing the traditional and the new learning in each of the seven arts and of joining them together in an imposing corpus to which, in analogy with the Pentateuch, he gave the name *Eptatheucon*. It was contained in two manuscripts of giant size, and it is stated in his obituary that, with forty-eight other volumes, he bequeathed this *Bibliotheca septem liberalium artium* to the Cathedral. As codices 497 and 498 of the Municipal Library of Chartres, they survived until the Second World War when, like many other books of that inadequately protected collection, they were destroyed.

Perhaps the most significant aspect of Thierry's teaching was his cosmological speculation, contained in his book *De sex dierum operibus*. Through the Latin translation of, and commentary on, Plato's *Timaeus* by Chalcidius, the scholars of the early Middle Ages had become acquainted with the classical formulation of the principle of causality, and the importance of this principle had been stressed by the numerous exegetes of the dialogue. The emphasis laid in these expositions on Plato's doctrine that "Whatever comes to be must be brought into being by the action of some cause," and on the necessity to "give the reason" (*reddere rationem*, Plato's λόγον διδόναι) taught the medieval scholar to look for the "legitimate cause" of every single phenomenon, as well as of the formation of the whole universe—a quest which, for him, was inevitably bound up with the search for the "legitimate reason."[2]

John of Salisbury, who speaks of the *series causarum vel rationum*, sums up this conviction (*Entheticus* 607–14, *P.L.* 199, col. 978):

> Causarum series natura vocatur, ab illa
> Sensilis hic mundus contrahit esse suum.
> Et si vicinis concordant plasmata causis,
> Tunc natura parens omne figurat opus.
> Si sit ab eventu vicino dissona causa,
> Contra naturam turba quid esse putat
> Et quia causa latet, dicit ratione carere:
> Sed plane nihil est quod ratione caret.

The consistent application of the principle of causality, in the earlier Middle Ages the privilege of a few outstanding minds, became in the twelfth century the common property of a large group of thinkers. The quest for the cause now seems to dominate men's minds. It helps to explain, on the one hand, such a phenomenon as the rapid success of astrology, the "matēsis" which appealed, by the apparent necessity implied in its system, to the scientifically minded as well as to the credulous. It leads, on the other hand, to the possibility of ordering vast materials in the most varied fields of intellectual life—in history, in law, and in theology—in a systematic whole, according to cause and effect.

It was, moreover, of great consequence that, as a result of the decisive selection which took place in late antiquity, the main literary source through which the principle of causality was handed down was not Democritus or the Epicurean tradition, but the *Timaeus* and its expositors. The balance between teleological and causal thought which distinguishes this dialogue, the myth with its "Father of the Gods," the emphatic statement that it is impossible to find language worthy to express him, made the work less foreign to Christian sentiment than any other pagan philosophical explanation of the world. Could not Plato's authority be claimed even for the origin of the universe in time? For a critical eye the fundamental issue dividing the revealed religions—Christian, Jewish, and Moslem—from ancient philosophy remains, viz. the belief in a *creatio ex nihilo*, but the repeated references in the Latin *Timaeus*, especially in Chalcidius's commentary, to a divine will as the cause of the existence of the world, tended to bridge the gap, drawing the attention away from the elements in the work which are incompatible with Christian doctrine.

Thus the main historical significance of the *Timaeus* becomes evident. The medieval scholar could read into this work his own conception of a divine being and, at the same time, learn the postulate of strict rational thought, thus finding a way to reconcile the claims of reason and faith. While trying to comprehend the universe in his mind, he could continue to believe in a personal God, without the sense that reason and faith were in conflict or even unrelated to each other. Rather, the very idea of a personal God who, out of his goodness, ordered the cosmos becomes the warrant for the possibility of understanding it. Reason acquires a new dignity from its function of retracing and revealing the art of the divine craftsman; and the search for knowledge of the causes of things becomes the service of God. Thus, those who were attempting, for the first time in the Christian era, by their interpretation of the visible world, to free cosmology from the trammels of theological dogma could justly claim they were not destroying the faith. Theirs was a new approach to the same faith, an approach that prepared the ground for modern scientific thought.

It was in this spirit that Thierry of Chartres, in contrast to the Fathers of the Church who, so he says, were concerned mainly with the moral or allegorical meaning of Scripture, attempted to interpret the Biblical account of the creation. His lecture on the creation of the world, in form a commentary on the first chapters of Genesis, is in fact one of the earliest attempts in Christian times to explain the formation of the world purely in terms of natural causes, in Thierry's words *iuxta physicas rationes tantum.* "God created heaven and earth," that is to say, the four elements. Given the fact of this creation, it is the task of the human mind to understand all consequent development in the cosmological process by natural reason without any further appeal to supernatural forces. From the properties of the elements, the whole process follows by natural steps. For example, taking the verse "... and God ... divided the waters which were under the firmament from the waters which were above the firmament" (Gen. 1 : 7), Thierry explains that fire, through its property of giving heat, warms the air which in turn warms the element water, causing part to evaporate and to rise as vapor above the air, thus forming the waters above the firmament. This account is proved by an observation from everyday experience, when the steam from a hot bath rises and hangs suspended above the air. In a similar way, by constant reference to common experience, to experiments which everybody could perform and test, the gradual formation of the world is explained. Naïve as his account may seem to the modern scholar and scientist, this first systematic attempt to withdraw cosmology from the realm of the miraculous, and to win for physical theory a relative independence from theology, gives Thierry an outstanding place among philosophers. For in the history of ideas we are concerned with those who dare to make a breach in the solid wall of prejudice which at all times dominates human thought, rather than with those who, the way once shown, follow the lead and secure the ground.

From his own assertion we learn that Thierry did not escape the charge of being a magician. This accusation, surprising at first sight, becomes understandable if it is considered in its wider context. For down to the very confines of modern times, almost all the great thinkers who by the power of their intellect moved on a mental plane above that familiar to the world they lived in, have been considered as magicians by succeeding generations, and sometimes also by their contemporaries. Thus Plato and Aristotle were in the later Middle Ages popularly believed to have been adepts in the black arts. Gerbert, who later became Pope Sylvester, Albertus Magnus, and Roger Bacon have come down in tradition as masters of the occult. Abailard, the logician, appears as necromancer and author of a book on magic, and even St. Thomas Aquinas was reputed to be the author of a treatise on the philosophers' stone. Many similar instances could be named down to the times of Leonardo da Vinci. If we now ask for the reason for these charges and try to understand what it was that induced men to ascribe a knowledge of magical arts to philosophers in particular—to those of former times as well as to those of their own generation—we shall have to realize that to the popular medieval imagination outstanding intellectual ability presented itself as an uncanny power and that therefore knowledge itself appears as a form of magic.

The influence of Thierry was far-reaching. Under him Chartres became the center of the liberal arts to which students came from all over Europe. In search of new sources of knowledge, his pupils crossed the Pyrenees and the Alps. They brought back mathematical and astronomical works in translations made from the Arabic, and new texts of Aristotle in versions made from the Greek. From Chartres this new learning was handed on to the Latin world.

While the emphasis thus laid on mathematics, physical science, and the classics is the distinguishing feature of the School of Chartres, this characterization is incomplete, even superficial, if we do not consider the purpose which these studies were to serve, viz., to attain, through knowledge of the structure of the created world, knowledge of the Creator.

As the world, in the words of the Book of Wisdom, is ordered according to number, measure, and weight, the sciences of the quadrivium—arithmetic and geometry, music and astronomy—are the instruments which the human mind has at its disposal for recognizing the art of the Creator. Thus the sciences are the indispensable organon of all philosophical and theological knowledge. But while the intellect gains insight into the world through the sciences, it would not be capable of expressing itself in an intelligible and, as Thierry says, elegant manner, without the help of the arts of the trivium: grammar, rhetoric, and logic. Thus the seven liberal arts together give man both knowledge of the divine and the power to express it. But, in so doing, they fulfil at the same time another purpose.

They serve *ad cultum humanitatis*, that is, they promote the specifically human values, revealing to man his place in the universe and teaching him to appreciate the beauty of the created world.

A pupil of Thierry who, in the dedication of his version of Ptolemy from the Arabic, calls him "the leading mind of the learned Latin world," claims that in his beloved master the soul of Plato has come down from heaven to show itself again among mortals. Indeed, in Thierry's works the memory of the Hellenic delight in the rational and harmonious order of the universe is kept alive, and the particular function which, as shown above, he allotted to science is to be understood in the context of a Platonic tradition.

The connection between this medieval Platonism and that of the fifteenth century has long been categorically denied; the continuity of the Platonic tradition in the West has thereby been obscured. And yet both the history of the manuscripts and an analysis of the sources prove conclusively how greatly outstanding thinkers of the "Renaissance," such as Nicholas of Cues, depend on the masters of Chartres in certain "Pythagorean" speculations about the universe, as well as in the fusion of the scientific, the aesthetic, and the religious elements which characterizes their glorification of the cosmos.

The full extent of the influence which the teachings of the School of Chartres exercised on the thought of later centuries cannot yet be adequately assessed. For it was often through devious channels that they reached the succeeding generations. Thus we find, for example, that Helinand, in his famous World Chronicle (MS British Museum, Cotton Claudius B IX), incorporates a large part of Thierry's account of the formation of the universe, word by word, without any mention of his source; and from Helinand the same account is taken over by Vincent of Beauvais in his *Speculum*—a source book for many centuries to come.

The history of the writings of another prominent master of the School, William of Conches, is equally complex. The zealous Cistercian abbot, William of St. Thierry, the influential friend of Bernard of Clairvaux, bitterly attacked him for reasoning about God in terms of natural philosophy: "Homo physicus et philosophus physice de Deo philosophatur." Nevertheless, the very large number of copies in which his main work, the comprehensive *Philosophia*, has survived and, above all, the extensive use made of it by scholars, poets, and popular writers, mostly without mention of his name, testify to its success. No less important was his activity as commentator on classical texts. None of his *Glosulae*—in

FIG. 1. Representatives of the Liberal Arts, *Voussoirs, South Doorway, West Front, Royal Portal, Chartres Cathedral*.

which, while expounding the text of the author, he frequently develops his own views—has been published in full. A systematic survey of his *œuvre* will show that it comprised commentaries on an extensive range of authors, and that not a few of them are still extant in manuscript form. Thus after a long search we found in Florence (Biblioteca Laurenziana, MS San Marco 310) his interesting exposition of Priscian, containing his grammatical theories, and in the Walters Art Gallery at Baltimore part of his Gloss on Juvenal (MS Walters 448). Of his large Commentary on Plato's *Timaeus* we have traced the full text in Cardinal Bessarion's copy in Venice (Biblioteca Nazionale di San Marco, fondo antico lat. cod. 225 [= Valentinelli classis X cod. 4]); from the collation of this and other manuscripts of the same work (Florence, Biblioteca Nazionale, Conventi soppr. E 8 1398; Vatican, Bibl. Apost. Vat., Urbinas lat. 1339; Paris, Bibliothèque Nationale lat. 14065; Avranches, Bibl. municipale 226), all differing from one another in their additions and omissions, it is manifest that William polished and revised this Commentary several times, as he did with various others of his writings. To these copies of the different redactions we may add extracts from the Commentary, abbreviations of some parts, and long verbal quotations, found, for example, in manuscripts at Munich, Berlin, Upsala, Prague, and Oxford; they strikingly indicate how widely known William's exposition of Plato was and how great a reputation it enjoyed.

Through William of Conches, who at one time was tutor to Henry II, the influence of the School is felt in England. As the extant catalogues show, there were few respectable libraries of the late twelfth and thirteenth centuries which did not possess a copy of one of his works.

The main link between Chartres and England, however, was John of Salisbury, the greatest writer of the age. In his youth a student at Chartres, and in his old age its bishop, John finds in the notion of *humanitas*, developed by Bernard and Thierry, the ideal for which he strives. Yet his interpretation differs in a characteristic way from that of his French masters. Whereas they, with logical vigor, seek to attain certainty in philosophical and theological speculation, the Englishman describes these efforts with great perspicacity, but views them with the detached attitude of the somewhat ironic sceptic. He is satisfied with probable solutions in questions of this nature, but lays the greater emphasis on the discussion of ethical and political values, mindful of the application to practical issues.

In contrast with the lucid masters of Chartres and their English pupil, superior perhaps in his appreciation of social and political life, but less interested in ambitious philosophical speculation, contemporary German writers appear as ecstatic visionaries, or as metaphysicians—forceful, profound, and vague. Are we justified in assuming that it is possible to detect, dimly foreshadowed underneath the apparent homogeneity of medieval Latin thought, certain national traits?

If we now turn to the opposition which formed the starting point of this paper, between dialectical reasoning and unreasoned reliance on authority, it will have become manifest that the teaching of the masters of Chartres cannot be adequately understood in terms of these antithetical categories. For they would agree with the logicians that, in philosophical argument, authority cannot be regarded as a fixed standard of judgment; it is "like a waxen nose" which can be twisted in any direction. But they would also maintain that the art of reasoning is not an end in itself. The old controversy between autonomous reason and an authority jealous of its rights now changed its character with the intervention of a new factor—the interest in a 'physical' explanation of the universe. Without being directed against religious faith, 'scientific' reasoning inevitably extended its scope and aspired to ever greater autonomy. On the other hand, philosophical speculation was, through its connection with the 'scientific' subjects of the quadrivium, preserved from the sterile self-sufficiency of a dialectic exercised *in vacuo*.

There is an apocryphal story, found in a Munich manuscript from St. Emmeram (cod. lat. mon. 14160), regarding the master of logicians, Peter Abailard, "a man of unbelievable subtlety" but without any training in the quadrivium. Conscious of this deficiency, so we are told, he applied to Master Thierry for some lessons in mathematics. Soon, however, he grew restive, repelled by the unexpected difficulty of the subject, and was teased by Thierry for his self-indulgence in desiring to pursue only that kind of learning which came easily to him—like an overfed dog wanting to lick the fat of the meat (*Baiolardus*) and spurning any less toothsome nourishment. The tale appropriately illustrates the feature which in the eyes of the contemporaries distinguished the teaching of Chartres, that is, the well-balanced interrelation of all the liberal arts within a single whole, as opposed to a one-sided emphasis on logic. This attitude is summed up in John of Salisbury's saying, "logic is of great value as an aid to other studies; but by itself it remains bloodless and barren," "*si sola fuerit, iacet exsanguis et sterilis*"—words which have not lost their aptness even in our day.

In this brief sketch we have dwelt on those tendencies which characterize the School of Chartres as a whole. A more detailed treatment will have to show that within the School, as with any group of men possessing vigorous minds and marked individuality, differences of doctrines and even tensions were not lacking. Thus a closer study of Thierry's Commentary on Boethius' *De Trinitate* reveals that in this work he attacks, with some vehemence, opinions which his contemporaries knew to be those professed by Gilbert de la Porrée, the master who had preceded him as chancellor. However, in standing up for a thorough and unhurried training in the whole cycle of the liberal arts, against the attacks of banausic utilitarians and pious obscurantists, all the masters of Chartres were at one.

To judge by the sayings and writings of these masters, the very foundations of learning, and even of civilized society, were threatened by the powerful tendencies of the day to abandon the course of studies developed in the schools of Chartres and Paris. Allowance may be made for some exaggeration—not uncommon, at all times, in the discussion of educational programmes. Yet there can be no doubt that many contemporaries disdained, or actively opposed, not only the thorough training in the trivium and the quadrivium but the very ideal it was to serve. These adversaries claimed that the end of education should be practical: "the fruit of wisdom should be wealth." With manifest relish John of Salisbury recalls in his *Metalogicon* how Master Gilbert used to scoff at those whom he saw forsake the study of the liberal arts for more lucrative and less exacting pursuits; he would counsel them to take up the art of bakery— one which did not require any special skill and yet assured its practitioners their daily bread. In John's account, the other distinguished masters of the School, Thierry of Chartres and William of Conches, are linked with Gilbert in their determined stand against the misguided stress on utility and the depreciation of the *artes* which it entailed.

The recognition of the liberal arts as a means to the knowledge of God finds visible expression in the cathedral of Chartres. The very year in which Thierry became chancellor, 1141, marked the beginning of the West front. It may perhaps at first appear surprising and arbitrary to relate these two facts. Yet if we bear in mind that it was the duty of the chancellor to supervise the fabric of the cathedral, we are not only allowed but even compelled to look for a connection between the architect's design for the sculptural decoration of the building and the philosophical conceptions of the chancellor. Here, on the Western or

Royal portal of the cathedral, the representatives of the seven liberal arts were for the first time fashioned in sculpture. Here for the first time, the principal teachers of pagan science—Donatus, Cicero, Aristotle, Boethius (the only Christian among them), Euclid, Pythagoras, and Ptolemy—became part of the Church's architectural imagery. In this significant innovation, which was a far from obvious step, we recognize the symbol of the endeavor to give the masters of ancient learning their place as necessary members in the structure of the Christian faith.

NOTES

1   See my note, "Standing on the Shoulders of Giants," *Isis*, XXVI (1936), 147–49.

2   It cannot be too strongly emphasized that the medieval scholar's conception of the *Timaeus* is derived, not directly from Plato, but from Chalcidius. Where Plato (*Tim.* 28a5) says that "without a cause (χωρὶς αἰτίου) nothing can come to be," Chalcidius renders the single Platonic term αἴτιον by "legitima causa et ratio." Here, as in many other passages (above all in that concerning "*voluntas dei*" as "*origo rerum certissima,*" *Tim.* 30a), the Latin translator of the second half of the fourth century alters Plato's thought by transposing it into a very different conceptual framework. A clear appreciation of the way in which Plato's text was thus transformed is essential for the understanding of Platonism in late Latin antiquity and in the Middle Ages. No detailed comparison between the Latin rendering and the Greek original has as yet been made. The Index to Chalcidius which, together with the critical edition of his work, is to appear in the *Corpus Platonicum* (Plato Latinus, Vol. IV) is designed to facilitate this task.

Urban T. Holmes, Jr.

Transitions in European Education

In the beginning the liberal arts were skills befitting the freeman, as defined by Plato in the fourth century B.C. Aristotle elaborated further upon this idea in his *Politics*, and Cicero spoke of them in his *De officiis* and *De oratore*.[1] Cassiodorus had much to say about them in the *De institutione divinarum litterarum*, and he was followed by Isidore of Seville, that great master of all seven of these arts, in the three opening books of his *Etymologiae*. They were no mere subject of speculation; they were the essence of general curriculum for the privileged Roman who wished to be a man of polite learning and of liberal education. We read in St. Augustine:

> And what did it profit me, that all the books I could procure of the so-called liberal arts, I, the vile slave of vile affections, read by myself and understood?... Whatever was written on rhetoric, or logic, geometry, music, and arithmetic... I found him [Faustus] utterly ignorant of liberal sciences, save grammar, and that but in an ordinary way...[2]

They are all here save astronomy. St. Augustine was a teacher of rhetoric: "I began then diligently to practice that for which I came to Rome, to teach rhetoric."[3]

These same liberal arts were the curriculum of the schools directed by Alcuin at the court of Charles the Great, and they enjoyed their important role throughout the Middle Ages. However, their emphasis and the textbooks used shifted considerably. Dialectic and rhetoric were paired together in Isidore and Alcuin as two phases of the doctrine of expression.[4] By the close of the tenth century Gerbert had rearranged the dialectic curriculum, basing its study more on the Old Logic of

Aristotle and on certain commentaries and treatises by Boethius "which had the effect . . . of translating the problem of distinguishing principles into the problem of discovering arguments . . . ."[5] Boethius distinguished between dialectic as presenting "theses" and rhetoric as offering "hypotheses." These new concepts spread slowly in the eleventh century, so that they could hardly be noticed. It was by the twelfth century that this need for differentiation produced revolution. Abelard thought of dialectic as a means of expounding the arguments of the Scriptures, and of rhetoric as the instrument of persuasion. After the advent of the New Logic (1141) rhetoric became still more assimilated to theology and edification and vanished as a handmaid to dialectic and proof.

As is often the case with revolution this struggle produced some monuments of lasting value: notably the great universities of Paris, Bologna, and Oxford. For these we are thankful.

The description of a cathedral school in the eleventh century can easily be surmised.[6] There was the trivium: grammar, rhetoric, and logic or dialectic, and the quadrivium: arithmetic, geometry, astronomy, and music—the seven arts with which we are concerned. Then there were the three practical sciences: theology, canon law, and medicine, which were considered most important but which remained unorganized because there was no systematic instruction in them in these schools. Just what was taught depended upon the *scholasticus*, the director of the school, appointed by the bishop's chancellor. The *scholasticus* was his own principal teacher, with one or more assistants. Basically he had classes in grammar and rhetoric, with some sermons on theology on Sundays and feast days. If arithmetic, geometry, and following the courses of the stars were particular interests of the master, he gave formal instruction in these also, as at Cologne and Liége. Logic was tied with rhetoric and it concerned itself mostly with the problem of the universals. Did a class or genus have "real" existence, before the creation of the individuals, in the mind of God? A properly educated man, supposedly including the *scholasticus*, professed to have acquaintance with all the arts, and some theology and medicine too, so that where advanced private instruction was desired it would seldom be refused. A monastic school was more or less similar, having as the director the librarian, or even the abbot or prior himself. Teaching in the cloister had greater continuity because excellence did not depend, as in the cathedral schools, upon the brilliance and versatility of some *scholasticus vagans* who was employed for a short time.

Excellent students knew that good instruction in all learning could not be acquired in one place; so, according to their tastes, they moved about. There was the case of Olbert of Liége:

> He had been brought up regularly at the Monastery of Liége since childhood; extremely learned in letters he showed what he was destined to become by the superiority of his natural ability. He had drunk from the lips of Abbot Heriger of Liége a taste for the seven arts. Abbot Heriger was a most eloquent man in his day. Olbert was not able to satiate his thirst for study. When he would hear of some one distinguished in the arts he flew there at once, and the more he thirsted the more he absorbed something delightful from each master. At Paris he worked at Saint-Germain and studied the Holy Faith which glowed there. In Troyes he studied for three years, learning gratefully many things from some, and others he himself taught prudently. He felt obliged to listen to Fulbert of Chartres who was proclaimed in the liberal arts throughout France. Afterwards just like the bees among flowers, gorged with the nectar of learning, he returned to the hive and lived there studiously in a religious way, and religiously in a studious manner.[7]

There was Raoul Mau-Couronné, a monk of Marmoutier, who about 1050 pursued his studies in this same diversified way. He attended schools in France and Italy, learning grammar, dialectic, astronomy, music, and medicine. (Note the lack of rhetoric and mathematics.) Ordericus Vitalis adds that "in Salerno, where they have had the greatest schools of medicine since ancient time, he found no one equal to him in the medicinal art except a certain wise woman (*matronam sapientem*)."[8]

From the catalogues of the time which list the books in the cathedral and monastic libraries we can observe the textbooks that were used. Donatus and Priscian were authorities for grammar; Cicero, Quintilian, Ovid, Vergil, Juvenal, and Fortunatus served in rhetoric, in addition to the histories of Gregory of Tours, Bede, Livy, Florus, and Josephus. For dialectic there was chiefly the *Isagoge* of Porphyry as translated by Boethius, but we know that they were now using all the Old Logic: the *Categories* and the *De interpretatione* in the Latin versions of Victorinus and Boethius. In arithmetic Bede was paramount, and in geometry use was made of Albinus and of the *Podismus* of Nipsius. For music there was Boethius.[9] Hucbald and Guido of Arezzo are not usually in the catalogues, which makes us suspect that music as an art was theoretical and not very much concerned with the practice of contemporary plain chant.[10] As John Cotton quoted from the *Micrologus* (1025) of Guido: "There is great distance between musicians and singers, the ones produce, and the others know what music consists of; he who executes what he does not know can be called a beast." [11] John was a musicologist. Theology based itself principally on the writings of the Fathers and the Old and New Testament. What little was done with canon law came from the conciliar canons and from Burchardt's *Decretum*. Theoretical medicine was read in the *Aphorisms* of Hippocrates, Galen, Surian, and in various *antidotaria* or collections of medical prescriptions. A little medicine was a social and professional asset for any teacher.

Grammar was "that grounde . . . of alle." Guibert de Nogent (d. 1124) commented upon the rarity of grammar schools in his youth but said in his later years, "I see towns and villages boiling with grammatical studies." [12] Rhetoric was approached in three ways, a fact that should be kept well in mind. Along with advanced grammar it could continue as an exposition of poetic art, an appreciation of literature *per se*. As a twin of dialectic it was a means of acquiring eloquence, and then, even at this date, its teaching was sometimes codified into the *ars dictaminis* to be an aid to effective letter writing. [13] In the eleventh century the schools at Le Mans, Angers, Tours, and Orleans were doing splendid work in teaching poetic art. [14] Three outstanding products of such schools were Hildebert of Laverdin, later bishop of Le Mans and then archbishop of Tours, Baudry de Bourgueil, later bishop of Dol, and Marbod who became bishop of Rennes. Literature flourishes best when it is half a trade and half an art, if we may quote Dean Inge.

During the first two thirds of the eleventh century abuses in the Church were stimulating renewed study of canon law, but theology still lagged behind. Simony and lay patronage were rife in many places, high and low. The reform party of Hildebrand, first chaplain under Gregory VI, and then chief adviser for temporal affairs until he became Pope himself in 1073, was both necessary and efficient in attacking these abuses. [15] Pier Damiani (1007–72), the hermit of Fonte Avellana, was deeply concerned with a revival of theology, but this was to be a theology not furthered by the application of argument—of dialectic. He was of great assistance in the reform efforts of Nicholas II (1059–61). [16] It was at the Abbey of Bec, in Normandy, that theology started to come into its own. Lanfranc who had begun as a lawyer, in Italy, taught this subject, and we may judge from his pupils Alexander II and Anselm of Aosta that his legal training made a potent combination with his devotion to theology and the law of the Church. It is of this Anselm of Aosta, or St. Anselm, that we must speak at greater length. [17] He was the key to the "new training" in the schools of the West. He entered the Cloister at Bec in 1063 and was soon prior and director of the monastic school. Lanfranc went to England as Archbishop of Canterbury in 1070 and the position of leadership at Bec was gradually assumed by St. Anselm, who held that theology can be proved by logic (dialectic), although there should be no element of doubt present in the mind of the theologian. From his instruction at Bec there went forth early masters of the dialectic method in theology and canon law, whose followers were fated to "shake the yoke of inauspicious stars" and nearly bring about the ruin of the liberal arts in England and France. It was in four little treatises that St. Anselm published abroad his faith in the new pedagogy, the *De grammatico*, the *De veritate*, the *De libero arbitrio*, and the *De potestate et impotentia* (his last work). In the Preface of the *De veritate* he adds:

I have made at various times three treatises pertaining to the study of Sacred Scripture which are similar in that they are based upon questioning and answering: the one who questions is called the pupil and the one who answers is the master. A fourth treatise I wrote in a similar manner which, I think, will be useful for an Introduction to dialectic; the beginning of this is "De grammatico etc. . . . "[18]

In this introductory primer for the newly expanded science of argumentation we have formal discussion as to whether a grammarian is a substance or a quality. (This was a risky subject for argument in any classroom where the master had prominent bad qualities!) Surely it was Anselm's intent to mingle some levity with the study of this arid and prosy subject matter. We will quote from the middle of the text.

Pupil. Do not contradict quickly what I have said; let me bring my argument to an end, then either approve it or correct . . . . In order to demonstrate that a certain grammarian is a substance it suffices to show that every grammarian is a man, and every man a substance. Everything that a grammarian has, which belongs to him as a substance . . . he has only because he is a man. Wherefore, when it is conceded that he is a man, anything that pertains to a man belongs to the grammarian. The philosophers declare this plainly, those who have treated of this matter, whose authority it is impertinent to question. Since it is essentia that a grammarian be either a substance or a quality—to the extent that he is one, he may not be of the other—insofar as he is not of the one, to that degree he must be of the other. Whatever is of value to show the one side, defeats the other; whatever weakens the one strengthens the other. Since one of these is true the other is false. I ask you that brushing aside the false you explain to me clearly what is true.[19]

The master complies and clears up the syllogism. This brings a further analogy:

Master: If a white horse is in a certain house, and you do not know it and some one says to you: "In this house is an *album* or *albus*," do you know from this that a horse is designated?

Pupil: No. If he says either a white whiteness, or something in which there is whiteness, I do not conceive the essence of anything clearly in my mind, even of this color . . . .

Master: If you see near you a white horse and a black ox and someone says to you, "Strike him," meaning the horse but not indicating by a sign which he means, would you know he means the horse? But if, when asked, the master responds "white" . . . .

At this point the pupil agrees that *horse* means a substance *per se* and not *per aliud*, while *white horse* designates a substance not *per se* but *per aliud*. The master closes proving that a grammarian may be a quality.

In the Preface to his *Liber de Fide Trinitatis et de Incarnatione Verbi*, directed against Roscellinus and the nominalist doctrine of the universals, St. Anselm justifies his use of dialectic in theology:

Since the Apostles, the holy Fathers, and many of our teachers have said so much on the reason of our Faith, in order to confound the weakhearted and to shatter the stubbornness of the unfaithful, and to feed those who delight in the purified Faith, we cannot hope to equal them today, or in the future, in this contemplation of Truth. But I do not think any one should be reprehended if, *firm in his Faith*, he wishes to exercise his *reason*. (The italics are mine.) Men, because their days are short, cannot say all that they wish to say, even though they may live very long, and the reasoning of Faith is so vast and deep that it cannot be exhausted by mortal men. . . . The Sacred Page urges us to investigate the reason when it says: "If you do not believe you will not understand"—it clearly bids us to extend our application to the process of discernment when it teaches how we should go about it. . . . Although I am a man of but little learning, who takes comfort in *reasoning* upon those things *which we believe*, as far as the Heavenly Grace deigns to allow it, I try to rise up at times and when I find what I did not behold before I proclaim this freely to others, so that what I myself believe I may teach to another's judgment.[20]

This is extremely important, and probably it continues something of what came from Lanfranc the "lawyer." Theology can be proved by dialectic. St. Anselm's *Monologion* (1076) was devoted to the Holy Trinity. The *Proslogion* (1077–79) elaborated upon the belief that "nihil maius cogitari possit Deo," 'nothing greater than God can be imagined.' The second chapter of this is concerned with the celebrated proof of the existence of God.

It is generally conceded that Anselm of Laon, a pupil of St. Anselm, came as master to the cathedral school of Paris and that he taught grammar, rhetoric, and theology there. Some believe that this constitutes the founding of the schools—and therefore of the later University of Paris. (However, we have already noted that Olbert of Liége read theology of a kind at the monastery of St. Germain des Prés.) This Anselm of Laon was a famous teacher and students flocked to his lectures wherever he gave them, but for some reason he, and his brother Radulphus, soon transferred to the school at Laon. Perhaps this was the proverbial "itchy foot" of the secular *scholasticus*. Afterwards a pupil of his, Guillaume de Champeaux, was the teacher at Paris. Anselm at Laon was a conservative man, despite his brilliance; he preached nothing anywhere close to heresy. He did not devote much time to the great problems of the Trinity and the Sacraments. Guillaume too was a conservative—extremely so in the problem of the universals.[21] He also was most attractive to the younger generation, and pupils flocked to Paris to be in his classroom. Among these was Peter Abelard who arrived around 1100.[22] Abelard came from Brittany, just east of Nantes, and he had attended lectures at Loches which were given there by Roscellinus, the nominalist heretic. Abelard was far from conservative and like many original thinkers he could make himself unpleasant to his teacher. We know, from Abelard's telling, that Guillaume was soon somewhat discredited. Abelard went away to teach on his own, and then returned for another try at Paris under Guillaume. This time Guillaume withdrew and, with the aid of King Louis VI, founded a cell farther up the river from Paris, intending to renounce all class instruction. Distinguished friends, among them Hildebert of Laverdin, urged and prevailed; in 1109 Guillaume de Champeaux taught again in his cell at St. Victor, the new Augustinian foundation. He subsequently was elected bishop of Châlons-sur-Marne in 1112—but the school at St. Victor had been founded. We will digress from the cathedral school at Paris momentarily in order to say more of this center at St. Victor which had a great future of at least a hundred years. It remained as a citadel of conservative strength even while the secular schools of Paris were flirting with deviationism. After Guillaume became a bishop his work was carried on by Gilduin and other pupils. In 1115–18 a young German from Saxony knocked at his doors. This was Hugh of St. Victor.[23] He was a teaching assistant by 1125, and in 1133 he was the *scholasticus* of the Abbey. Hugh's *Didascalion*, based upon the "Aristotelian" definition of the arts according to their purpose, and upon St. Augustine and Isidore, is a fine presentation of a balanced medieval curriculum.[24] Traces of it are found in many places, among others in the theory and practice of Alexander Neckam. Hugh died in 1141; he was followed shortly by a Scotsman, Richard of St. Victor, who taught until 1173.

In the *De Vanitate Mundi* Hugh presents a picture of the activity within a school. It may be that he is depicting the activity at Mount Ste. Geneviève, above Paris; but then again he may have had his own studium in mind. The Teacher asks the Questioner to look around and say what he sees. He describes students who are exercising their tongues in the reading and pronunciation of letters. He sees still others who are practicing inflections for the sake of obtaining eloquence (for "talking and eloquence are not the same; to speak, and to speak well, are two things"). There are individuals engaged in dialectic dispute, endeavoring to trick one another slyly. Some are employed in calculating, doubtless with counting boards before them like little tables. Others are applying themselves to a monochord, working on the theory of music. Some have various instruments, quadrants no doubt, with which they are describing the orbits of the heavenly bodies; others are explaining geometric figures; and last of all there are some who are discussing plants and the properties of things. These last are engaged with Physica.[25] We assume that these exercises were not all taking place at the same time, in the same hall. Ordericus Vitalis tells of classes held in the town of Cambridge by monks of Croyland. The monks rented a granary. Between dawn and the First Hour Odo taught grammar; at Prime, in the same hall, Terric held forth on rhetoric; at Tierce, William gave lessons in dialectic. On Sundays and on feast days Gilbert spoke on the Fathers and on elementary theology.[26] A schedule of this sort was probably followed at St. Victor in the hall allotted to the school.

After Guillaume de Champeaux withdrew from the cathedral schools to the comparative quiet of his new cell it is not known who was his immediate successor on the Cité. At that time Abelard began to teach on the hill, with permission from the abbot of Ste. Geneviève. Soon he was called to the Cité and he held the post of *scholasticus* from about 1112 to 1118. It was during this time that he was associated with Héloïse, the niece of Canon Fulbert, and he wrote his commentaries on Porphyry in which he argued for dialectic as a major branch of the arts. If Guillaume had had brilliant pupils Abelard excelled him in this also. The reputation of the Paris schools began to be acclaimed everywhere, especially after the death of Anselm of Laon in 1117. After his personal tragedy and departure from Paris in 1118, Abelard surely left much of this momentum as a carry-over for his successors during the next ten or fifteen years. His glosses on Porphyry and his new *Dialectica* were used as texts and must have haunted his pupils. It would be from some of them that he received the urging to compose a handbook on theology. A petition from schoolmen requested that he use his methods in making such a compendium:

> Since they had read many writings by us on philosophic matters and secular letters which had pleased them, it seemed that our talent could penetrate easily the meaning of the divine page, and the arguments for Holy Faith, since it had drawn from the deep wells of philosophy.... As they believed me capable of solving the difficulties, me, who they knew had been brought up from the very cradle in philosophic studies, and especially in dialectic which appears to be the mistress of all reasoning... unanimously they asked me not to delay in increasing the talent which had been committed to me by God. They added also that it is suitable for our age and our profession, as well as to ethics and our monastic habit, that I change studies and prefer divine volumes to the human; for when I left the secular world I proposed to transfer myself completely to God. Although at one time I began to study for the acquiring of money, now I change this to acquiring souls, that I may come in at the eleventh hour to cultivate God's vineyard, as far as I can....[27]

The resulting introduction to theology, in three books, contains some startling allegations, which provoked more difficulty for its compiler. St. Bernard of Clairvaux could see nothing orthodox in a passage such as this:

> We learn from many testimonials of the Saints that the Platonic sect is often in agreement with the Catholic Faith. Wherefore, not without cause, Plato is held by all to be the greatest of the philosophers before all others, not only by those trained in the secular arts, but truly by the saints....[28]

and at this point he quotes St. Augustine.

But Abelard's great contribution to the new learning which was thrusting aside the other ancient arts which he loved so much was his *Sic et Non* which handled theology in a special way. The "Aristotelian" concept of the role of logic was there. This was the incomparable tool which was destined to help alter the character of instruction in all schools. Again, we will cite a few lines from the Preface. It is in the opening sentences to his work that an author is wont to declare his purpose and originality, as well as the names of those who inspired the effort. The *Sic et Non* has this preamble:

> Since in a great multiplicity of words some of the observations of the Saints are inconsistent at times, even contrary, the right of judgement is not to be feared among those who in turn will judge the World; for it is written "The holy nations shall judge" and again "You will sit in judgement." May we not presume to

treat them as speaking falsely, or condemn them for being in error, of whom the Lord has said: "Who hears me, hears you; who spurns you spurns me...." Having tasted all this, we have been pleased, as just said, to gather the differing remarks of the holy Fathers, when they occur to us, formulating questions which may provoke young readers to the greatest exercise of inquiry after Truth, assiduous and frequent questioning, the desirability of which that most perspicacious of all philosophers, Aristotle, urges upon students who are in doubt over anything. It is difficult to speak confidently about such things until they have been perused frequently. It is useful to have doubts about many things.[29]

Then Abelard quotes from St. Matthew: "Seek and you will find; knock and it will be opened to you."[30]

In this methodology opinions from differing authorities are cited in succession and the learners are encouraged to debate, while the compiler often gives his own position on the problem. This system has considerable merit, but it tends to make a "project" out of learning and thereby lessens the amount of subject matter. The method led to a further step in the dialectical resolution of contradictions, although at this stage it was rhetorical rather than dialectical. Abelard owed much of his system to these predecessors, Hincmar of Rheims, Bernold of Constance, and Ivo of Chartres. The immediate influence of the *Sic et Non* method was to encourage students in the task of discovering arguments rather than principles. John of Salisbury in his *Metalogicon* is deeply concerned with the cheapening of presentation in the lecture rooms, and in discussion, which is attributable, we feel, to the *Sic et Non* system. In the *Policraticus* also he speaks of the decrease in subject matter. He finds the leading teachers of philosophy arguing in the midst of noisy crowds of pupils. They have only a few basic problems on which to invite debate. In the classrooms the masters draw the students into combat and, when pressed hard, they deal in subterfuge, twist words, and become as slippery as Proteus, or the proverbial eel. They know either much about very little or very little about too much. The problems are passed on to their successors enveloped in still greater obscurity. John insisted upon wide reading in history, oratory, and even mathematics, although he asserted that not all of such reading can edify us. Eventually one must make a choice from those matters which benefit health, the State, and one's soul. John had great regard for the State. He is a founder of political theory.[31]

It has been said that grammar was taught in the lower schools for the boys and dialectic in the studia for the men, and that rhetoric received sparse treatment somewhere in between. It seems that even the lower schools began to develop the dialectic method to an extreme. Schools at London in the period 1170–80 would have been of the lower type since there was no important studium there. A description by Fitz Stephen is most enlightening on the number of these grammar schools and the "progressive" nature of their instruction.

The three principal churches possess, by privilege and ancient dignity, celebrated schools; yet often, by the favor of some person of note, or of some learned men eminently distinguished for their philosophy, other schools are permitted upon sufferance. On festival days the masters assemble their pupils at those churches where the feast of the patron saint is solemnized; and there the scholars dispute, some in the demonstrative way, and others logically; some again recite enthymemes, while others use the more perfect syllogism. Some, to show their abilities, engage in such disputation as is practised among persons contending for victory alone; others dispute upon a truth, which is the grace of perfection. The sophisters, who argue upon feigned topics, are deemed clever according to their fluency of speech and command of language. Others endeavor to impose by false conclusions. Sometimes certain orators in their rhetorical harangues employ all their powers of persuasion, taking care to observe the precepts of the art, and to omit nothing apposite to the subject. The boys of the different schools wrangle with each other in verse, and contend about the principles of grammar or the rules of the perfect and future tenses. There are some who in epigrams, rhymes, and verses, use that trivial raillery so much practised amongst the ancients, freely attacking their companions with Fescennine license, but suppressing the names, discharging their scoffs and sarcasms against them....[32]

There we have the London schools and their local contests at a time when dialectic, and the method of the *Sic et Non*, were flourishing well.

Abelard taught again in Paris in 1137–39(?) on Mount Ste. Geneviève. We should like to be able to pinpoint why the upper schools of Paris took on a more general character at this date.[33] Some evidence of this is offered by John of Salisbury. John came there in 1136–37 and studied with Abelard, on the hill. After Abelard's going he remained there with Alberic and the Welshman Robert of Melun; in 1138–41 he was at Chartres, studying with Guillaume de Conches, Gilbert de la Porrée, and Richard l'Evêque. He migrated again, this time to the Cité, in 1141 and studied another year with Gilbert de la Porrée, until the latter was elected Bishop of Poitiers. From this date on John was concerned only with theological courses. His next master was Robert Pullen until 1144; thereafter he was with Simon de Poissy. In these later years John revisited former associates near Ste. Geneviève and commented upon their stagnant interests and lack of progressiveness. And yet the school on the hill continued with reputation, for Gerald the Welshman and William de Monte were there at the same time, presumably in the 1160's.³⁴ In 1176 Stephen of Tournai, a distinguished master, was abbot. Probably the teachers at Ste. Geneviève were tending to specialize more in the fundamental arts and their students were the "freshmen," the very young, who intended later to descend to the Cité and Petit Pont, when ready for advanced work. It is Abbot Stephen who writes most bitterly against the beardless youths who are teaching in this cathedral studium.³⁵ Whatever may have been the reason, the Paris studium began to boom and flourish greatly after 1140. It is certain that the Chancellor of the Bishop of Paris was then offering *licentiae docendi* very freely to qualified persons who wished to teach within his jurisdiction. (Pope Alexander III, in 1170 and 1179, ordered that these licenses be given without charge.)

The *Metamorphosis Goliae Episcopi*, probably composed around 1142, gives a list of famous teachers.³⁶ Of these the following were certainly at Paris: Adam of Petit Pont, Peter Lombard, Mainerius, Bartholomew, Robert Pullen, and Robert of Melun. In this period Aristotle's New Logic was now making itself strongly felt. We know that this New Logic was read at Chartres by 1140–41, and we must assume that it was soon basic in Paris, giving renewed impetus to the schools. Theology, and dialectic and practical rhetoric (as attendant disciplines), were ready for a distinguished future. An ideal textbook was needed for theology, and this was supplied by the *Sententiae* of Peter Lombard.

Peter Lombard was a native of Novara (Italy) who came to the schools of St. Victor in 1142–43.³⁷ His great *Libri IV Sententiarum* were compiled in the interval 1148–52. He had been one of the *magistri scholares* who sat in judgment at Rheims (1148) on Gilbert de la Porrée. He was elected bishop of Paris just prior to his death in 1160. His *Sententiae* follow the *Sic et Non* methodology, and he was conscious of filling a growing need:

> We have been happy to present the Truth; but the immensity of the task terrifies us.... However, we could not resist the earnest desires of studious breth-ren who have urged us vigorously to serve Christ in praiseworthy studies with tongue and stylus. This labor must not appear superfluous to the lazy and to the learned, because it is needed by many active unlearned folk like myself—bringing together in a short volume the sayings of the Fathers, with their testimonies added, that it may no longer be necessary for a student to handle an immense number of books. This brevity is offered to him without labor.... For this treatment I desire not only the pious reader; I want the critical reader, particularly where deep questions of Truth are involved.³⁸

So Peter knew that he had composed a handbook which would be a labor saver. It became so popular that for many it took the place of the Bible. There were, of course, savage attackers, in 1163, 1179, and again in 1215; but this book had constant support and eventually it was given official approval by Innocent III.

The principal threat to the basic arts did not come from dialectic, nor from the practical pursuit of theology. There was something else far more pragmatical which began to overwhelm schoolmen, particularly about the middle of the twelfth century. This was the laws, with special reference to canon law. Master Mainerius, one of the best students of Peter Abelard, stood in his classroom and spoke a prophecy of Sibyl: "The day will come, Woe be to them, when the Laws will obliterate the memory of Rhetoric." Gerald the Welshman reports this twice and says that he heard Mainerius say it. Probably Gerald studied rhetoric with this master.[39]

We must retrace our steps and reveal how the laws rose in popularity. They lent themselves, even better than theology, as meat and material for the dialectic passion. Isidore of Seville, master of all learning, had collected some of the False Decretals of the Apostles. Then there were minor groupings of the canons as in the *Collectio Anselmo dedicata* and the *De Synodalibus Causis*. There was the collection of Reginon of Prum, and above all the Decretum of Burchardt of Worms (compiled in 1008–12). These and other collections of the decretals (papal letters) and acts of the Councils were incomplete and unsystematic.[40] They were rendered positively insufficient by the recovery of the Roman civil law in the mid-century: the Digest of Justinian, the Novellae, the Institutes, and the Codex.[41] A thorough appreciation of canon law presupposes acquaintance with the Roman civil law. In the last years of the eleventh century Bishop Ivo of Chartres undertook to codify the canons and decretals.[42] It is beside the point whether he did this in person, with or without assistants. The result was three works: the *Collectio Tripartita*, the *Decretum*, and the *Panorma*. The Prologue to the *Decretum* shows that Ivo wished to bring together hard-to-get materials from many sources in the *Sic et Non* style, rather than make a synthesis:

I have tried to bring together into one corpus, with much labor, excerpts of ecclesiastical regulation, partly from the letters of the Roman Pontiffs, partly from the Acts of the Councils of Catholic Bishops, partly from the writings of the orthodox Fathers, partly from the Institutions of the Catholic kings—all these in order that any one who cannot have at hand the books from which I have drawn may find here easily what is applicable to his case.[43]

By the Institutions of the Catholic kings Ivo meant the Theodosian Code, the Digest, and the capitularies of the French kings.

This gigantic effort on the part of Ivo was soon dimmed by what was transpiring in the Italian city of Bologna.[44] This city had a good school in the arts from an early date. The discovery of the Civil Code produced an instant effect there. One of the teachers in the arts named Pepo displayed an amazing knowledge of the law by 1076. In 1085–87 Bishop Walter II of Siena referred to him as the "clarum Bononiense lumen." Perhaps he had set up a school of his own by 1088, reading law to his pupils.[45] After 1113 he was succeeded by Irnerius, another teacher of the arts, who, perhaps on the urging of Countess Mathilda, began to gloss upon the Roman law and teach.[46] This new interest spread like wildfire and hosts of young men came from everywhere to study the Laws in Bologna. The independence of this legal study was guaranteed by Frederick Barbarossa after the Diet of Roncaglia in 1158. The students were divided between the Citramontani (Italians) and the Ultramontani (foreigners). Arts and sciences were not included in this law studium—not until the thirteenth century when the student body was divided between lawyers and artians. One form of rhetoric, the ars dictaminis, flourished in Bologna. This was a necessity for the notaries.

A Camaldolese Benedictine who was attached to the school at Santi Felice and Nabore in Bologna undertook a tremendous task. This was Gratian who between 1140 and 1151 compiled his celebrated *Concordia discordantium Canonum*, which was commonly known as the *Decretum* of Gratian, imitating the title from the works of Burchardt and Ivo.[47] This masterpiece followed the *Sic et Non* methodology of Peter Abelard. Gratian was no mere compiler. He went back to originals where he could—to the canons from the fourth to the eleventh centuries, to the papal decrees from Anacletus to Innocent II, to the Fathers, to the Theodosian Code, the Visigothic, and the Capitularies of the French kings. When teachers of canon law moved from Bologna to Paris and elsewhere they carried this classic handbook with them. The master who taught canon law to Gerald the Welshman at Paris was an Italian from Bologna:

After Gerald had given his own first lecture on the Decretals, on a Sunday as was the custom, his success was very great. He visited his teacher after the [inaugural] dinner and the master said: "I would not take a hundred sous in exchange for your having spoken so well today, in so great an assembly of scholars."[48]

Gerald apologizes for his master's exuberance, adding, "For his language was that of Bologna." One of the auditors on this great occasion was Master Roger of Normandy who "had read in arts at Paris and had studied law for long at Bologna." No wonder that the studium at Paris now specialized in law and theology with these splendid texts of Peter Lombard and Gratian at the students' disposal. The teaching of civil law never reached the same proportion at Paris. After all it was not the basic law of the French or English king. Because of Papal disapproval it ceased to be taught there in the thirteenth century.[49] Peter of Blois wrote: "Till now, though I have not yet extended my steps in God's Law, I employ vacation time with reading the Codex and the Digest, etc., for amusement, not for any practical use.... It is dangerous to be ensnared by human laws."[50] In another letter Peter complains that he had left an order for a set of the Digest, etc., with a bookseller in Paris and that the fellow had sold it to someone else.[51]

With all this concentration on canon law and theology there had grown the feeling that these were the ultimate goals for all worthy minds and that concentration upon the pagan classics should not be encouraged beyond the earlier years. This had always been a matter for struggle in the minds of earnest churchmen. St. Augustine had phrased very plainly that "only the eternal meanings and realities are important; knowledge of temporal things and of the arts is chiefly useful for the interpretation of the language and symbolism of Scripture."[52] John of Salisbury and Hugh of St. Victor admitted definitely that cultivation of the delights of poetry beyond schoolboy years could be an invitation to the devil, because such writings hold a snake hidden in the grass. Theology, and not even the canon law, should be the eventual goal for a cleric whose mind turned in the right direction. There is a letter written by Peter of Blois to another Peter of Blois, a Canon at Chartres, in which he upbraids the Canon who has consumed his time till old age on "the fables of the pagans, the study of philosophers, and on civil law." The Canon has made matters worse by insisting that the narratives of the Church are boring. Peter says that he had warned his own brother, William of Blois, and that he had already brought this wandering sheep back to the steep and thorny path.[53] In another scathing letter Peter denounces Raoul of Beauvais, teacher at Oxford, who had criticized him for wasting his time with the King's Court. He denounces Raoul for continuing to teach grammar and rhetoric among the boys when his contemporaries have mounted to higher places. In still another letter Peter remonstrates with a student who has completed his liberal studies and insists upon resting for a while before beginning theology.[54]

On this same subject Gerald remonstrated with Walter Mapes at Oxford who had clung to belles-lettres at an advanced age. Gerald quotes Cicero as saying that if he had his life to live again he would never read any lyric poetry.[55] Elsewhere he gives a quotation from Origen to the effect that the songs of poets are like the croaking of frogs.[56]

While emphasizing the inadequacy of advanced grammar and rhetoric as an end in life these more mature thinkers insist with bitter zeal that grammar and rhetoric are essential for the beginning of a proper education. In a proper sequence of studies the boy should begin with psalter (elementary letters), pass to a grammar school, and then to a studium for further cultivation of the arts.[57] Dialectic was a most important tool, but it tended to be overdone. Gerald the Welshman accused Archbishop Hubert of having jumped from his Donatus and Cato (grammar school instruction) to the laws and then to public affairs. The man, he said, was positively illiterate.[58] The *Metalogicon* (1159) of John of Salisbury seeks to give a clear evaluation of the trivium, especially of the teaching of dialectic. Many critics were complaining of the new masters who sought licenses to teach after only three or four years in the studium generale.[59] Raoul de Beauvais, at one time in Oxford, coined the term *superseminati* for these superficial clerks.[60] Gerald attacks them very specifically:

Scholars in these days when they study the trivium omit almost entirely the two most necessary subjects: the first of which teaches how to speak correctly and the second teaches one to speak with charm and eloquence. Instead they pass to the study of logic and a sort of chattering loquacity.... [61] Like the spider these dialecticians eviscerate themselves to form a web in which they can catch fleas and flies.[62]

Speaking of the bad grammar of his present generation:

Not only those errors just listed but others far greater and more enormous you will hear and catch from contemporary priests. How can they instruct others when they have been so "instructed," or rather, how they "distruct" others when they have been thus "distructed."[63]

Still more specifically he says:

It will be noted that abuse of dialectic science does not open locks rather it hinders and involves, sometimes it brings on immoderate delay and suffocates and enervates literature.[64]

Then Gerald uses a most interesting comparison. When scholars disputed *circa artem* they were like players of *scacci* (draughts or chess) who prefer long games with all the pieces in use; now such long competitions are omitted as being too long and tedious and they have turned to games with only a partial number of pieces, which they consider less boring and more expeditious.[65] Gerald considered himself as a model, having studied in the schools for twenty years, not including the infinite number of hours he had put into private study in his own lodgings.[66] He said, speaking of himself in the third person:

In due time for advanced study he crossed over to France three times, making three stays there of several years each at Paris in the liberal arts; finally coming to equal the best masters he taught the trivium there with distinction, and he got special praise in rhetoric.[67]

Gerald returned to England in 1172. The English students were called home because of hostilities in 1167–70, and he was certainly in Paris in 1165.[68] To these six years we should add the three years from 1177 to 1180 and six years spent with William de Monte on theology at Lincoln in 1192–98. This makes fifteen years of attendance under masters. We assume that he studied for some five years in Wales before going to France in the first place. Probably he was assisting as a teacher of the trivium in 1170–72, and this would mean that by that time he had received the baccalaureate, a degree of which we know very little. These figures, then, would indicate a proper attendance at the schools.

Peter of Blois studied at Chartres and Tours (certainly in the trivium) and then went to Paris and Bologna. He must have been in these schools for some twelve years which, with four years at elementary level, would total sixteen years.

Alexander Neckam, whose taste for formal learning was insatiable and who first came to Paris about 1177, specialized in all the arts, including some of the mechanical ones thus classified by Hugh of St. Victor in the *Didascalion*.[69] Alexander gives a list of textbooks for use in the schools, for each of the seven arts, and for theology, medicine, and canon law.[70] He mentions Gratian, Burchardt, and Ivo of Chartres for the law; but a gloss in the Caius College MS adds that Burchardt and Ivo may be omitted. A great team of translators at Toledo, headed by Gerard of Cremona, had translated some of the *Physics* and *Metaphysics* of Aristotle. At the end of the century Gerald the Welshman expressed some approval of the fact that these so-called Aristotelian works were being banned. He saw in this a return to the arts.[71]

The fact that John of Salisbury, Gerald, Peter of Blois, and most of their colleagues found it necessary to insist upon devotion to theology as the only end for a Christian education is evidence that there were always some who persisted in their primary devotion to belles-lettres. Hilarius had been a pupil of Abelard, and yet he wrote some plays—religious to be sure—which he staged professionally: the *Daniel*, the *Lazarus*, and the *Image of Saint Nicholas*. (A variation of the first of these is now presented annually in New York City.) At Tours and at Orleans such men as Bernard Sylvester, Hugh Primatus, and later Arnoul of Orleans continued their emphasis upon profane letters. Among their distinguished pupils was Matthieu de Vendôme who wrote the oldest *Ars Versificatoria* of the time. In England, and surely at Oxford, as evidenced by Raoul de Beauvais and later by Walter Mapes, one did not feel so squeamish about belles-lettres. There was the Englishman Geoffrey de Vinsauf who composed a *Poetria Nova* around 1200.[72] But these men were highly criticized and called many harsh names for their worldly attitude. Alexandre de Villedieu, from his distant vantage point at Dol, wrote a grammar, the *Doctrinale*, around 1200 which was directed against the poetic rhetoricians. This work became popular and prevailed. Alexandre says in his *Ecclesiale*: "Orleans teaches us to sacrifice to the gods, pointing out the festivals of Faunus, of Jove, and of Bacchus. This is the pestiferous chair of learning in which ... sits no holy man, ... avoiding the baleful doctrine, which, as at Orleans, is like a disease spreading contagion among the multitude."[73] Alas, the disease was fairly conquered. How could a few followers of the "Muses on admired themes" hold out against such blasts as these? This grammar of Alexandre became the accepted text, replacing Priscian. And yet Orleans persisted in the poetical arts till at least the middle of the thirteenth century when the laws prevailed there also. St. Richard of Chichester went to Orleans after 1229 to perfect himself in practical eloquence.[74]

John of Garland who taught at Paris, exept in the years 1229–32 when he migrated to the newly formed studium at Toulouse, also composed a *Poetria*, and gave classes in grammar and in poetical rhetoric to the best of his ability. He expressed the hope that some legislation could be made to protect these arts while there was still time.[75] By 1250 Henri d'Andeli in his vernacular *Battle of the Seven Arts* proclaims in sorrow the defeat of the arts but expresses the pious hope that they will return in thirty years. Jehan le Teinturier d'Arras wrote his *Marriage of the Seven Arts* just about thirty years later. The arts had not returned any stronger, but they were still there and were being married to the Seven Virtues.[76] Another hundred years and they commenced their rehabilitation.

Till now we have said very little about the quadrivium as it was studied in the twelfth century, except to quote from Hugh of St. Victor. The quadrivium—arithmetic, geometry, astronomy, and musical theory—was joined in the minds of men with Physica—inquiry into the nature of things. Physica, in turn, merged gracefully into theoretical (not practical) medicine. At any given time it is not always possible to determine whether the medieval author has in mind the science of nature or that of medicine when Physica is mentioned. We observed earlier in this paper how some knowledge of theoretical medicine was a matter of pride to masters whose common tasks lay in a different direction. Even so Peter of Blois astounds us in one of his letters. He spent three days at Amboise ministering to the sickness of a knight named Geldewin. When he was obliged to leave he wrote to a professional physician, a friend named Peter, and advised him on the nature of the disease and the treatment in the most technical language.[77] He was no practicing physician himself. For practical medicine the wise student turned to Salerno, Montpelier, or to an apprenticeship with an empiric.

The best musicologists of the time were in England, and at St. Martial in Limoges—perhaps also at Saint James of Compostella. But Paris kept well in the current at the Schools of St. Victor. We have described the teaching there with the monochord. It was Adam of St. Victor (d. 1192) who demonstrated his achievements with his Collection of Sequences. The twelfth century saw a breakdown of the stricter rules of Gregorian chant, under popular inspiration. Thirds were no longer dissonances, the keys of F major and D minor were popular, arpeggios were common, the range or ambitus was increased. The restriction of the number of modes was probably influenced by the more and more constant use of the organ and other fixed-tone instruments which could not adjust the semitone.[78]

A sort of general science, in the name of the quadrivium, was certainly maintained in Paris and nearly everywhere; but this was not specialization.[79] For one who really cared for mathematics and astronomy, and the science of nature, the place to go was where there was a mingling with Arab learning: Toledo, Sicily, and even the Holy Land. Adelard of Bath did exactly that, after study at Tours and teaching at Laon. When he returned he wrote on the abacus or counting table, on the astrolabe, on Euclid, on falconry, but particularly on the astronomical tables of Al-Khawarismi. [80] His *Perdifficiles Quaestiones* should have set men to thinking—not on such questions as "Why men get bald on the forehead" or

"Why the living are afraid of the dead," but re the force of his remarks on authority. He observed that a title had only to be old to be accepted as the truth. Nothing modern was taken as worthy of consideration. The Arabs, he said, are obedient to reason while the Europeans have authority for their halter. Adelard died in 1144. Despite his concentration on science his principal work had to do with the universals. Surely his science teaching had some effect upon the thinking of King Henry II of England whose tutor he was. Daniel of Morlai in the latter part of the century went to Toledo for a long residence. On his return he commented adversely upon the stupid creatures who sat in the Paris schools, poring vapidly over their huge volumes of the Codex.[81] The public in France and England may have appreciated the real nature of what was being done at Toledo, but in legend and literature Toledo is called disparagingly the center for the teaching of necromancy. In the *Roman de Renart*, *Wistasse li Moine*, *Renaut de Montauban*, and so on, this is a recurrent and somewhat jesting theme.

Perhaps it was because of ideas first spread by Adelard of Bath, perhaps it was a general inclination, but England had more interest in the quadrivium than one observes at Paris. How else can we explain the vulgarizations of pseudo science which are extant in Anglo-Norman— perhaps also the enthusiasm of Alexander Neckam—and above all the *Topographia hibernica* of Gerald the Welshman? This last, written after 1185, is filled with original observations on the fauna of Ireland. There is much on the natural phenomena of Wales in the same author's *Itinerarium Kambriae*. The *Topographia* was a source of great pride for Gerald. He read it on three successive days at Oxford where it was much admired by Walter Mapes and Richard of Belfeu. We have noted a copy of it listed in the Hamo catalogue (*ca.* 1200) of the books in the Cathedral library at Lincoln, where it is indicated that the book was given by the Archdeacon of Brecon, that is, Gerald himself. But still more important is the concern with science at Oxford around 1200. There was John of London, the master of John of Garland and of Roger Bacon. John of London was a self-made man who lectured on weather phenomena, earthquakes, eclipses, and winds. He did a little forecasting of the future for the common people. He was also a splendid mathematician, and so was his colleague Peter of Maricourt. When the Franciscans were established at Oxford they were ardent disciples of this scientific movement —the greatest among them being Roger Bacon and Robert Grosseteste. The Franciscans stressed also the need for additional language study.[82]

If time and space permitted we would now like to discuss the growth of the areas in which these great studia had their physical location. Something can be said about expansion of halls and the construction of the colleges. Oxford furnishes the best evidence for this because details on individual houses, and even exact measurements, for the whole town are available.[83] The schools in Oxford began adjacent to Saint Mary the Virgin, extending up Cat Street, and then to School Street. All Saints and Brasenose Colleges now occupy much of the site. We can form some idea of the number and size of the academic halls which came first into use. There is almost no information of this kind for Paris and Bologna. The founding of the various colleges is a subject of keen interest. These were doubtless inspired by the Franciscans and other communities, although we must not forget the "Dix-huit Clers" at Paris in 1180.[84] Much can be said about the formal organization of the university communities—their regulations, statutes, and privileges. In this connection we call attention to the requirements for a university of masters and students as formulated in the *Siete Partidas*, inspired by Alfonso X of Castile.[85] This last has received considerable attention by many predecessors. It belongs more with the study of the growth of institutions than it does with the survey of curricula. It was a product of a new Spiritus which blew strongly in the thirteenth century.

NOTES

1   Plato, *Republica*, 405a; Aristotle, *Politics*, VIII, 2; Cicero, *De officiis*, I, 42; *De oratore*, III, 32.

2   *Confessions*, IV, 16, 30; V, 6, 11; Migne, *Patrologia Latina*, 32, cols. 705, 710.

3   *Conf.*, V, 12, 22; Migne, *P.L.*, 32, col. 716.

4   *Etymologiae*, Bks. I–III; Alcuin, *Didascalica*, in Migne, *P.L.*, 101, cols. 950–75.

5   Richard McKeon, in *Speculum*, XVII (1942), 10. This article, entitled "Rhetoric in the Middle Ages" (pp. 1–32), is a profound analysis of the intellectual currents which produced the transition in twelfth-century education.

6   L. Maître, *Les écoles épiscopales et monastiques de l'occident depuis Charlemagne jusqu'à Philippe-Auguste* (Paris, 1865, 1924); Loren C. MacKinney, *Bishop Fulbert and Education at the School of Chartres*, The Mediaeval Institute, No. VI (Notre Dame, Indiana, 1957).

7   Sigebert in MGH SS, VIII, 536.

8   Ed. Le Prévôt, II, 69–70.

9   MacKinney, *Bishop Fulbert*, pp. 59–60.

10   Boethius on Music is rather a meager reference. Besides, his eighteen-tone gamut does not prepare one for the modal structure of plain chant.

11   Migne, *P.L.*, 150, col. 1394.

12   *Ibid.*, 156, col. 844.

13   C. H. Haskins, *The Renaissance of the Twelfth Century* (Cambridge, Mass., 1928), p. 138.

14   The eleventh-century schools at Orleans are praised in Migne, *P.L.*, 188, col. 366.

15   A. Fliche, *La réforme grégorienne*, I, II (Paris; Louvain, 1924).

16   F. Neukirck, *Das Leben des Petrus Damiani* (Göttingen, 1875).

17   M. Rule, *The Life and the Times of St. Anselm* (2 vols.; London, 1883); Migne, *P.L.*, 158, cols. 49–118.

18   Migne, *P.L.*, 158, col. 467.

19   *Ibid.*, col. 561.

20   *Ibid.*, cols. 259–61.

21   G. Robert, *Les écoles et l'enseignement de la théologie pendant la première moitié du XIIe siècle* (Paris, 1909); H. Weisweiler in *Beiträge zur Geschichte der Philosophie und Theologie des Mittelalters*, I–II (Münster, 1936).

22   L. Tosti, *Storia di Abelardo e dei suoi tempi* (Naples, 1851).

23   H. Weisweiler, in *Scholastik*, XX–XXIV (1949), 256–66; *Dictionnaire théologie catholique*, VII, cols. 239–306.

24   Migne, *P.L.*, 176, cols. 739–839. For our present purpose the most significant sections are in cols. 751, 751–53, and 768–69.

25   *Ibid.*, col. 709. We quote the description of those studying Nature: "...Alii de natura herbarum, de constitutionibus hominum, de qualitate rerum omnium et virtute pertractant."

26   *Ibid.*, 175, lxxvff.

27   *Ibid.*, 178, col. 979.

28   *Ibid.*, col. 1028.

29   *Ibid.*, col. 1338.

30   *Ibid.*, col. 1349.

31   *Policraticus*, ed. Webb, II, 622. The same idea is frequently expressed throughout the *Metalogicon*, II, 17, and *passim*.

32   In John Stow, *The Survey of London* (Dent, 1945), pp. 503–4.

33   John of Salisbury gives details on his schooling in *Metalogicon*, Bk. II, ch. 10. We supplement this from R. L. Poole's "The Masters of Paris" in the *English Historical Review*, XXV (1920), 321–42.

34   Gerald, ed. Brewer (Rolls Series), I, 92.

35   Letters of Stephen as Abbot are in Denifle et Chatelain, I, nos. 41–49. The bitter letter is no. 48. Pope Alexander III's letters on nonpayment for the licenses are nos. 4 and 12.

36   Ed. Thomas Wright in *Latin Poems Commonly Attributed to Walter Mapes*, pp. 21–30.

37   J. de Ghellinck in *Dictionnaire théologie catholique*, XII, cols. 1941–2019.

38   Migne, *P.L.*, 192, cols. 521–22.

39   Gerald the Welshman, ed. Brewer, II, 349; IV, 7.

40   A general description of the growth of canon law is given by Gabriel Le Bras in *The Legacy of the Middle Ages* (Oxford, n.d.), pp. 321–61.

41 A similar discussion on civil law is given by E. Meynial, *ibid.*, pp. 365–99.
42 A. Sieber, *Bischof Ivo von Chartres und seine Stellung zu den kirchen-politischen Fragen seiner Zeit* (Königsberg, 1885); P. Fournier in *Bull. Ec. des Chartes*, LVII (1896), LVIII (1897).
43 Migne, *P.L.*, 161, col. 47.
44 Albano Sorbelli and Luigi Simeoni, *Storia dell'Università di Bologna* (2 vols.; Bologna, 1940–47).
45 H. Fitting, *Die Anfängen der Rechtschule zu Bologna* (Berlin, 1888).
46 There are thirteen documents mentioning him between 1112 and 1125. See reference in note 41 above.
47 E. Niccolai, *Graziano da Chiusi* (Rome, 1933); *Graziano, Testi e studi camaldolesi* (Rome, 1949). See Dante's *Paradiso*, X, 1035.
48 Ed. Brewer, I, 48.
49 Forbidden by Honorius III in 1219.—Denifle et Chatelain, *Chartularium Universitatis Parisiensis*, I, 97.
50 Migne, *P.L.*, 207, Epistle 26; Denifle et Chatelain, no. 27.
51 Migne, *P.L.*, 207, Epistle 71; Denifle et Chatelain, no. 28.
52 McKeon, *loc. cit.*, p. 7.
53 Epistle 76.
54 Epistle 9; Denifle et Chatelain, no. 26. There is also Epistle 81 addressed to Canon Simeon of Chartres who, having studied for four years, is preparing to go into business.
55 Ed. Brewer, I, 288. "Tullius ait: si mihi etiam duplicaretur aetas, nunquam lyrica legerem."
56 Ed. Brewer, I, 271 ff. "Ranae significant carmina poetarum, quae inani et inflata modulatione velut ranarum, sonis et canticis mundo deceptionis fabulas intulerunt."
57 *Vie de saint-Thomas* of Guernes de Pont Sainte-Maxence, vv. 201 ff.
58 Ed. Brewer, II, 38; II, 344, 349.
59 Peter of Blois, Migne, *P.L.*, 207, Epistle 101; Denifle et Chatelain, I, 24, 25, 48; Gerald, IV, 7. See note 35 above.
60 Quoted by Gerald, II, 348.
61 *Ibid.*, IV, 7. Some of this is reconstructed from Anthony Wood.
62 *Ibid.*, II, 348.
63 *Ibid.*, p. 357.
64 *Ibid.*, p. 351.
65 *Ibid.*, p. 356.
66 *Ibid.*, IV, 3.
67 *Ibid.*, I, 23.
68 An old woman called to him on the night Philip Augustus was born.—Gerald, VIII.
69 Migne, *P.L.*, 176, cols. 760–63.
70 Published by C. H. Haskins in *Harvard Studies in Classical Philology*, XX (1909), 75–94. Cf. also Denifle et Chatelain, *Chartularium Universitatis Parisiensis*, I, 78.
71 Ed. Brewer, IV, 9.

72   L. Delisle, "Les écoles d'Orléans," in *Annuaire-Bulletin de l'Histoire de France*, VII (1869); Edmond Faral, *Les arts poétiques du XIIe siècle* (Paris, 1924).

73   Quoted by L. J. Paetow in his *The Battle of the Seven Arts* (Berkeley, 1914), p. 28. Professor Paetow made eminent contributions to the subject that is now being discussed in the Introduction to this edition (pp. 5–30), and in his "The Arts Course at Mediaeval Universities" in *University Studies of the University of Illinois*, III (1910).

74   Peter of Peckam, *Vie de Saint Richard*, ed. A. T. Baker, in *Rev. Lang. Rom.*, LIII (1910), 245–396.

75   *Morale Scolarium*, ed. L. J. Paetow (Berkeley, 1927), vv. 371–72.

76   Ed. A. Långfors (Paris: Champion, 1923). There is also an anonymous version, in quatrains, of the same era. This is included in Långfors' edition.

77   Epistle 43.

78   Armand Machabey, *Genèse de la tonalité classique* (Paris: Richard-Massé, 1955), Ch. IV.

79   While speaking against excesses in the teaching of logic Gerald says that men used to study *ex arte* and talk *circa artem*. Now they learn a little of the quadrivium which is a part of the seven arts that flourishes better in the East (meaning among the Moslems, no doubt) than it does in the West (II, 355).

80   C. H. Haskins, *Studies in Mediaeval Science* (Harvard Univ. Press, 1927), pp. 20–40.

81   Ed. Brewer, II, 356.

82   The information on John of London comes from the *Morale Scolarium*. See the Paetow edition, pp. 83–84.

83   H. E. Salter in *History*, n.s. XIV (1929–30), 57–61, 97–105. We cannot say with Dr. Salter that the early halls had four rooms to a floor. Our observation has been based upon visits to most of the extant ruins.

84   Denifle et Chatelain, I, no. 50. The "Dix-huit Clers" were followed by a foundation for thirteen poor scholars at St. Honoré in 1209, and there was a similar hospice at St. Thomas du Louvre in 1210.

85   Titulo XXI, Leyes I–XI.

Adolf Katzenellenbogen

The Representation of
the Seven Liberal Arts

If one studies the representations of the Seven Liberal Arts in the twelfth century one realizes that they are only a link in the whole chain of representations of this subject, and that a long tradition of ideas and forms lies behind their images. On the other hand, one becomes also aware of some essentially new aspects in their portrayal. First of all, it is in the twelfth century that the Liberal Arts enter the programs of sculptural decoration for church façades. Their places within these systems of decoration indicate in different ways the relation of secular learning to theological truths. Furthermore, the representations of the Liberal Arts in miniatures become sharply articulated and even develop into a whole philosophical system of a comprehensiveness and clarity not found until that time. One should also not forget that in the twelfth century Liberal Arts were chosen for the first time as decoration for candlesticks. Finally, it is important to keep in mind that the significance of the Liberal Arts varies according to the context in which they appear. On church façades they are seen as part of the whole program of representation, on manuscript pages in relation to specific texts, on candlesticks in relation to the light shed by the candles.

It is well known that the Royal Portal of Chartres Cathedral, decorated between about 1145 and 1155, is, in all likelihood, the first façade on which the Seven Liberal Arts were represented. Personifying the rational endeavors of man, they form part of an iconographical program that was rationally organized by the men who planned it.

On no other church façade of the twelfth century were the main christological dogmas represented with greater clarity. The two lateral tympana balance each other in meaning. On the right-hand side the Incarnation of Christ is shown by a number of scenes, on the left-hand side His Ascension. The central tympanum contains the second Coming of Christ at the end of time.

Two of the three tympana remain firmly rooted in the iconographical tradition. The ascending Christ had been represented before among archivolts with the Signs of the Zodiac and the Labors of the Months. Antecedents can be found likewise for the apocalyptic Christ surrounded by the twenty-four Elders. It is the right-hand tympanum that has an essentially new character (Fig. 2).

For the first time, as far as I know, Jesus enthroned on the Virgin's lap, that is to say the Seat of Wisdom incarnate, is brought into a definite axial relation to the Child in the Nativity scene and to the Child of the Presentation in the Temple. That Jesus is enthroned and adored by Angels while He is also lying on an altar-like table or standing on an altar expresses the idea of Godhead and manhood united in His person and the idea of His sacrifice.

The tympanum is not only surrounded by worshipping Angels but also by the Seven Liberal Arts. Underneath each Art a philosopher is portrayed who had excelled in that particular discipline.

The Liberal Arts are easily identifiable. The identity of the philosophers can only be suggested, as Emile Mâle has done,[1] according to the authors whose writings or theories were primarily used in the study of the arts at that time. We see arranged in circular sequence at first the Trivium: Grammar with Priscian or Donatus (on the lower right-hand side of the outer archivolt), Dialectic with Aristotle (on the lower left-hand side of the outer archivolt), and Rhetoric accompanied by Cicero. Then follow the members of the Quadrivium: Geometry and Euclid, Arithmetic and Boethius, Astronomy and Ptolemy, and finally, Music and Pythagoras.

The literary sources for the cycle of the Liberal Arts go ultimately back to antiquity. Greek philosophers had taught the various disciplines and thus provided their substance. Varro was most likely the first one to classify them in the first century B.C. He had established a system of nine disciplines, including in addition to the Seven Liberal Arts, Medicine and Architecture which were counted among the mechanical arts later on. Martianus Capella had taken another important step. He had personified the Liberal Arts in his allegorical-didactic treatise *De Nuptiis Philologiae et Mercurii*, written between 410 and 439. Thus he had lent actual forms to mere concepts and inspired artists to do likewise. By describing the appearance and the attributes of the Arts, he had provided a rich vocabulary of representation. Artists and their learned advisers selected attributes for the Liberal Arts from those mentioned by Martianus Capella and a strong pictorial tradition developed. But they also chose attributes from other literary sources and even invented attributes wherever it seemed desirable.

Finally, it was Boethius who, early in the sixth century, had given structure to the system of the Liberal Arts. He had called the four mathematical disciplines (Arithmetic, Geometry, Music, and Astronomy) the Quadrivium. This fourfold path to wisdom, he thought, should be followed by the student of philosophical disciplines if he wanted to reach the height of perfection.[2] The three other Arts were accordingly termed Trivium from Carolingian times.

The earliest representation of the Liberal Arts which has come down to us is a miniature of the Quadrivium in the Boethius manuscript written for the Emperor Charles the Bald (Fig. 3).[3] Arithmetic, the science of numbers, stands next to Music who deals with the proportional relation of tones. Geometry, the science of immobile magnitudes, is paired with Astronomy (labeled Astrology in the miniature), the science of mobile magnitudes. The miniature is obviously based on an earlier model. It embodies the literary tradition of Martianus Capella and an even older pictorial tradition, namely the representation of Muses in classical art. The arrangement of the figures, their attire, and the use of a small column to serve as stand for the tablet of Geometry bear witness to the influence exerted by the portrayal of the Muses.

As far as we can judge from *tituli*, the Seven Liberal Arts and their human representatives had served in all likelihood as wall decoration in one of Charlemagne's palaces.[4] Their portrayal was obviously stimulated by the educational reforms of the emperor and was meant to make known in his own residence the important part he had played in the restoration of learning.

The cycle on the Royal Portal owes its existence in a similar manner to a specific stimulus, this time provided by the School of Chartres. Here the studies of the Liberal Arts were thriving in the first half of the twelfth century. We have only to remember the names of Bernard of Chartres and William of Conches, of Gilbert de la Porrée and Thierry of Chartres. The figures of the Seven Liberal Arts and of their retinue of sages were carved at a time when Thierry was chancellor of the School. He had finished composing his *Heptateuchon*, the handbook of the Seven Liberal Arts. In its prologue he had succinctly defined the specific roles of Trivium and Quadrivium, one illuminating the mind, the other making its expression elegant, rational, and ornate. Thierry had explicitly stated that he was not collecting his own inventions in the handbook, but those of the principal teachers of the arts. In his own writings Thierry had stressed the importance of proofs directly derived from the Quadrivium for an understanding of the Creator. And he had used a mathematical figure, the square, to explain in a rational manner the creation of the Son by the Father and the equality of the Son with the Father.[5]

A poetical epitaph dedicated to Thierry's memory praises him for his relentless search in both Quadrivium and Trivium whereby he made them known to everyone.[6] The author of the poem goes still further in his desire to extol Thierry's success as a teacher. Philosophy, we read, hitherto chaste and reserved, gave herself up to Thierry. Married to him, she brought forth many illustrious men for the whole world. These words smack of exuberant oratory. Nevertheless, they are true in essence. Men like John of Salisbury or Clarenbaldus of Arras had been among Thierry's pupils.

Thierry's responsibility as chancellor of the School, his intense concern with the Liberal Arts as instruments of Philosophy, his trust in their usefulness for a rational explanation of theological truths must have caused their representation around the Incarnation cycle of the Royal Portal. His strong admiration for the philosophers of the past must have led to the decision that their images should be added to the group of the Liberal Arts. About twenty-five years earlier, an Incarnation cycle had been carved in a more expressive style for a tympanum at Vézelay. Here exclusive emphasis was given to the religious scenes. Rosettes and plant motives were deemed sufficient to serve as frame.

The place accorded the Liberal Arts at Chartres has special significance. Decorating the archivolts, they were brought into a direct relation to Jesus enthroned. The instruments of human wisdom exemplified at the periphery of the tympanum are thus bound to Divine Wisdom in the center. This makes it clear that man's striving for knowledge is dependent on, and directed towards, Divine Wisdom.

With the exception of Dialectic whose essence could best be represented by symbols of good and evil, a flower and a dragon equipped with the head and the forelegs of a sharp-toothed dog, the Liberal Arts are actively engaged in their specific tasks. Grammar, for instance, teaches two boys. Music creates tones by striking bells with a hammer. The philosophers, on the other hand, are less sharply differentiated from each other. They are either meditating or writing. Thus the concept that there are different branches of learning with separate methods is made real by the activity of ideal figures and not by the activity of their human representatives.

The lucidity with which an intricate system of theological truths is represented here within the framework of rational endeavors is the result of the fortuitous coöperation between a learned cleric suggesting a clear system of ideas and sculptors working with a vocabulary of forms equally clear due to the rise of the Gothic style at that time.

On other church façades of the twelfth century, the realm of secular studies was likewise made part of the iconographical program, namely about 1160 on the north portal of Notre Dame in Déols, destroyed in 1830, and about the end of the century on the west façade of Laon Cathedral. On both façades the Liberal Arts retain their peripheral places in archivolts but they are by no means mere copies of the Chartres group. First of all, both cycles include Philosophy, the personification of the general concept that embodies the Liberal Arts. The particular position of Philosophy in relation to the Arts becomes, therefore, significant. New possibilities of meaning are explored and various definitions given to Philosophy are reflected. Other personifications were also added, Natural Science at Déols, Architecture and Medicine at Laon. The philosophers, on the other hand, were eliminated.

We know from descriptions that at Déols the group of the Liberal Arts surrounded the apocalyptic Christ in majesty.[7] Here their subordination to Philosophy was emphasized. Her figure was placed at the apex of the archivolt. She gave scrolls to two of the Arts, Grammar and Dialectic. This made it clear that the Arts receive their substance from her. That Natural Science is added to the cycle and follows Music seems to show the influence of Hugh of St. Victor's *Didascalion*. In this work he had dealt with Natural Science right after he had discussed the Quadrivium.[8]

The cycle at Laon decorates an archivolt framing a window on the second story of the façade.[9] Philosophy forms the beginning of the whole group. Her representation was obviously shaped after the description Boethius had given in *De Consolatione Philosophiae*.[10] A ladder is placed against her breast and her head reaches partly into clouds. That part of the head which is hidden from view symbolizes the highest part of philosophy, namely theology, extending into the sphere of Divine Reason. Thereby the wide range of philosophy is shown. The spectator looking at the whole sequence of personifications from left to right, sees the image of Philosophy, an introductory figure as it were, and the nine spokes of the ladder indicate that there are Seven Liberal Arts and two additional Arts according to Varro's classification.

About 1200 the Liberal Arts received a new place on the façade of Sens Cathedral (Fig. 4). No longer do we find them, as at Chartres or Déols, in archivolts close to Christ. Instead, they decorate the lower part of the façade, namely the socle zone to the left of the central portal underneath saints whose statues have since been destroyed. Now the sequence of the Liberal Arts implies the gradual progression of secular studies. In contrast to Laon, Philosophy forms the end of the group. The cycle begins with the Trivium, farthest away from the door. Then comes the Quadrivium and finally Philosophy. Once again philosophers were added to the group but without exact numerical relation. Two masters precede Grammar. Two others come after Philosophy.

As in Laon the representation of Philosophy is indebted to the description Boethius had given of her. The sculptor of Sens disregarded the motives of cloud and ladder, but borrowed from the text the letter Π as ornament for the lower border of Philosophy's garment, and the letter θ as decoration for the upper border of her robe. Philosophy was thus defined according to the Aristotelian concept of practical and theoretical philosophy as Boethius had transmitted it to the Middle Ages in the graphic image he had used.

The particular location of the Liberal Arts and of Philosophy at Sens shows now their exact position within a hierarchical system of values. Their superposition over animals and other creatures denotes their superiority over the lower animal world. Their place in the socle zone indicates that they represent fundamental knowledge and are subservient to theological doctrines.

John of Salisbury had used architectural concepts of the same kind in order to explain the relation of reason, the instrument of the Arts, to faith: "As it is necessary for buildings to have some fixed and stable base on which the structure to be erected can rest, so in every doctrine well considered reason requires by necessity some stable starting point." [11]

If we look just one decade ahead into the thirteenth century we will find that still another place was assigned to the Liberal Arts on the west façade of Notre-Dame in Paris. The original reliefs no longer exist but, according to Viollet-le-Duc,[12] they decorated the pedestal underneath the statue of Christ in the central door. Remaining within the lower zone, the group of the Arts was compactly drawn together. Once more they were brought into direct relation to Christ, the Wisdom of the Lord. Thus ideas expressed at Chartres and Sens were harmonized here. As at Sens, the Liberal Arts were shown as the foundation of higher knowledge, subservient to theological truths. As at Chartres, their place close to Christ indicates that they are dependent on, and directed towards, Divine Wisdom.

The only other figure decorations in the socle zone of the central portal are twelve Virtues enthroned above Vices. This cycle is represented underneath the statues of Apostles on the jambs. Seen together, the Liberal Arts and the Virtues exemplify the idea that knowledge and virtue by which man is similar to God can give integrity to human life.

On church façades the Liberal Arts were visible to the whole congregation as it entered the church. Miniatures of the Liberal Arts were painted for the learned reader. Whatever the location of the Liberal Arts on church façades may be, they form but a small part of the whole iconographical program. In book illuminations, on the other hand, the Liberal Arts are independent of religious connotations where they illustrate treatises on particular Arts and derive their substance from the text in which they are embedded. Only where their representations are determined by more general philosophical concepts are they apt to indicate the dependence of human wisdom on Divine Wisdom.

Miniatures of the Liberal Arts vary from decorative designs to highly organized ideological systems including intricate inscriptions to clarify the meaning. They represent the realm of studies on various levels ranging from a more specific to a more general plane. They illustrate the practice of the Arts. They portray the masters who were instrumental in originating them and they represent the personifications of the Liberal Arts themselves.

A South German manuscript of Isidore's *Etymologiae*, to be dated about 1150, may serve as an example for the illustrations of the practical use made of the different Arts. The initial of the word Arithmetic shows a man counting numbers. The initial of Music encloses a musician plucking an instrument. The *A* of Astronomy contains a man gazing at the stars.[13]

On a higher conceptual level miniatures portray outstanding representatives of a single discipline, either alone or in conjunction with the Art. A miniature in a French manuscript of about 1140 precedes the commentary of Boethius to Porphyry's *Isagoge* (Fig. 5).[14] Exalted on a pedestal and crowned, *Dialectica domina* holds in her left hand a snake manifoldly knotted because the problems of Dialectic are complicated. Her right hand grasps a floral scepter. It forms vines enclosing in the center the names of genera, in the lateral scrolls those of species according to the text of the treatise. This stemma appears in other copies of the treatise only in the text, in order to clarify for the reader the proper sequence of genera and species. In the miniature it is appended to the scepter.

By size and place Dialectic dominates four outstanding representatives of her discipline, Plato and Aristotle at the top, Socrates and a Magister Adam in the lower corners. Magister Adam is in all likelihood Adam of Petit Pont. He had treated the *Analytica priora* as early as 1132 in his *Ars dialectica*. Thus a contemporary master is accorded the honor of joining the group of great philosophers and of participating in their dialectical arguments.

The miniature gains its precision of meaning by the ideographical stemma rather than by figure representation. This was obviously the best way of making the substance of Dialectic visible.

To represent the field of Music offered different possibilities to a book illuminator. An English miniature of about 1160—it decorates a manuscript of Boethius' *De Musica*—does not show Music herself but gives a very graphic representation of four philosophers who had laid the theoretical foundations of the Art: Boethius, Pythagoras, Plato, and Nicomachus (Fig. 6).[15]

The miniature clearly shows the different ways used by the philosophers to arrive at certain truths. Separated by vertical bands of inscriptions, Boethius and Pythagoras play instruments. Joined as a group, Plato and Nicomachus are disputing. This differentiation goes even further, due in part to elaborate marginal inscriptions. Plucking the string of a monochord, Boethius judges the sound with his ear in order to understand tonal intervals. Pythagoras goes beyond mere judgment by listening as the text of the treatise explains and tries a more valid experiment. He uses a pair of scales, some hammers, and a set of bells for this purpose. By finding out about the right weight of the hammers and by striking bells he discovers the proportional relationship of consonances. Both men derive knowledge from experiments with different instruments,

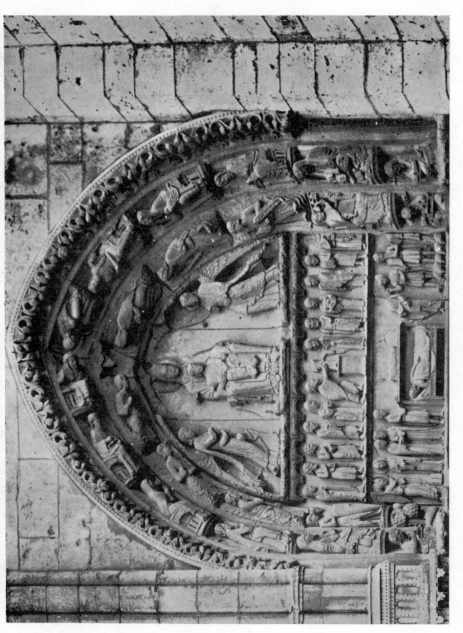

Fig. 2. Incarnation Tympanum and Cycle of the Liberal Arts, *Chartres Cathedral, Royal Portal.*

MVSICA · ARITHMETICA · GEOMETRIA · ASTROLOGIA

Fig. 3. Quadrivium, *from a Boethius Manuscript, Bamberg.*

FIG. 4. Astronomy, Philosophy, and a Philosopher, *Sens Cathedral, West Façade, Detail.*

FIG. 5. Dialectic and Philosophers, *from a Boethius Manuscript, Darmstadt.*

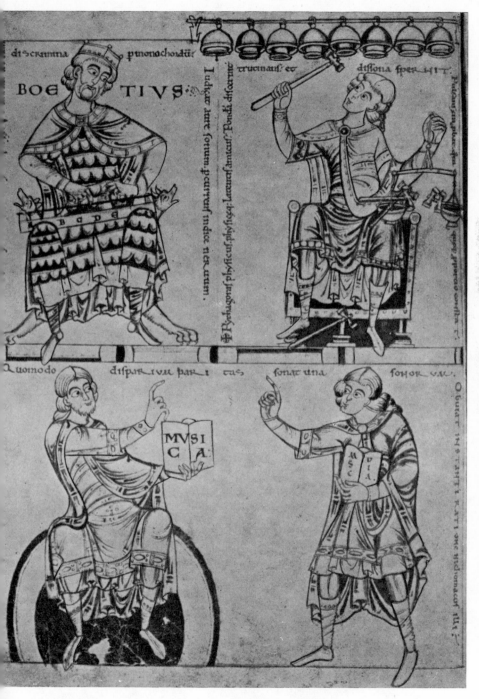

6. Boethius, Pythagoras, Plato, and Nicomachus, *from a Boethius Manuscript, Cambridge.*

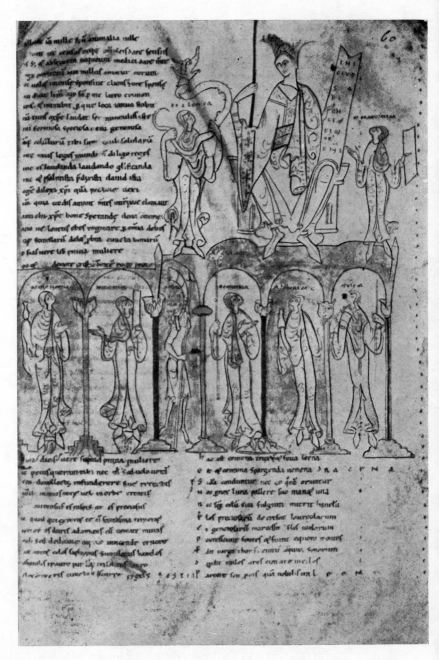

FIG. 7. Philosophy and Her Seven Daughters, *from a French Manuscript, Paris.*

Fig. 8. Philosophy and the Liberal Arts, *Collection R. v. Hirsch, Basle.*

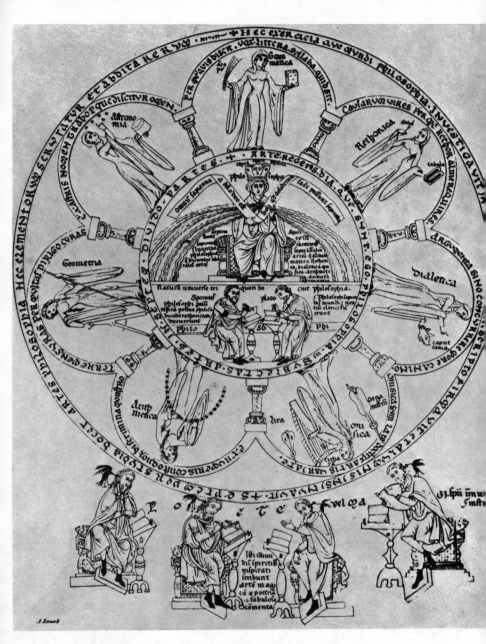

Fig. 9. Philosophy and the Liberal Arts, *Miniature, Hortus Deliciarum.*

Fig. 10. Candelabrum, *Detail, Milan Cathedral.*

FIG. 11. Candelabrum, *Detail, Milan Cathedral.*

the monochord producing tones by plucking, the set of bells by percussion. Plato and Nicomachus, on the other hand, deal with the mere concepts of music. Their methods exemplify *lectio* and *disputatio*. Plato teaches (*edocet*) about the consonance of different sounds. Nicomachus is arguing with him. As the inscription says, he opposes Plato by instant argument.

In an ingenious manner the painter has made this clear. Strong emphasis is given to the book held by Plato. It is large in size and bears the prominent inscription *Musica*. Plato is obviously teaching. The book in the hand of Nicomachus is much smaller as is the lettering on it. His gesturing right hand is stressed, strongly expressing his argument.

Finally, three of the philosophers are characterized through by-names. Boethius is called an investigator of the most exalted philosophy, while Pythagoras is named a student of nature and a lover of nature's secrets. Plato is given the title of the highest of the philosophers. He does not sit on a chair like Boethius and Pythagoras but on an orb corresponding to the spherical shape of the world according to the *Timaeus*. This ideal seat may well symbolize the throne of wisdom which, in the words of John of Salisbury, Plato, the prince of the philosophers, had occupied for a long time.[16]

The miniature is more than a portrayal of four philosophers concerned with music. It has been sharpened into a system that clarifies the various problems of the discipline, the diverse methods used by the sages, and the different types of philosophers.

Where the Liberal Arts are represented on an allegorical level as a whole group in relation to Philosophy or Wisdom, a definite change from a rather loose configuration to a tightly organized system can be observed.

A miniature of the late eleventh century, first published by M.-Th. d'Alverny, illustrates a poem that fuses didactic and bucolic elements (Fig. 7).[17] Wisdom is shown as the mother of the Liberal Arts with her seven daughters. Gracefully enthroned, she holds a floral scepter and a scroll with the inscription: "The fear of the Lord is the beginning of wisdom" (Prov. I, 7). Secular knowledge is thereby programmatically linked to the teachings of the Bible about the basic condition of human wisdom. Two Liberal Arts stand next to their mother, the other five are represented underneath in an arcade. The arrangement is by no means systematic. Dialectic and Grammar flank Wisdom, but Rhetoric, the third member of the Trivium, appears in the lower group among Geometry and Music. One half-arch even contains a shepherd who in the poem came to greet the group on Mount Parnassus.' The miniature, therefore, adds an incidental figure to the personifications of the Liberal Arts. Only Dialectic is identified by a special symbol, a large snake. The other Arts have attributes of a more general kind, scrolls, urns, and scepters. Their identity depends solely on the inscription of their names The artist was obviously not concerned with a clear didactic differentiation of the seven disciplines.

In two miniatures of the second half of the twelfth century a more rational composition and a more definite characterization of the Liberal Arts has become the aim of the artists.

A German miniature of about 1160 in the collection of Robert von Hirsch in Basle shows the coherence of the whole figure group with great clarity (Fig. 8). Philosophy is made the dominating figure in the center. She holds a scepter and two books, one small, the other large, probably referring to the Trivium and the Quadrivium. She is represented only as a half-figure. The lower part of her body dissolves as it were into seven streams that flow from her breast into the mouths of the Liberal Arts. Thus they are all equally connected with her. Furthermore, they receive their substance from her, according to the age-old idea of streams exemplifying nourishment and the emanation of enlivening powers. The Arts are arranged in a continuous curve. Their attributes clearly differentiate them from one another. Grammar holds a key and a box that, according to Martianus Capella, contains all the instruments she needs. Rhetoric is clad in arms as Martianus describes her. Dialectic partly hides a dragon-like snake under her mantle. We see only its body and claws. In her right hand she holds a disc with circles, probably representing the little forms of which Martianus speaks. Arithmetic holds a tablet with mathematical figures. Next to her is Music playing the psaltery. Geometry bears a square and a sphere, and Astronomy is winged.

The illuminator has further enhanced the validity of the philosophical system. He has created an ideal space for all the figures within cloud edges. He makes the spectator aware that only Philosophy reaches into the higher sphere of the sky illuminated by the sun, the moon, and the stars.

Even more comprehensive in scope, clearer in its geometrically conceived composition and by accompanying inscriptions is the famous miniature in the *Hortus Deliciarum* of Herrad of Landsberg (Fig. 9). Herrad had compiled and illuminated her gigantic encyclopedia after she had become abbess of the convent of Hohenburg in Alsace in 1168.

Organized according to the architectural shape of a rose window, the miniature illustrates the relation of the Liberal Arts to Philosophy and to one another. In addition, it shows their relation to the right philosophers and to false arts. Circular schemata had been used in antiquity and since that time for the representation of cosmological or other ideological cycles. Herrad might well have derived the general layout of the miniature from an engraved liturgical bronze bowl, but she sharpened and expanded composition and meaning into an intricate philosophical system.[18] She conveys definite ideas through the mere arrangement of the figures in different sections of the geometrical schema: within the inner circle, inside the outer ring, and outside the circle.

The central circle is divided into uneven segments, the larger one allotted to Philosophy herself, the smaller one to the realm of ancient philosophy. Philosophy is enthroned in the upper part. The three heads on her crown denote her threefold division into Natural Science, Ethics, and Logic. This division had been ascribed to Plato by Cicero and St. Augustine, and afterwards by many authors. The scrolls in her hands refer with basic precision to cause and effect of wisdom: "All wisdom is from the Lord God" (Eccl. I, 1) and: "Only the wise are able to do what they wish." The seven streams emanating from her do not flow directly into the mouths of the Liberal Arts. They are mere symbols explained by the inscription: "Seven fountains of wisdom flow from Philosophy. They are called Liberal Arts." A corresponding inscription establishes once more a link between human wisdom and Divine Wisdom: "The Holy Spirit," it says, "is the inventor of the Liberal Arts."

At the top of the lower segment the achievements of ancient philosophy are stated: "Philosophy has taught how to investigate the nature of the universe." This concept is illustrated by the figures of Socrates and Plato. They are accorded places underneath Philosophy, in a separate realm but still within the inner sanctum. The two philosophers are not related to any two particular Arts but to Philosophy as a whole. Their fundamental role is made evident by their particular places and by the inscription: "They taught at first ethics, then natural science and finally rhetoric." That their wisdom transcended the secular sphere is stressed by the sentence: "They were the sages of the world and the clerics of the gentiles."

The inscription around the inner circle describes Philosophy as the ruler over the Seven Liberal Arts. The inscription surrounding the outer circle explains more specifically the proper sequence of exercises: first to investigate, then to explain the investigation, to confirm it in writing, and finally to teach it to the pupils.

With finite precision the Arts are so arranged in the outer ring that they radiate equally from the center and form a complete circle. Each is enclosed by an arch and thereby accorded a realm of her own. This perfect geometrical layout expresses the idea of their equal validity and their interdependence. One might think here of a postulate made by Hugh of St. Victor: "In such manner are they [i.e., the Liberal Arts] interdependent and in mutual need of each other's principles that if one is missing the others can not make a philosopher."[19] Each figure is given significant attributes. These are often labeled so as to exclude any misunderstanding. In addition, the functions of the Arts are explained by inscriptions. Their methods are, therefore, precisely defined, for these should not be mingled, as Hugh of St. Victor had pointed out.[20]

Outside the circle four writers of magic arts and poetry in the sense of fictitious ideas are inspired by black birds, symbols of evil spirits. Hugh of St. Victor held that the magic arts are outside philosophy and do not form part of it.[21] In a comprehensive manner the four figures illustrate different stages of activity. The first one meditates, the second one writes, the next man explains the text, and the last one sharpens his quill with a knife. Their benches, covered by rugs and cushions, compete in richness with the seat of Philosophy. Socrates and Plato, in contrast to them, sit modestly on a plank.

This beautifully lucid composition illustrates graphically the essence and validity of secular studies, but one should not forget that the didactic miniature is inserted in a whole sequence of Biblical scenes. With loving care Herrad has spared no efforts to clarify the most subtle ideas for the intellect. Painted as instruction for nuns, the miniature differs strongly from another earlier miniature, likewise designed for the use of nuns and equally concerned with the acquisition of knowledge. The miniature to which I am referring illustrates the *Speculum Virginum*.[22] This treatise was in all likelihood composed by Conrad of Hirsau early in the twelfth century. Copiously illustrated, it remained very popular throughout that century as a great number of copies bears witness. The miniature is called *Mystical Paradise* by the author. The four Rivers of Paradise as they went forth from the fountain are set in parallel to the four Gospels and to the ecclesiastical doctrines as they flow from Christ, the source of all wisdom. Arranged like the four arms of a cross around the central figure of Paradise holding a medallion with the figure of Christ, the personifications of the Rivers bear discs containing the symbols of the Evangelists and the four Fathers of the Church. The text of the treatise urges the nuns to drink from these fountains in order to imitate both the eight Beatitudes and the four Cardinal Virtues, for they encompass the whole essence of spiritual discipline. Personifications of the Beatitudes stand between the Rivers. Four trees radiate from the center towards the corners of the miniature. They bear the Cardinal Virtues in their crowns. Nowhere in the text is there an indication that the study of the Liberal Arts should be a preparatory step for achieving these aims.

These two miniatures are indicative of two different concepts about knowledge, the *Mystical Paradise* conforming to the ideas of those who, like St. Bernard, did not put much trust in the Liberal Arts, the miniature of the *Hortus Deliciarum* corresponding to the ideas of those who, like Hugh of St. Victor, stressed the importance of secular studies as preparation for the Sacred Scriptures.

The belief in the importance of the various philosophical disciplines even reshapes the content of a Bible miniature. Traditionally the beginning of Ecclesiasticus: "All wisdom is from the Lord God" had been illustrated by the initial *O* containing the figure of Wisdom personified. It was, indeed, a bold step when about 1160 Philosophy took over the place of Wisdom. In the Bible from St. Thierry at Reims she holds half-circles that enclose the figures of Natural Science and Logic.[23] Another segment of a circle is placed at the feet of Philosophy. It contains the figure of Ethics. The filiation of definitions becomes even further ramified according to Alcuin's division of philosophy.[24] Natural Science holds four discs with the names of the Quadrivium. Logic holds corresponding discs with the names of Grammar and Rhetoric. Discs with the names of the cardinal virtues are joined to the figure of Ethics. The importance of rational concepts is thus stressed within the Bible itself and the gradual filiation is made clear by the decrease in figure size and, geometrically, by the diminution from a large circle to smaller circle parts to still smaller circles.

Where the Liberal Arts decorate candlesticks, another facet of their meaning is made visible. There had been a long tradition for representing on candlesticks symbolically the conflict between light and darkness which is the conflict between good and evil. On a candlestick made for Bishop Bernward of Hildesheim early in the eleventh century, for instance, human figures try to extricate themselves from sin and to strive toward the light.[25] Other candlesticks include the Evangelists or their symbols and the four Rivers of Paradise likened by medieval writers to the four cardinal virtues and to the four Gospels. The Sacred Scriptures and moral forces that can help man in his desire to reach the light are thus visibly stressed or implied. Dragons serving as feet are functional not only structurally but also symbolically.

In the second half of the twelfth century personifications of philosophical concepts enter the program of representation for the first time, as far as I know. They proclaim visibly that intellectual endeavors, too, can enlighten man. A candlestick in the Cathedral of Hildesheim, a work of the Mosan School of about 1170, has at its base the personified parts of Philosophy as Hugh of St. Victor had defined them.[26] Philosophy herself holds small busts of Theoretical and Practical Philosophy. She is accompanied by Logic and by Medicine who represents the mechanical arts. Calmly seated, the three figures triumph over the dragons that serve as feet and over others that try in vain to raise their heads.

On the famous candelabrum in Milan Cathedral of the end of the twelfth century the idea of the struggle between light and darkness is more fully and dramatically spun out.[27] With its seven branches it is shaped after the candlestick made by Moses on God's command. This candlestick had been interpreted by medieval writers as a symbol of Christ, "the true Light, which lighteth every man that cometh into the world" (John I, 9), so that the sinner will be able to see his own darkness. On the shaft of the Milan candelabrum Christ is worshipped by the three Magi. He is the Light and Divine Wisdom. The lower part of the candelabrum contains a complex system of figures. They pertain to the realms of nature, of knowledge, of ethics, and of religious history with the explicit or implied idea of the victory of light over darkness, of good over evil, of wisdom over ignorance.

The doom of evil forces is dramatically shown by the fall of the four large dragons (Fig. 10). Their heads are attacked by figures likewise symbolizing evil so that the forces of sin destroy each other. The spiral tails of the monsters, devoid of all energy, contain the four Rivers of Paradise and four of the Liberal Arts. In the intermediary sections the eye may recognize within exuberantly spiralling vines the twelve Signs of the Zodiac, eight Virtues overcoming Vices, and eight scenes from the Old Testament. Similar cycles were used in the twelfth century as floor decoration for churches as we know from descriptions, thus forming "fundamental" systems because of their location.

At first glance, the dynamic design of the Milan candelabrum seems to have absorbed completely any clarity of the iconographical program. Each figure is entwined in vines and subordinated to the total decorative effect rather than having an importance of its own. A closer look, however, reveals that a definite iconographical substructure exists underneath the decorative effect. The sequence of the Signs of the Zodiac runs in the same direction as the historical sequence of the biblical scenes. The four Rivers represent the four ages of man, when viewed in the same way.

Of the four Liberal Arts two belong to the Trivium, two to the Quadrivium. They are so arranged that each pair is coördinated with one of the two epochs of Old Testament history. Rhetoric belongs to the Temptation and Expulsion, Logic to Noah in the Ark and to the Sacrifice of Isaac, that is to say to the era before the Law. Geometry is coördinated with scenes from the life of Moses. The next section (Fig. 11) shows in the upper left Music, and below, Esther and Ahasuerus as well as David's victory over Goliath.[28] The two members of the Quadrivium are, therefore, linked with the epoch under the Law. Consequently, the progression from the Trivium to the Quadrivium corresponds to the progression from the era before the Law to the epoch under the Law.

Here the Liberal Arts are made part of an intricate program. They demonstrate their importance for overcoming the darkness of ignorance. At the same time, they complement the Rivers of Paradise who imply the four ages of man and the flow of the Gospels. As on the central portal of Notre Dame in Paris, they are coördinated with Virtues.

Most of the works I have discussed were created between about 1140 and 1200. It was during this period that new tendencies came to the fore. In sculpture and miniature painting alike we witness the probing of ever different possibilities to clarify the system of learning for the eye and the mind. The Seven Liberal Arts were included in programs of representation where up to that time no place had been given to them; but more than that, Philosophy was accorded different places in relation to the Liberal Arts. Above the group of seven she was shown as a supereminent concept (Déols, Basle miniature), at their beginning as a primary concept (Laon), at their end as a final concept (Sens), and in their midst as a central concept (*Hortus Deliciarum*). Each change emphasized a new aspect of their relationship and kept the representations of the Liberal Arts from becoming a mere formula.

Adjacent or subordinated to theological doctrines, the Liberal Arts proclaimed the importance of secular learning on church façades while the emphasis remained centered on the religious scenes in the tympana and on the large statues of holy figures. It was left to the art of a still distant future to create a balance between the realms of theology and philosophy.

Illumination of darkness through rational endeavors became apparent in the decoration of candlesticks. The realization of this concept proved fruitful for the future. In the Pisa pulpit finished by Nicola Pisano in 1259, the dark region underneath the pulpit is still inhabited by figures symbolic of ignorance and evil. In the Siena pulpit begun six years later, the same area of darkness is "illuminated" by Philosophy and the Seven Liberal Arts clustered around the central base.

And when we see living personalities related to the Liberal Arts in paintings of the Renaissance we should remember that one root of this type of representation goes back to the twelfth century. We might think here of Adam of Petit Pont who had belonged, however modestly, to the retinue of Dialectic.[29]

NOTES

1   *L'art religieux du XIIIe siècle en France* (6th ed.; Paris, 1925), pp. 82ff.
2   *De institutione arithmetica*, I, 1 (Migne, *P.L.*, 63, col. 1079).
3   Bamberg, Staatsbibl., Ms. H. J. IV, 12, fol. 9v.
4   *Monumenta Germaniae Historica, Poetae latini medii aevi*, I, 408ff.
5   W. Jansen, *Der Kommentar des Clarenbaldus von Arras zu Boethius' De Trinitate* (Breslau, 1926), p. 13*.
6   André Vernet, "Une épitaphe inédite de Thierry de Chartres," *Recueil de travaux offert à M. Clovis Brunel* (Paris, 1955), II, 66off.
7   Jean Hubert, "L'abbatiale de Notre-Dame de Déols," *Bulletin monumental*, LXXXVI (1927), 5ff.
8   *Didascalion*, II, 17 (Migne, *P.L.*, 176, col. 757).
9   Lucien Broche, *La cathédrale de Laon* (Paris, 1926), Fig., p. 75.
10   I, prose 1 (*Boethius*, ed. H. F. Stewart and E. K. Rand [London, New York, 1926], p. 136).
11   *Policraticus*, VII, 7, ed. C. C. J. Webb (Oxford, 1909), II, 116.
12   *Dictionnaire raisonné de l'architecture française* (2nd ed.; Paris, 1859), II, 8.
13   Stuttgart, Württemb. Landesbibl., Cod. poet. et philol. fol. 33, fols. 29r, 26v, 31r (Karl Löffler, *Schwäbische Buchmalerei in romanischer Zeit* [Augsburg, 1928], pl. 42b–d).
14   Darmstadt, Landesbibl., Ms. 2282.
15   Cambridge, Univ. Libr., Ms. Ii.3.12, fol. 61v.
16   *Policraticus*, VII, 5, ed. C. C. J. Webb, II, 105.

17 Paris, Bibl. nat., Ms. lat. 3110, fol. 6or.—M.-Th. d'Alverny, "La Sagesse et ses sept filles. Recherches sur les allégories de la philosophie et des arts libéraux du IXe au XIIe siècle," *Mélanges dédiés à la memoire de Félix Grat*, I, (Paris, 1946), 245ff., especially 261ff.

18 For the relation of the miniature to a bowl in Angermund, see Josepha Weitzmann-Fiedler, "Romanische Bronzeschalen mit mythologischen Darstellungen," *Zeitschrift für Kunstwissenschaft*, XI (1957), 1ff., especially 30ff.

19 *Didascalion*, III, 5 (Migne, *P.L.*, 176, col. 769).

20 *Ibid.*, III, 6 (*P.L.*, 176, col. 769f.).

21 *Ibid.*, VI, 15 (*P.L.*, 176, col. 810).

22 Adolf Katzenellenbogen, *Allegories of the Virtues and Vices in Mediaeval Art* (London, 1939), p. 69f., Fig. 68.

23 d'Alverny, *op. cit.*, Pl. II.

24 *De dialectica*, I (*P.L.*, 101, col. 952).

25 Francis J. Tschan, *Saint Bernward of Hildesheim*, III (Notre Dame, Indiana, 1952), Figs. 107, 110f.

26 Otto von Falke and Erich Meier, *Bronzegeräte des Mittelalters*, I (Berlin, 1935), p. 99, Pl. 21. For the division of philosophy, see *Didascalion*, II, 2 (Migne, *P.L.*, 176, col. 752).

27 Otto Homburger, *Der Trivulzio-Kandelaber* (Zurich, 1949).

28 The particular relation between some Arts and personalities of the Old Testament can be explained for the most part by St. Augustine's *City of God*. Rhetoric is placed next to Adam and Eve, because the fallen Angel used the serpent to insinuate his persuasive guile into the mind of man (*City of God*, XIV, 11). When the dove returned with an olive leaf, Noah drew the conclusion that the waters had receded (Gen. VIII, 11). Abraham obeyed the Lord, but he knew that his son would rise again because of the earlier promise about Isaac's seed (*City of God*, XVI, 32). Noah and Abraham, therefore, exemplify Logic. Geometry accompanies Moses because he was learned in all the wisdom of the Egyptians who took delight in geometry (*City of God*, XV, 27). The relation of Music to David is obvious.

29 Illustrations 1 and 3 are reproduced with the kind permission of the Bildarchiv Foto Marburg.

 Part II TRANSITIONS IN ECONOMY AND SOCIETY

Hilmar C. Krueger

Economic Aspects of
Expanding Europe

Views and interpretations of the twelfth century carry number, indeed, if not always clarity and conviction. In these respects economic historians are not at all different from their more learned colleagues. Fortunately, however, the dates of the twelfth century permit this essayist, first, to disregard the controversies that pertain to the rise of towns and the beginning of trade and, secondly, to eliminate from his discussion the later medieval culmination of several other economic developments. However, no one is to assume, as far as economic matters go, that the twelfth century offers a judicious balance between paucity and plethora of sources and that the economic historians write and speak of the century in pleasant agreement.

The expansion of Europe in the twelfth century occurred in all directions, but the time limit of presentation makes it advisable to select but three areas of this expansion. It is possible, I think, to indicate the most significant economic forces at work in western Europe on the basis of the selected examples. In the century under review French and Spanish feudal barons extended their domains south of the Pyrenees at the expense of the Moslems, while English kings and their feudal armies brought parts of Wales, Ireland, and Scotland under royal authority. We will not concern ourselves with these ventures nor with the exciting heroic overseas expeditions to Iceland and Greenland and the more gradual penetration of northern Scandinavia. Instead, we will review the expansionist movement overseas into the Near East, the movement of the Crusades. It, after all, was the most influential of the numerous expansionist movements of the twelfth century and cannot easily be eliminated from our discussion. Secondly, we will concentrate on the colonization movement in northeast Germany that pushed the German frontier beyond Mecklenburg and Brandenburg into Pomerania, lands formerly held by the Slavs, omitting the less striking German expansion in the southeast. And, thirdly, we will occupy ourselves with an expansion movement within Europe itself, the expansion of the city over the adjacent countryside. The Crusades, the frontier, and the city will be the focal points of our discussion. It is not at all inappropriate on this campus to pay our respects in that fashion to Munro, Turner, and Stephenson. We will discuss the three phenomena in reverse order.[1]

By the twelfth century most towns of western Europe had already started and in the twelfth century they were expanding far beyond their original limits.

Pirenne, Stephenson, and others have discussed the military and economic reasons for the general location of medieval cities.[2] The hopes for security, the natural advantages for defense prompted the feudal barons to erect their castles or *bourgs* and ramparts in localities surrounded by hills and mountains, at river forks and on hill-plateaus. In each case the new settlements had the protection of natural barriers and fortified ramparts against attacks of foreign invaders, rival barons, and aggressive rulers. Often the military considerations also served economic purposes. The nearby mountains perhaps had a pass through which an attacker had to invade and the single passage made defense easy. But the pass also induced the itinerant merchants and weary travellers to stop at the castle, to do and bring business. In the winter both the merchant and traveller sought rest and protection at the feudal castle. Within the shadow of wall and towers, within call of the feudal lord, the merchants settled down in their own community outside the castle walls, a community that was therefore called *faubourg*. The confluence of rivers and tributaries became the meeting and stopping places of merchants who floated their goods down the rivers by barge or who transported them along the river routes by horse and mule. In other instances the bend of a river that increased the potential water front, the shallows of a stream that facilitated a crossing, the mouth of a river that invited river and sea traffic became sites of new towns. Names like Oxford, Cambridge, Toledo, and Nueremberg indicate origins of this type. The same reasons prompted medieval people to continue or revive ancient Roman settlements often at the crossroads of the great highways. Wherever people met in considerable numbers for protection, out of social habit, and for business, a medieval town grew up. It was Pirenne who suggested that towns originated "in the footsteps of trade."

The reasons that prompted the original settlement also prompted the expansion of the medieval cities. The geographical aspects, which afforded the protection, and the communal settlement itself, which increased the military strength, encouraged others to shift their residence from less fortunate and more isolated areas to the new centers. Every additional family affected the economy of the group to the extent that it added manpower and technical skill and in the degree to which it demanded goods and services. And the merchants who at first had been temporary residents of the *faubourg* became its permanent inhabitants, while the *faubourg* which at first had been merely an outside quarter of the old *bourg* gradually encircled it on all sides. The expansion of the *faubourg* into a city may be indicated by the appearance of entirely new economic and social classes, first, the commercial middle class and, later, the industrial proletariat.

The growth and expansion of medieval cities had the same effects which we note in our own day. In the construction of new houses, in the furnishings which they needed, in the extension of the city walls, in the making of their new gates and towers, in the building of new and larger churches the cities had need of materials, manpower, and skills. The influx of new residents, the wages in the new jobs, the comforts and standards of urban living increased the business of the shopkeepers, retailers, and provisioners. While some items could be provided by the immediate locality and could be bought and sold at the local market, many had to be bought by the merchants from other communities and fair centers. Industry, commerce, and related economic pursuits became urban means of livelihood. The extension of the city walls to provide room for new shops and residences, the extension of urban authority to control those who raised foodstuffs nearby, the policy of the municipal consuls of guarding the routes of trade exemplify the expansion of medieval cities.

The maritime cities of Italy were probably more aggressive than the inland cities of western Europe, but their expansion generally took a different form from that of the cities of the interior. Like all cities, the Italian towns were interested in defense and security, and consequently they built and extended their walls and gates just as did other cities.

But the economic factors were stronger than elsewhere and these factors created a more aggressive expansionist policy. The mountain pass through which an enemy might invade was actually used by their own and other merchants. In it, on all roads to the cities, on all bridges, the cities collected a fee from every individual, on every horse or mule load, or they leased out the right to collect a fee to an individual or syndicate. Over the hinterland the cities established a monopoly over natural products and human resources, over markets and business affairs. If the hinterland included feudal nobles who had military levies at their command, the towns demanded that the nobles become city residents for several months each year and that they furnish military aid to the city. The sea merchants who wanted to continue their profitable commerce relied upon others for the usual military defense.

In the coastal areas the city merchants also showed their prime interest in economic matters. The communal consuls placed the small ports along the sea under strict commercial restrictions. They subjected them completely to their own interests. The merchants of these small coastal towns could travel only in convoy with the ships of the mother city, the ships of these communities had to depart from and return to the mother city, and, in turn, no foreign ships or merchants were allowed to trade in these centers. At the same time the small communities had to furnish a quota of ships, barges, and men to the navy of the mother city and at times timber to its shipyards. Salt trade and distribution was a monopoly of the home city or of a syndicate to whom the mother city had sold or leased the monopolistic rights. These practices spelled out a twelfth-century mercantilism.

Another economic feature of the expanding cities must be mentioned. The growth of the cities in all its manifestations—the influx of people, the creation of new jobs, the increase of wages, the appearance of trade— was both the cause and effect of the organization of economic life. Industrial and merchant gilds had existed before 1100, but by the end of the twelfth century virtually every town had numerous industrial gilds and every small town a merchant gild. The complexities of urban life necessitated law and order. The regulations of the industrial gild fixed the quality and quantity of manufactured goods, the wages of workers and prices of goods, the hours and conditions of labor. The rules of the merchant gild regulated the sales and purchases of goods by local and alien merchants, fixed the prices of imported goods, controlled the weights and measures, and the general business of the fair if one existed in the community. Both gilds were aristocratic in nature since they included only the masters of industry and the wholesalers in trade, but they regulated the life and work of the entire population and the merchant group often directed the expansionist movement of the cities.

The expansion of medieval cities, whether inland or coastal, was caused by economic interests. It is true, in the foundation of the cities attention was given to military matters because of the hope for security, but once the location was established, the need for existence and the ambition for gain were dominant. The need for residence caused the increase in the extent of the cities and the addition to the city walls, while the need for existence and the hope for profit caused the expansion of municipal authority over the countryside and the adjacent area. Within the cities the municipal government and the gilds, which strongly influenced the government, regulated economic life to such a degree that the urban worker, although personally independent, was considerably restricted both as to means of livelihood and mode of life. Beyond the cities, the rural population generally gained from the growth and expansion of the nearby town. The congested urban community needed more food, so that the landowner and landworker gained from increased prices and wages. In the urban community living conditions were more comfortable than on the manors and life itself was free, so the landworkers had good reason to flee to the new cities, which offered these great opportunities. Consequently, since the landworker had the chance for flight to the city, the landowner found it advisable to improve the conditions of rural life and work, often to grant freedom to his serfs and to retain them as farm tenants. Not until after 1200 did the urban worker and the nearby peasant rebel against the domination of the cities and their administration. In the twelfth century all welcomed and enjoyed the new prosperity that had come with the expansion of the cities.

The European expansion into northeast Germany was a long, continuous movement that began with the campaigns of Charlemagne.[3] In the eleventh century Adam of Bremen (d. 1076) reviewed the earlier exploits and narrated extensively the expeditions of the Baltic Europeans to the northwest and northeast. He has given to us the first reference to Vinland, a contemporary account of a polar expedition into the Arctic, his archbishop's jurisdictional claims to Iceland, Greenland, the Orkneys, and Hebrides, and to the Scandinavian peninsulas themselves. Adam also related the travels of Danish merchants into the Baltic and along the Neva and Dvina in northern Russia and along the Dnieper into southern

Russia, which they followed to the Black Sea and eventually to Byzantium. But these travels often implied mere exploration rather than expansion and settlement and it is with expansion for purposes of settlement that we are concerned.

Northeastern expansion and settlement in the twelfth century were quite extensive in themselves. The starting point for the expansion began in the northwest with the Elbe River and in the southwest with the Saale River, the Thueringerwald, and the Erzgebirge. From the Elbe and Magdeburg on the Elbe the expansion moved directly northeastward across the Oder up to the Vistula and a little beyond that river to the east of Danzig. This push covered about 350 miles. It stayed north of the Netze River, a tributary of the Oder. From the Saale River, a southern tributary of the Elbe, and the Thueringerwald the movement south of Magdeburg carried eastward about 150 miles to the Bober River, also a tributary of the Oder. The expansion added Mecklenburg, and most of Brandenburg and Pomerania to Christian Europe.

Actually, of course, many parts of this area had been explored, traversed, and settled before 1100, but not until the twelfth century was the area settled permanently and Christianized uninterruptedly. On three occasions, in 983, 1018, and 1066, the pagan Slavs revolted against their Saxon conquerors and oppressors, lay and clerical; their repeated revolts indicate the renewed efforts at settlement and Christianization, which often led to exploitation. But by 1100 the Baltic Slavs had worn themselves out and the Saxons successfully established Christian authority thereafter.

Not only had an earlier expansion taken place, but economic matters had a strong influence in the explorations, settlement, and revolts. Both Adam of Bremen and Helmold, the best sources for this area in the period, denounced vehemently the economic exploitation of the Slavs by the Saxon clergy and barony. The former has the Danish king say "that the Slav people would long since have been converted to Christianity if it had not been for the avarice of the Saxons." Helmold echoes the same opinion: "The princes divided the tribute among themselves. But no mention was made of Christianity. From which the insatiable avarice of the Saxons may be appreciated. They excel all other peoples in arms and the art of war; but they care more for tribute than they do for the winning of souls." Tithe-collecting rather than soul-saving was the reason for the conquest and conversion of the Slavs; more thought was given to conquest than to conversion. The tithes of the Church were in grains, flax, linen, hemp, honey, cattle, and silver. The serfs on the extensive church lands were declared unfree forever and bound to church soil.[4] Saxon feudality carved out their estates without the excuse of religion and they and their peasants soon enjoyed prosperity in the early eleventh century. Along the Baltic coast the Danish kings aimed to extend their land and sea empire to include the mouths of the Elbe, Oder, and Vistula. Coastal cities like Wollin and Stettin in the delta of the Oder, and Danzig on the Vistula, all mentioned in the tenth century, suggested the possibilities of commerce and wealth. And merchants resident in Magdeburg travelled eastward into Slavic territory to buy agrarian goods for the border settlements. So it was that all elements found economic reasons to extend Christianity toward and beyond the frontier of 1100.

The twelfth-century expansion from the Elbe to the Vistula was organized and directed by three princes, Count Adolph II of Holstein (1128–1164), Duke Henry the Lion of Saxony (1129–1195), and Margrave Albrecht of Brandenburg (1100–1170). It may be noted in passing that the men were local feudal princes, significant but still local, and that the ruling families of Germany, whether royal or imperial, Salian or Hohenstaufen, did not bother about the expansionist movement. Since the days of Otto I the central rulers had surrendered the project, important though it was, to the local barony. Although there was less antipathy between the secular barons and the churchmen in regard to the expansion in the twelfth century than in the preceding period, the secular princes overpowered their ecclesiastical contemporaries in this work.[5]

Of the three men, Adolph and Albrecht resembled one another in policy and direction. Both spoke and wrote Slavic well, knew Slavic customs, and appreciated Slavic traditions. They favored friendly diplomacy and patient negotiation with the Slavic chieftains and gained tremendous successes by their methods. Count Adolph had his success in the area immediately to the east of Holstein and the Elbe as far as the Baltic. Here he persuaded the Wendish leaders to accept his feudal overlordship, to enter the status of vassalage to him, and, more important for our purpose, to permit a gradual colonization by the immigrants whom he brought in. That he was similarly successful in regard to his own people may be gathered from the praise of Helmold: "He did justice unto his people, suppressing turmoil and liberating the oppressed from the land of feudality." Albrecht the Bear directed the expansion eastward toward and across the Oder and toward the Vistula. In 1134 he received Brandenburg as an independent fief and in 1150 he received part of it as a legacy from the Christian Wendish chieftain. However, Albrecht pressed eastward toward Pomerania to avoid open military conflict with Count Adolph and King Henry. His expansion over Brandenburg and Pomerania was carried out with relatively little bloodshed. Both Albrecht and Adolph avoided direct leadership and prominent participation in the Crusade of 1147 through which the Slavs suffered much loss and devastation.

Henry the Lion was a different type. When St. Bernard preached the Second Crusade to Emperor Conrad III, Henry and his Saxon nobles argued that it was senseless to go overseas to fight the Moslems when they could crusade against the pagan Slavs right next door. St. Bernard agreed and released them from the overseas venture. The incident initiated the Saxon Crusade against the Wendish Slavs in 1147, much more successful than the debacle of Conrad III and Louis VII. Henry was a conqueror and a crusader, very successful, but also quite ruthless. He paid little attention to the pagan customs and traditions of the Slavs.

This difference in the political and military aspects of the expansion also created a difference in economic matters, although the variation in the latter did not cover all spheres. Henry the Lion in his appeal for crusaders played upon the land needs of his barons in Saxony, in which unoccupied land was already scarce. The greater barons needed no new lands, but the lesser barons and the younger sons of feudal nobles were less well off. In the distribution of the conquered lands, after the Saxon Crusade of 1147, Henry, nevertheless, seems to have favored the greater barony and the creation of large estates. At least, the lesser barons complained: "Is not the land which we have devastated our land?" Their complaint was all the more poignant because they and many free peasants had suffered from the pressure of the great land proprietors west of the Elbe in Saxony and in Thuringia and for that very reason had joined the Crusade. Nevertheless, the new occupants cultivated the Slavic lands more efficiently than had the Wends and reaped better and larger harvests. Helmold wrote: "The Slavs little by little failed in the land, and the Saxons came in and dwelt there."

The three men appealed strongly to the Dutch, Flemings, and Frisians, in addition to their own subjects, to settle and colonize the lands beyond the Elbe, once Slavic and pagan, but now German and Christian. They had good reasons to call to the Lowlanders and others to the west of the Elbe. For several generations the secular and ecclesiastical nobility had increased their agrarian holdings at the expense of the lesser barony and free peasantry and had laid claims to the forests in which many of the dispossessed and landless peasants had established squatters' rights. The pressure of increasing population and of recurring famines in this older area made the bid of the princes more inviting. The dominant economic appeal appeared blatantly in a proclamation of 1108: "They [the Slavs] are an abominable people, but their land is very rich in flesh, honey, grain, birds, and abounding in all products of the fertility of the earth, when cultivated, so that none can be compared to it. So they say who know. Wherefore, O Saxons, Franks, Lotharingians, men of Flanders most famous—here you can both save your souls, and if it please you, acquire the best of the land to live in." In regard to Count Adolph, Helmold wrote: "In 1143 because the land was sparsely settled Count Adolph sent messengers into all regions roundabout, even into Flanders and Holland, Utrecht, Westphalia, and Frisia, to proclaim that all who were in want of land might come with their families and receive the best of soil, a spacious country, rich in crops, abounding in fish and flesh, and of exceeding good pasturage." And the colonists came "with horses and oxen, with plows and wagons." The call to the Lowlanders was also made because their experience with deep plowing of heavy soils and their knowledge of drainage techniques could be put to good use in lands of similar composition. Upon Henry's invitation numerous Lowlanders settled around Mecklenburg and Ratzeburg and upon Albrecht's to the east of Magdeburg in a district still called Fläming. Because the land was arid here, the new settlers dug ditches for irrigation rather than for drainage. In Brandenburg and Pomerania the new immigrants occupied plots of land rather than great estates; they were free peasants and small barons and no great landlords. Already in the eleventh century the workers who had developed the polders in the Lowlands were free peasants; in the twelfth century the same custom prevailed in the new Germany.[6] All peasants and barons were directly landowners under Albrecht and he favored the little man.

The influx of the Lowlanders stopped around 1181. Possibly the exile of Henry the Lion had some influence upon the stoppage. However, it is also probable that the increased prosperity in the Lowlands reduced the need and desire for migration and that the more extensive marshlands in Pomerania required the coöperative efforts of groups like the Cistercians rather than the efforts of individual workers.

In their expansionist movement the three princes gave considerable impetus to the town movement and trade. In 1143 Adolph founded Luebeck, whose quiet rise and lasting fame indicate the farsightedness of the count. Shortly it supplanted the old Saxon city Bardowick as the commercial center in the area, so that Henry seized it in 1158. He established a mint there and moved to it the markets formerly held at Bardowick and Ratzeburg. It was shortly visited by the merchants of England, Denmark, Sweden, and Russia, and soon it became the great center for the Hanseatic League. Albrecht set up his capital at Berlin, an older Slav settlement, and in it the first Christian church was dedicated to St. Nicholas, the patron saint of the merchants. To the mercantile communities he granted town charters with commercial privileges and in them established his official mints to facilitate the use of money. On the Spree and Oder he stationed guards to protect shipping against the Wendish attacks and in cities like Wittenberg on the Elbe and Potsdam and Heiligensee on the Havel he granted warehouse privileges to the merchants who stopped to pay their tolls. For him the merchants were a source of income.

Economic factors in the northeastward expansion of Christian Europe were significantly causal for and in turn the expansionist movement itself was contributive to economic development. Of the three leaders in the movement two certainly relied upon peaceful, nondestructive penetration and occupation rather than upon wasteful war and conquest. Their projects for conquest and/or colonization were attractive, because they offered relief from disturbing and disheartening economic and social developments in the west. Whatever the skill of the leaders may have been, the crusading and migrating forces in the main were made up of men who possessed too little land in the west or none at all. They were pushed into the ventures by population pressures and feudal aggrandizement to improve their lot beyond the Elbe. These men and their families gave the expansionist movement a popular character; they came as colonizers, settlers, landowners, and landworkers. In those capacities they increased the cultivable land to serve and support the growing population of western Europe. In the main, the princes promoted and encouraged these small but free peasants and the lesser barons. As long as they encouraged the far distant Lowlanders to come eastward, they were hardly in a position to do otherwise; they could not invite them into agrarian serfdom when they already were free. Although the urban and commercial factors were present, they held a secondary position in the aims of the promoters and in the immediate consequences. The potentialities for urban life and urban means of livelihood existed in the new Germany, but in the twelfth century they were embryonic. Once the Germans were in control of the southern shores of the Baltic Sea, they were in a position to clear the North and Baltic seas of the Scandinavians just as the Italians had cleared the Mediterranean of the Arabs. Thereafter the Hanseatic League developed and maintained a position which in many respects was similar to that of the Italian cities in the Mediterranean.

The economic factors and forces existent and operative in the expansion of the city and plain were significantly present in the more extensive, overseas ventures into the Near East. Similarly, these economic forces were at work for a long time before the twelfth century.

The Crusades were part of a pan-European expansionist movement that pushed into all directions, partially under the impetus or guise of Christianity. The conquest of England by Duke William of Normandy, the foundation of another Norman Kingdom in the Two Sicilies, the Spanish campaigns of the Christian knights of Spain and France, and the Saxon Crusade across the Elbe, the expeditions of the Scandinavian sailors into the northern seas and the Christian settlements in Iceland and Greenland, the acceptance of Roman Christianity by St. Stephen and his Hungarian subjects were all parts of the same expansionist movement, some antecedent, others contemporary, to the more phenomenal overseas expansion. To a great degree this general development made the Crusades possible and acceptable. In all areas the developments continued beyond the end of the twelfth century.

The economic aspects of the Crusades were as varied as the participants. There is little need and no method to weigh and evaluate the varied causes for this overseas expansion. Admittedly, religious, political, and social forces existed in addition to the more material economic factors. Pope Urban II appealed successfully to all interests and by no means did he overlook the economic and material aspects. That these economic interests influenced considerably the activities of some of the crusading elements may be gathered from the denunciations of them when some of the crusades failed to reach the expectations of the more spiritually minded.

In a measure the Crusades were evidence that the Peace of God and the Truce of God had failed. The varied accounts of Pope Urban's speeches refer to bloody strife, plundering and pilfering, homicide and sacrilege, hatreds and dissensions. These actions were economic liabilities for western Europe and any diminution of them was of economic profit to the communities and groups among whom they existed. Urban's references to the actions were couched in terms of religion, humanity, and social conscience, but the economic losses from war and plunder cannot be denied and the gains from their absence cannot be overlooked.

To the feudal barons, "aforetime robbers" who were to become soldiers of Christ, the pope gave promise of material gains. He promised to the overseas crusaders what the bishops and princes of the north had offered to the Saxon colonists and settlers. "The possessions of the enemy will be yours, too, since you will make spoil of his treasures. . . ." "Wrest that land from the wicked race, and subject it to yourselves, that land which, as the scripture says, 'floweth with milk and honey.'" He obviously hoped to gain the support of the landless or land-poor barony, who possessed little property because of the rules of inheritance or the ill fortune of the feudal wars. He knew, too, the inevitable result of increasing population whose land "is too narrow. . . . nor does it abound in wealth; and it furnishes scarcely enough food for its cultivators."[7]

The economic gains that were promised to the feudal barons were also obtained by them. The great princes at the head of their feudal levies carved out the largest estates, but lesser barons established themselves as well. As the crusading armies marched southward from Asia Minor into Syria and Palestine, individual leaders conquered and claimed their personal principalities. In that fashion Tancred established himself in Cilicia, Baldwin in the County of Edessa, and Raymond of Toulouse in the County of Tripoli. They often quarreled with one another in complete disregard of the common cause and the Kingdom of Jerusalem and certainly not in the interests of the Holy Sepulcher and the papal see. With them their own personal ambitions ranked first, and they demanded before anything else the establishment of their own political authority along feudal lines which gave them the customary economic returns in fees, services, fines, and products. The lesser barons generally became vassals and enjoyed similar gains, but on a smaller scale. Many of the barons, who had nothing to return to in western Europe, established residence in the Levant and their descendants became part of the Frankish aristocracy of the East. Fulcher of Chartres exclaimed: "He who in Europe owned not so much as a village is lord of a whole city out here. He who was worth no more than a few pence now disposes of a fortune. Why should we return to the West when we have all we desire here?"

While the feudal barons formed the majority of the fighting men in the crusading campaigns, the Italian townsmen and merchants were so essential to the whole movement that it would have collapsed without their support. After the First Crusade all western armies travelled eastward, by sea, and even in the First Crusade the naval and military support of Genoa and Pisa was considerable. Pope Urban II recognized the importance of the towns and merchants for the movement and accordingly sent itinerant propagandists into the cities to preach the crusades or had local preachers perform the job.

Since the Italian towns had been fighting the Moslems for several centuries, the papal preachers had no difficulty persuading the Italian merchants to coöperate. The Italians had fought the Arabs for three hundred years before 1095, at first defensively, then offensively. All the great Italian cities, Naples, Rome, Pisa, and Genoa in the west, Bari, Ancona, and Venice on the Adriatic, had been attacked and plundered by the Arabs. In the early tenth century the south Italian cities had wiped out the last Arab base in Italy, and in the early eleventh century Genoa and Pisa had driven the Arabs from the Tyrrhenian Sea. In 1087 a combined force of Italian cities, under the leadership of a papal legate, attacked Mehdia in North Africa, plundered a merchant suburb, gained compensation for damages done to their ships by Arab pirates, and obtained free access to the area for their merchants. The victory cleared the western Mediterranean of Arab pirates and competitors. To the Italian cities the call of Pope Urban II sounded like an invitation to help clear the eastern Mediterranean as well and to obtain similar commercial privileges.[8]

To the Italian merchants the Crusades always appeared to be extraordinary economic opportunities. From the very start the Italians gained financial rewards. Their ships carried the crusaders and their equipment, even their horses, to the Holy Land, and then supplied the crusaders with food, drink, and, on occasion, with timber, manpower, and siege machinery. Genoa and Pisa commandeered all possible ships in their domains for transport purposes and ordered the construction of more and larger vessels. The transport services were a source of immediate income for the communes, merchants, and shipowners. The Fourth Crusade is good evidence that financial return loomed large in the aims of the shipowners and merchants. The Crusades gave to the Italian cities much of the liquid capital that was needed in the capitalistic developments that were just beginning. Furthermore, this capital came from sources unrelated to the Italian towns, from western feudal barons and kings. It was money which the Italians could not have obtained otherwise.

In addition to these immediate monetary returns Genoa, Pisa, and Venice received promises of quarters in the coastal towns of Syria and Palestine. These promises were generally made in private agreements between the Italian cities and the baronial leaders, the kings of France and England, and the kings of Jerusalem. Often they were made under pressure of the moment and then forgotten when the pressure was lifted. However, the Italians, especially the Genoese, established themselves well enough to enjoy long-term rewards and profits. In at least a dozen coastal towns of the Levant the Italians possessed throughout most of the twelfth century residential and commercial quarters, from which they gained an income from rentals, leases, harbor dues, and court fines. In these centers the Italian merchants carried on their trade with the European colonists and feudal residents, with Arab traders, and with their associates and agents who worked in the area. The Italian quarters of the Levant became the centers of exchange for Oriental and European goods and the markets for the western imports that increased as the century wore on. The Oriental trade was highly profitable and another source of capital in the new money economy of the period. The Crusades were the strongest influence on the development of medieval trade and industry.

Something needs to be said about the Crusades and the general structure of medieval business and capitalism. First of all, the Crusades created a situation in which capital appeared and circulated. Feudal, clerical, and royal participants mortgaged and sold their holdings to obtain money to buy equipment, hire soldiers, and pay for passage. In some instances they melted down their plate and jewelry. Occasionally, the peasants brought out their hoards and bought their freedom from their anxious and hard-pressed lords. Guibert de Nogent wrote: "As everyone hastened to take the road of God, each hurried to change into money everything that was not of use for the journey, and the price was fixed not by the seller, but by the buyer." Generally, as already indicated, this capital went to the Italian merchants and shippers for transportation or other services connected with the venture. Eventually, numerous other people received jobs and wages, including armorers, shipbuilders, ropemakers, and vintners. Obviously, much of the capital paid to the Italians covered the cost of materials and labor, but a considerable part was profit and gain. In turn, much of the profit was reinvested in the Levantine trade, which also was extremely lucrative. The Crusades had promoted the capitalistic cycle of capital, investment, profit, and reinvestment of profit for further profit and capital. The Crusades, cities, and commerce initiated a money economy which threatened and certainly modified the older land economy of western Europe.

Another capitalistic instrument given impetus by the Crusades was credit. Credit, after all, was based on the expectancy of income and profit by the borrower. Many participants in the Crusades bought their equipment or obtained loans on credit, expecting to profit from the material rewards which Urban had promised. In the Holy Land many again resorted to loans from the Templars and Hospitallers, hoping to repay from their ventures in the Near East or from their properties in western Europe. The rulers, of course, could expect to pay their loans from tax receipts or new crusade aids. The merchants seemingly did less business with the banking orders, partially because they had capital, primarily because they had their own banking systems and credit arrangements. Nevertheless, the Crusades helped to establish credit on an international scale and gave to credit instruments an international operation between the Italian bases in the Levant and the fairs of Champagne and Flanders in the West.

Similarly, the Crusades gave to commerce an international aspect. They again opened up the entire Mediterranean Sea to Christian ships and trade and provided an entry into the trade with the Near and Far East. The crusaders' acquaintance with Arab and Moslem customs created a demand for Oriental goods in Christian Europe, so that dyes, spices, woods, silk, cotton, precious stones, pearls, and alum became regular western imports from the Italian quarters in the East. Henry of Champagne acknowledged some gifts of Saladin with: "You know that your robes and turbans are far from being held in scorn among us. I will certainly wear your gifts." At the same time the growing industries of the West gave the Italian merchants the chance to carry western goods, especially cloths, eastward to exchange them for the Levantine goods, and the continued residence of westerners in the East created a demand for those western wares. While the Italian quarters served as the *entrepôt* in the Levant, the fairs of Champagne and Flanders served a similar function in the West. The famous fairs of Troyes, Lagny, Provins, and Bar-sur-Aube were instituted in the twelfth century. But between the two distant points the sea merchants of maritime Italy and the land merchants of North Italy and France carried on a regular cycle of purchases and sales, usually on credit. They thrived on a commerce that had become international. Even though the crusader states and the Kingdom of Jerusalem lost heavily to the Moslems toward the end of the century, the trade relations continued, the coastal cities and the Mediterranean Sea remained open to the European merchants.

Finally, within this international commerce on land and sea, partnerships and associations developed which reflected the expansionist movement within the maritime cities and promised more complex capitalistic institutions and instruments. In the early twelfth century the usual commercial partnership, the *societas*, consisted of two men, a stay-at-home investor who contributed two-thirds of the capital and received one-half of the profit, and a traveling factor, who gave one-third of the capital and received one-half of the profit. Eventually, several investors often made up the two-thirds portion and received their prorated profits. By the late twelfth century another partnership, the *accomendatio*, was formed. In it one or several stay-at-home investors contributed the entire capital to the commercial venture and received three-fourths of the profit, while the active traveling merchant contributed no capital, but gave his skill, time, and knowledge, ran personal risks, and received one-fourth of the profit. The growing use of *accomendatio* was concomitant to the popular movement within the cities. Since no definite ratio of capital was required, anyone could contribute capital, in large or small amounts. The investors need not be merchants of wealth and nobility, but could be orphans, widows, dyers, cobblers, bakers, weavers, and mercers; they could come from the nonmercantile section of the populace. In Genoa between 1155 and 1164 several hundred nameless, occasional, small-time investors contributed almost as much capital to the overseas commerce as did the merchant capitalists.[9] Commerce like expansion was popular in the twelfth century. In another direction, some partnerships among investors, and between investors and factors became continuous, extending over several years. Permanent or almost permanent associations, with the possibility of partners being resident in foreign ports, were in the offing around 1200. Not only commerce and credit, but commercial and capitalistic organizations, too, had become international.

In summary, the economic life of Europe in the twelfth century exhibited an extraordinary vigor and gave promise of longevity. In the growth and expansion of the cities industry and commerce provided an increasing population with new means of livelihood, greater comforts, and wider experiences. These improvements in daily living resulted from the flow of capital into the new centers, a capital that came in part through the expansion of the city over the countryside and in part through the expansion of Europe beyond the seas. The complexities of community life and work, of expanded industry and commerce called for mercantilist regulation and coöperation. In turn, on occasion the regulations curbed, the coöperation promoted the capitalistic temper and organization. These phenomena appeared first in the older Mediterranean section of Europe, but the expansionist movement in north Germany offered the possibility of similar developments along the Baltic. Generally, agrarian life and conditions improved, too. The colonists and settlers of the frontier were a courageous, adventuresome, and independent group, not the type to submit readily to manorial regulations. Nor did the needs and conditions of the frontier fit into the older agrarian mode of life and work. Not always, but usually, the expansion of the frontier encouraged the free peasantry and lesser barony. Within older Europe the manorial peasant and manorial lord gained through the expansion of the city. The former gained from reduced services and fees, often from freedom, the latter from greater markets and higher prices. The characterization of creativeness, development, and vigor, given in the term *renaissance*, but generally applied to the intellectual and artistic aspects of the twelfth century, should be applied to the economic aspects as well.

NOTES

1 Professor Robert L. Reynolds, one of the planners of this symposium, has given attention to this development in "The Mediterranean Frontiers, 1000–1400" in Walker D. Wyman and Clifton B. Kroeber, *The Frontier in Perspective* (Madison, 1957), pp. 21–34.

2 Pirenne's synthesis of his ideas and arguments can be found in *Medieval Cities* (Princeton, 1925) and *Economic and Social History of Medieval Europe* (London, 1936). Cf. also Carl Stephenson, *Borough and Town* (Cambridge, 1933). The most extensive bibliography at the present time can be found in *Cambridge Economic History*, II (Cambridge, 1952), 531–56.

3 This expansion was of special interest to James W. Thompson. Cf. his "East German Colonization in the Middle Ages," in *Proceedings of the American Historical Association*, 1916, pp. 125–50; "The German Church and the Conversion of the Baltic Slavs," in *American Journal of Theology*, XX (1916), 203–30, 372–89; "Dutch and Flemish Colonization in Medieval

Germany," in *American Journal of Sociology*, XXIV (1918), 159–86; *Feudal Germany* (Chicago, 1928); they are the basis for my remarks. On the sources of the movement see his *A History of Historical Writing* (2 vols.; New York, 1942), I, 200–203. Indicative of the recent German interest in the problem is *Vom Mittelalter zur Neuzeit, zum 65. Geburtstage von Heinrich Sproemberg* (Berlin, 1956), which has several studies on the problem. See also Bryce Lyon, "Medieval Real Estate Development and Freedom," in *American Historical Review*, LXIII (1957), 47–61.

4   Thompson, "The German Church and the Conversion of the Baltic Slavs," pp. 203–30, discusses this aspect thoroughly. He also indicates that the Saxon nobles opposed the missionary efforts of the Church because they feared a loss of their income just as soon as the Church collected its tithes.

5   Thompson, "The German Church and the Conversion of the Baltic Slavs," pp. 372–89, also points out that the high churchmen of the area were of higher stature than their predecessors, but that their humane and moderate approach "was out of temper with the spirit of the twelfth century." Certainly they were not in sympathy with the crusading temper of Henry the Lion and St. Bernard of Clairvaux.

6   Lyon argues that such reclamation projects in Flanders had more to do with the growing freedom of the common man than did the towns and the commutation of labor services.—Lyon, "Real Estate Development," p. 61. It would seem that this argument can be applied to northeast Germany as well.

7   Other promises of an economic nature, but not concerned with the expansion into the Levant, were made. The participants were promised that their properties and families at home would be protected and that their debts would be cancelled. For an analysis of Pope Urban's plea at Clermont see Dana C. Munro, "The Speech of Pope Urban II at Clermont," in *American Historical Review*, XI (1906), 231–42. Extensive and very recent bibliographies on the Crusades may be found in *A History of the Crusades, I: The First Hundred Years* (Philadelphia, 1955).

8   All of this may be found in extended form in the writer's "The Italian Cities and the Arabs before 1095," in *A History of the Crusades*, I, 40–53.

9   Cf. the writer's "Genoese Merchants, their Partnerships and Investments, 1155 to 1164" in *Studi in Onore di Armando Sapori* (Milan, 1957), I, 257–72.

Joseph R. Strayer

The Development of
Feudal Institutions

Because feudalism in the twelfth century is a large subject which obviously cannot be covered in all its aspects in a brief paper, I have imposed
three limitations on my discussion. First, I am using the narrowest
possible definition: feudalism as a method of government, a way of
accomplishing certain essential political acts. I am not sure that any
broader definition makes much sense, but we need not examine this
problem now. Feudalism as a method of government is a sufficiently
complicated topic in itself and will more than fill up our time. Second,
I am considering feudalism only as it existed in England, France, and
Germany. There are many interesting aspects of the feudalism of Italy
and Spain, but feudalism was less complete in these countries than in
the north and it was modified by peculiar political conditions and
events, so that Italian and Spanish feudalism differs in many ways
from that of the northern countries. Third, I am not going to discuss
all the changes which took place during the twelfth century in the
feudalisms of England, France, and Germany. One of the remarkable
things about feudalism was its extreme flexibility. It was constantly
being modified to fit individual needs and local conditions, and it is impossible to trace all these adjustments. On the other hand, even if we
look at it in most general terms, it is clear that the feudalism of 1200
was not the feudalism of 1100. It had changed in both theory and practice; it had a different impact on men's minds and it could be used to
achieve new political results. It should be possible to separate basic

changes in the nature of feudalism from temporary adjustments to immediate problems, and I am going to discuss only basic changes in this
paper.

It is hardly necessary to say that even in the north feudalism was not
uniform. There were great differences in the political structures of England, France, and Germany in 1100. There was the obvious contrast of
an England which was united and relatively homogeneous, a France
which was a loose confederation of feudal lordships in varying stages of
development, and a Germany in which the old pattern of government
was being disrupted by the Investiture Conflict with no new pattern
yet discernible. There were less obvious contrasts: the presence of
numerous allods in Germany and southern and eastern France as opposed
to their virtual absence in England and northwestern France, or the greater
importance of fighting men who were not knights in German armies as
compared to those of France. But with all these differences the three countries had one thing in common; the essential work of government could
not be performed without recognizing and using the power of the local
lords. There was no possibility of establishing a centralized, bureaucratic
administration; no ruler had enough money to pay and supervise local
officials. Therefore, local administration and justice, which is the essential
work of any government, had to be left to the leading men in each
district, that is, the lords. It was equally impossible to establish a single,
centralized army which could defend all regions threatened by war or
disorder; local defense had to be left to the local lords. And to carry out
these responsibilities the lords in all countries had hit upon much the
same formula. They had acquired groups of retainers or vassals; they
had fortified key defensive positions, and they defended their districts
and carried on the work of local government with the assistance of their
men. This is the essence of early feudalism, and feudalism of this sort
existed everywhere. The local lord, with his vassals and his court, was
the basic political unit of the early twelfth century.[1] He could not be
eliminated, and, in fact, no one wanted to eliminate him. Many people
were not at all sure that any larger political unit than the local lordship
was either desirable or possible. Assuming that it was, the only practical
question was whether a political system could be developed which recognized the special position of the local lord and yet permitted a certain
degree of central control. Was feudalism necessarily synonymous with
localism? Could it be used to build larger and more effective systems of
government?

No one, in the year 1100, could have given an unqualified affirmative answer to this last question. Until very recently, the largest effective political unit in western Europe had been the kingdom of Germany, but Germany was far less feudalized than either England or France and the power of the king of Germany had certainly not been built on his position as supreme feudal lord. In France, the country where feudalism was most fully developed, the king was profiting very little from his theoretical lordship over his dukes and counts, and the latter, in turn, seemed to have little authority over their own vassals. The peripheral counties of the duchies of Aquitaine and Burgundy, and the viscounties of the county of Toulouse were becoming independent of their nominal suzerains. The same thing was happening in the duchy of Lorraine, the most thoroughly feudalized part of Germany. In short, it must have seemed to many people that feudalism could be an effective system of government only within very narrow geographical limits, the area of a single castellany or at most two or three castellanies. Early feudalism depended so much on close personal relations between lord and vassals that a distant and seldom seen lord had little influence over his nominal subordinates. Up to 1100 most attempts to hold together or rebuild large political units on a feudal basis had failed.

It is true that in the north there were a few exceptions to this rule, the county of Flanders, the duchy of Normandy, the kingdom of England. But it could be argued that each one of these states had developed under exceptionally favorable circumstances which were not likely to recur elsewhere. A series of early wars had eliminated many of the local lords in the lands of the count of Flanders, and the precocious growth of Flemish towns had given the count such wealth that the balance of power remained permanently shifted in his favor. Normandy had been conquered by a group of invaders who knew nothing of feudalism, so that feudal institutions must have been established there at a comparatively late date, perhaps not until the end of the tenth century. Scattered evidence also seems to indicate that Norman feudalism grew from the top down, or at least was regulated and guided by ducal grants, a circumstance which would give the duke an unusual degree of control over his vassals.[2] There is no doubt that feudalism had been imposed from the top in England and in any case England was a very recent addition to the rank of feudal states. The Conquest was only a generation old in 1100, and the ties between the king and his vassals were still strong.

Moreover, a dispassionate observer in 1100 might well have wondered how long Normandy and England were going to remain strong, united states. Normandy, under Robert Curthose, was not a spectacle to excite any confidence in feudal institutions. In England a king who had been trying to make the most of his position as feudal lord had just been assassinated, and his successor had gained the throne only after making extensive concessions to his vassals. Of all the great feudal states, only Flanders was making steady progress, and one special case was scarcely enough to justify a belief that feudal institutions could be effective over wide territories.

Yet by 1200 the whole picture had changed. England, Normandy, and Flanders had more than fulfilled their early promise and had developed into strong, well-organized states. Other French provinces, such as Champagne, were not far behind these leaders. The king of France had begun to profit from his rights as supreme feudal lord, and he was about to give a most convincing demonstration, at the expense of King John, of the great advantages of this position. Most striking of all, one of the ablest rulers Germany ever had, Frederick Barbarossa, had spent a long reign in deliberately strengthening and perfecting the feudal bonds between himself and the German princes, because he was convinced that this was the best way to re-establish the unity of his weakened kingdom. Obviously certain things had happened to feudalism during the twelfth century which made it far more effective as an organizing principle in politics. Some of these modifications will be discussed in the following paragraphs. They may be summed up as the "réalization," the systematizing, and the bureaucratizing of feudalism.

In the first place, during the twelfth century feudalism ceased to be an intensely personal relationship between lord and man. There was what Ganshof calls a "réalization" of the feudal relationship,[3] an emphasis on the fief and its income rather than on the vassal and his service. Vassals wanted to hold on to their old fiefs, to accumulate new ones, and to pass all their holdings on to their heirs. At the same time, they strove steadily to reduce the amount of personal service which they rendered for these fiefs. Lords began to act as if service were owed by the fief rather than by the man, and therefore became more willing to accept women, minors, and remote collateral relatives as heirs of their vassals. Many vassals held fiefs from more than one lord. This did not greatly distress the lords, even though it was obvious that in such a case they would receive little personal service. Liege homage did little to redress the situation; it merely recognized that the secondary lords would receive little service without ensuring the liege lord of the undivided loyalty of his vassal.[4]

There was a general tendency, during the twelfth century, for the importance of personal service to decrease. As it decreased, the lords tried to make up for its loss by securing money payments from their men. Thus military service could be bought off, in England and Normandy, by payments of fines and scutages.[5] The feudal aid, almost unknown in the eleventh century, became an important source of revenue in the twelfth.[6] The lord's right to wardship was by no means universally recognized in the eleventh century and where it existed was used more to protect the lord's military and political position than as a source of revenue. In the twelfth century it became more common and more profitable; wardships were exploited as a source of income.[7] These changes were, of course, not uniform throughout Europe, but it is significant that the tendency to substitute money payments for personal service was most marked in the states where feudalism was most complete, that is, in Normandy and in England. Conversely, in Germany, or even in the duchy of Burgundy, where feudalism was in an earlier stage of development, some of the Anglo-Norman payments from vassal to lord were unknown.[8]

At first sight, this weakening of the personal bond might seem to make feudalism less, rather than more effective as a means of political organization. But a little reflection will show that those who lost most by the change were the local lords, and that those who gained most were the rulers of provinces and kingdoms. The power of the local lord depended on his ability to secure personal service from his knights, many of whom lived with him in his castle or at least spent long weeks there every year doing castle-guard. As these men acquired fiefs and became more attached to their own lands, as they tried to reduce or evade personal service, the military power of the local lord declined. He found it difficult to compensate for this loss by securing money payments because the greater lords tried to monopolize such payments, or at least took from him almost as much as he collected. Thus in England the king developed the doctrine of prerogative wardship, whereby he took possession of all the holdings of a minor heir if that heir held even the smallest fief from the crown.[9] This rule deprived many lords of their most profitable wardships, since their richest tenants were almost certain to hold something of the king as well. Again in England, royal policy, not always successful, was to make tenants-in-chief pass on to the king all the scutage which they collected from their men.[10] Even if the local lord succeeded in making some money out of feudal obligations the total sum was usually too small to enable him to hire mercenaries to replace the knights who were no longer giving him service.

Kings, and the greater dukes and counts, on the other hand, gained greatly by the introduction of money payments. Most vassals were glad to give money instead of military service, and while they grumbled more about other payments, such as aids and reliefs, they could seldom refuse them entirely. The stronger rulers of the twelfth century developed other sources of revenue, but a very large part of the income of a king such as Henry II came from strictly feudal payments. Large sums of money were raised from reliefs and wardships, aids and scutages, and these sums could be used to build up centralized governments. Mercenaries who served for months at a time could be hired in place of vassals who disliked serving at all. Paid functionaries could be used to enforce the orders of the king or provincial ruler throughout his territories. New castles could be built to hold down rebellious districts; neighboring lords could be bribed so that they would not support rebels. In short, once money was available it was possible to begin to create a territorial state.

The second great change in twelfth-century feudalism was the creation of feudal systems. Even in the Anglo-Norman states feudalism was not very systematic in the year 1100. There were many unsolved questions, for example the one which Henry I tried to settle concerning the court which was to have jurisdiction in disputes between vassals of different lords.[11] But at least in England and Normandy there was a complete feudal pyramid; all fiefs were held directly or indirectly of the king or the duke. Elsewhere feudalism had far less of a hierarchical character; it revealed clearly that it had grown out of a series of improvisations required to meet immediate emergencies. In much of France and most of Germany it was possible for a lord to have vassals and yet to possess his lands as an allod, free from any feudal obligations to a superior.[12] Thus there could be many small feudal groups which had no connection with each other and which escaped almost entirely from the control of higher authorities. Even where the feudal chain of command existed in theory, it might be broken in fact. The count of Toulouse might be a vassal of the king of France, but he rendered no service to the king and did not expect the king to intervene in any way in his county. At the same time, he had powerful subordinates, who were very nearly as independent of him as he was of the king of France.

During the twelfth century most rulers made a deliberate effort to pull these scattered pieces together, to force lords who were virtually independent to recognize that they had feudal superiors. Dubious or half-forgotten claims to suzerainty were revived and were often made good by legal or military pressure. Lords such as the king of France made more of an effort to secure the homage of their great vassals and to tie each homage to a specific fief.[13] They gained little immediate advantage by this policy, but they established their legal superiority and so laid a basis for later intervention. In Germany, where feudalism had been especially disorganized, Frederick Barbarossa tried to make it into a coherent system and to ensure that all the lay princes and bishops of the Empire recognized him as their lord.[14] Pressure against allodial lordships began to increase. This pressure reached its height in the thirteenth century, but even in the twelfth rulers such as the duke of Burgundy persuaded some allodial lords to surrender their lands and receive them back as fiefs.[15]

It was also in the twelfth century that the franchise theory of justice began to be stressed by some of the stronger lords, such as the king of England.[16] This theory held that all rights of justice must originate in grants from a superior; it was probably bad history, but it had obvious political advantages. The man who granted justice could define the terms of the grant, or intervene to see that it was not abused. Frederick Barbarossa was obviously attracted by these possibilities and tried to make the franchise theory of justice a basic rule of German feudalism.[17] This is fairly good contemporary evidence of its significance, since Frederick was trying to build a neatly organized feudal system at a comparatively late date and presumably emphasized only ideas that seemed to be producing useful results elsewhere. He gained little by his action, but other lords found the franchise theory very useful. It laid a basis for appeals from the courts of local lords, or for requests to the overlord to make the local lord do justice. Such appeals and requests had been almost unknown earlier; they became relatively common in the second half of the twelfth century. Henry II used the writ ordering the local lord to do right in his court as one of his most effective weapons in increasing his control over his tenants-in-chief.[18]

By systematizing and universalizing feudal relationships and by insisting on their rights as feudal superiors, the lords at the top of each feudal pyramid acquired more opportunities to interfere in local affairs. And the more the overlord intervened, the weaker the bonds between the local lord and his vassals became. The protection of the rear-vassal by the superior lord is one of the great innovations of the twelfth century. These men had been almost entirely at the mercy of their immediate lords; now they could ask for judicial or military protection from higher authority. Perhaps the most important result of the legal reforms of Henry II was that the tenure of rear-vassals was protected by the king's court.[19] The growth of the power of the French monarchy began when Louis VI and Louis VII started to protect lesser vassals and weaker lords against their powerful neighbors.[20] And perhaps the greatest weakness in Barbarossa's feudal system was that in creating the estate of princes he blocked direct contacts between himself and rear-vassals and so deprived himself of opportunities to intervene in local disputes.[21]

In most regions, however, the systematizing of feudalism reinforced the effects of its "réalization." The power of the greater lords over their vassals increased. Local lords, on the other hand, had to pay more attention to the orders of their superiors and had less authority over their inferiors. Rear-vassals who could count on the protection of the courts of the overlord were more independent of their immediate lords; they could insist on defining and limiting the amount of service they rendered. They often entered into direct relations with the overlord and some of them became important officials of the suzerain. All these changes aided the growth of relatively large, territorial states.

The third great change was the development of specialized administrative, judicial, and financial officers—the bureaucratizing of feudalism. Here again, the twelfth century offers a striking contrast with the preceding period. The feudal lord of the eleventh century had only his vassals and a few clerks to assist him in the work of government. The real trade of the vassals was fighting; most of them were not particularly good administrators, and in any case, when they received an administrative post they promptly tried to turn it into an hereditary fief. The clerks were at least literate, which is more than could be said of most vassals, but they often had little more skill in administration than laymen. They did not have the longing for order and routine, the love of precedents and records, the passion for legal forms which are the marks of a good bureaucrat. (This is not said in sarcasm; a government which lacks the spirit of routine, has no records, relies on no precedents, and is uncertain about the legality of its orders is apt to be an inefficient, disorderly, confused, and unpopular government.) The lack of specialized administrative personnel helps to explain why the effective sphere of government had been no larger than the castellany. A lord who tried to control a larger area could not be everywhere at once and he received little help from his vassals and household clerks. If he delegated authority he would probably succeed only in creating a new lordship; if he did not delegate authority he might lose all control over outlying districts. In the twelfth century, on the other hand, many lords succeeded in developing staffs of trained administrators. They could now delegate authority without losing it and therefore could keep control over wide areas.

The great increase in the number of educated men and the improvement in the quality of education during the twelfth century certainly facilitated improvements in feudal administration. More clerks were available and many of them had had some training in law. This meant that records were better kept, that precedents were remembered and used, that fixed procedures were gradually substituted for the informal actions of early feudal courts. This in turn increased both the revenues and the authority of the greater lords who were the only ones able to secure the services of a large number of clerks. Great lords usually had a number of ecclesiastical benefices at their disposal which they could use to pay their clerical administrators; in some cases they even established new foundations as a means of securing a supply of trained clerks. For example, the duke of Burgundy founded a collegiate church (the Chapelle-le-Duc) about 1184 in order to train clerks for his service.[22] Obviously, lesser lords would have more difficulty in finding enough benefices to support an adequate staff of clerks, so here again the change was to their disadvantage.

Clerks could do a great deal to improve administration, but they could not enforce the rules which they proclaimed, nor expect local lords to share their enthusiasm for precedents. The indispensable element of force had to be added by laymen. Laymen were needed as local governors, judges, and collectors of revenue, and it was much more difficult to find capable and trustworthy lay administrators than capable and trustworthy clerks. The tendency to turn offices into fiefs was still strong in the twelfth century. Even in so well organized a state as Flanders the receivers of the count's revenues were vassals—"feodales homines ratiocinatores"[23]—and even so strong a ruler as Henry II found his seneschalships of Anjou and Poitou turning into hereditary possessions.[24] Loyal and efficient lay administrators could not easily be found; they had to be chosen by hit-or-miss methods and trained by apprenticeship in minor offices.

Yet in spite of all these difficulties lay administrative officials did begin to appear in the twelfth century. The circuit judges of England, the *baillis* of Normandy, Flanders, and the French royal domain are the outstanding examples of this group.[25] They held office for limited periods; they could be moved about from place to place; they usually received salaries, though they might also be rewarded by the grant of small fiefs. But the important point was that their power was derived from their offices, not their fiefs, and that when they ceased to hold office they lost their power. Most, though not all, of these men belonged to the class of small feudal tenants; they were either lesser vassals or rear-vassals of the lord whom they served. This was another proof of the value of the protection given to this class by the greater lords. Small vassals could now hope for greater rewards from entering the administrative service of a suzerain than from staying on their estates and serving a local lord. And they no longer had to fear that they would lose their lands to rapacious neighbors if they left home to serve in a distant court.

The German solution to the problem of finding lay administrative officials was a little different from that of the western countries. In Germany, lay officials came largely from the class of *ministeriales*, hereditary servants of the lords.[26] The *ministeriales* were of servile origin, but they rose steadily in the social scale as they acquired lands and offices. By the end of the twelfth century many of them could hardly be distinguished from the lesser free vassals. Thus they were not unlike the men who held administrative posts in the western states, and they received equally important positions. In the long run, they proved less reliable than the *baillis* in France or the circuit judges in England, but this was largely a result of the civil wars and political confusion of thirteenth-century Germany. In the twelfth century they served their lords faithfully and enabled German rulers to build up reasonably effective administrative systems.

Not all feudal lords developed a staff of lay administrative officials during the twelfth century. The lords of small districts obviously had less need for this kind of assistance; they also had fewer opportunities to secure capable men. Some great lords were equally backward in this respect; thus the duke of Burgundy had no *baillis* until the middle of the thirteenth century.[27] But the advantages of the new system were clear; the lords who had lay administrative officials had more effective courts, drew greater revenues from their lands, and had a better chance of making permanent additions to their possessions. Their competitive position was so much improved that in the end all lords had to follow their example if they hoped to retain any rights of government.

The changes which I have been discussing were, of course, not uniform throughout western Europe. They went farthest in England and in Normandy, and it is precisely in England and Normandy that we find the strongest and most unified feudal states. They were observable, but less complete in France, notably in matters of finance and judicial administration. Moreover, in France many lesser lords retained a large degree of autonomy well into the thirteenth century, and real centralization came after, rather than before 1200. These changes were also felt in Germany, where Barbarossa tried to create a feudal system which would give peace and a certain degree of unity to his realm. But he began late, and his work was vitiated by his need to secure the support of the greater lords for his Italian policy. This led him to accept a too rigid feudal system, in which the princes of the Empire intervened effectively between him and lesser vassals, and in which he renounced the possibility of adding any great fief to the royal domain.[28] Thus in the end the real beneficiaries of the new type of feudalism in Germany were the princes rather than the king.

Difference in the degree and effectiveness of changes in feudalism in the twelfth century should not obscure the fact that the direction of change was clear and irreversible. The thirteenth century is the best proof of this assertion. During the thirteenth century the importance of personal service from vassals to lords continued to decline; the power of overlords continued to increase, and the number of professional and semiprofessional administrative agents grew. The states which came out of the thirteenth century with reasonably strong and efficient governments were the states which had been able to profit from these changes.

NOTES

1   See the discussion of local lordships in J. Boussard, *Le gouvernement d'Henri II Plantegenêt* (Paris, 1956), pp. 229–33.

2   C. H. Haskins, *Norman Institutions* (Cambridge, 1925), pp. 11–12, 22; Michel de Bouard, "Le Duché de Normandie," in Lot and Fawtier, *Histoire des institutions françaises au Moyen Age*, I (Paris, 1957), 7–8, 13.

3   F. L. Ganshof, *Qu'est-ce que la féodalité?* (Neuchâtel, 1947), p. 171. Cf. the section in Heinrich Mitteis, *Lehnrecht und Staatsgewalt* (Weimar, 1933), pp. 522–27, which is called in the table of contents "Verdinglichung des Lehnsvertrag."

4 On liege homage see Marc Bloch, *La société féodale: la formation des liens de dépendance* (Paris, 1949), pp. 330–36; and Mitteis, pp. 556–69.

5 Sidney Painter, *Studies in the History of the English Feudal Barony* (The Johns Hopkins University Studies in Historical and Political Science, Series LXI, no. 3, Baltimore, 1943), pp. 30–37, 125–28.

6 Mitteis, pp. 615–16; Bloch, pp. 343–45. The first clear cases of the feudal aid come in Normandy and Anjou in the first half of the twelfth century; it develops later in the French royal domain and is almost unknown in Germany.

7 Bloch, pp. 311–13.

8 Mitteis, pp. 615, 674, generally no reliefs or aids in Germany; Jean Richard, *Les ducs de Bourgogne et la formation du duché* (Paris, 1954), p. 106, no reliefs in Burgundy.

9 Glanvill, *De Legibus et Consuetudinibus Regni Angliae*, ed. G. E. Woodbine (New Haven, 1932), lib. VII, cap. 10 (p. 108): "...si quis in capite de domino rege tenere debet, tunc eius custodia ad dominum regem plene pertinet, sive alios dominos habere debeat ipse heres sive non."

10 Painter, pp. 34–37, 125–26.

11 Stubbs, *Select Charters* (9th ed.; Oxford, 1921), p. 122.

12 E. Chénon, *Étude sur l'histoire des alleux en France* (Paris, 1888), pp. 34–42; Richard, pp. 102–7; J. W. Thompson, *Feudal Germany* (Chicago, 1928), pp. 293–94; *Sachsenspiegel*, Lehnrecht, ch. 65, para. 4; ch. 71, paras. 6, 7.

13 A. Luchaire, *Histoire des institutions monarchiques de la France* (Paris, 1883), I, 35–38; J. Declareuil, *Histoire générale du droit français* (Paris, 1925), pp. 188–89.

14 Mitteis, pp. 427–49, and especially pp. 428, 448–49.

15 Richard, p. 105.

16 Julius Goebel, *Felony and Misdemeanor* (New York, 1937), I, 281, 287, 290, 391.

17 Mitteis, pp. 426–27; Freiherr von Dungern, "Die Staatsreform der Hohenstaufen," in *Festschrift für Ernst Zitelmann* (Munich, 1913), p. 28.

18 Frederick Pollock and Frederic Maitland, *History of English Law* (Cambridge, 1923), I, 386; W. S. McKechnie, *Magna Carta* (Glasgow, 1914), pp. 347–49.

19 Pollock and Maitland, I, 146–48.

20 Luchaire, I, 273; II, 31–32, 34–35; Ch. V. Langlois, *Textes relatifs à l'histoire du Parlement de Paris* (Paris, 1888), nos. 5, 7, 11, 12, 15.

21 Mitteis, pp. 441–42.

22 Richard, pp. 398–99.

23 F. L. Ganshof, "La Flandre," p. 393, in Lot and Fawtier.

24 Boussard, p. 357.

25 For the first appearance of *baillis* in Normandy and Flanders see M. de Bouard and Ganshof in Lot and Fawtier, pp. 32, 404. There were *baillis* in Champagne by the year 1189.—*Ibid.*, p. 132. For the royal domain in France see Ch. Petit-Dutaillis, *Feudal Monarchy in France and England* (London, 1936), pp. 184–86.

26 Mitteis, pp. 445–48; von Dungern, pp. 24–26.

27 Richard, pp. 459 ff.

28 Mitteis, pp. 440–42, 448.

Ernst H. Kantorowicz

Kingship under the Impact
of Scientific Jurisprudence

Participants* of a Symposium which was arranged to demonstrate from various points of view the characteristic features of "Twelfth-Century Europe," will be inclined, despite the additional heading "and the Foundations of Modern Society," to fall under the spell of Charles Homer Haskins' great vision and ingenious thesis of "The Renaissance of the Twelfth Century." Although the subject I have proposed to discuss tonight would seem to confirm rather than refute Haskins' thesis it is not at all my intention to deal with "Renaissance" features or analyze twelfth-century kingship *sub specie iurisprudentiae renatae.*[1] It is my intention to stick more closely to "the Foundations of Modern Society" and point out certain effects which a disciplined scientific jurisprudence—reborn or not—seems to have had upon the idea of medieval kingship.

What unquestionably distinguished, in the public sphere, the twelfth century from the preceding centuries was the sheer existence of a learned jurisprudence.[2] Law, of course, there always existed, even in the darkest of the so-called Dark Ages. It will be quite sufficient here to recall the impressive sets of Dooms of the Anglo-Saxon kings, the Lombard edicts, the Visigothic law collections, or the *Capitularia* of the Carolingians in order to understand that the earlier Middle Ages were anything but lawless. These *leges barbarorum*, however, were characterized by the fact that according to their claims and their applicability they all were provincial and not universal; second, that they were the work not of professional jurists, but of jurisprudential laymen even though many a feather may have been borrowed from scientific, that is, Roman law; finally, that those laws, which represented the customs of a tribe or a region, were administered by jurisprudential laymen (kings, counts, clerics, noblemen, or *missi* of any kind) and not by learned and scientifically trained judges. A similar situation prevailed within the realm of ecclesiastical law. True enough, the canons of the councils, decrees of popes, and certain laws of the Christian emperors—apart from Scripture and patristic tradition—formed *a priori* a body of ecclesiastical law which, however, was as yet unsifted and unorganized. A period of regional-provincial collections of canonical material (African, Hispanic, Gallican, Italian) was followed by a period of private collections of a more universal character, of which a respectable number was produced between the Carolingian age and that of Gregory VII. Thereafter, however, the forces released by the Church Reform and the Struggle over Investitures broadened the universalistic outlooks. After the efforts of Burchard of Worms and Ivo of Chartres, a compendious and organized body of canon law was privately composed, around 1140, by the Bolognese monk Gratian, the *Decretum Gratiani*.[3] Nor can we doubt that it was by the power of the same forces that the body of Roman law was reactivated which, in its turn, was not without influence on the work of Gratian.[4] Hence, a universal ecclesiastical law and a universal secular law made their appearance, within a generation or two, in the early twelfth century.

The intricate problem of the survival of Roman law during the Middle Ages and the process of its so-called revival shall concern us here as little as the question who first made Bologna the home of legal studies, Pepo or Irnerius.[5] It is quite sufficient for our present purpose to know that in the pamphlet literature of the Struggle over Investitures Roman law was not infrequently, if only sporadically and unsystematically, applied to bolster the imperial position as well as to undermine it;[6] further, that around 1100, or a little later, Irnerius taught Roman law at Bologna; finally, that around 1140 Gratian composed in Bologna his *Decretum*. At any rate, two independent, though eventually interdependent, sets of law, both universal according to claims and applicability, came into existence in the twelfth century. The scientific interpretation of these sets of law became a "must" owing to the numerous contradictions and other difficulties, and it gave birth to a methodical study of sources and parallels, and therewith to a legal science which, in the course of time, mothered our modern historico-philological method. That is to say, once the two bodies of law, Roman and canon, were placed before the scholar, there resulted also the challenge to understand, interpret, and apply the law scientifically—comparable to the effects issuing from Holy Scripture and leading to numerous expositions on the books of the Bible or, as happened later, to the effects of the *corpus Aristotelicum* and its commentation in the age of scholasticism. Canonistic studies (hitherto a branch of theology) and secular jurisprudence (hither-to a branch of rhetoric) became each a science in its own right. Legal science acquired the rank of "moral philosophy"; it became autonomous and soon rose to be a challenge to theology.[7]

Moreover, through the concentration of the new legal studies in the city of Bologna and their combination with the study of the notariate and with the *ars dictandi*, a broad layer of legally trained men and minds began to spread, especially in Italy where the jurists became the foremost representatives of the Italian intelligentsia, a legal profession the like of which did not exist in the earlier Middle Ages. This change did not escape contemporary observers who in prose and in jingling verses began to complain that the study of the two lucrative arts—jurisprudence and medicine—tended to eclipse the study of literature, and of letters in general, as well as of theology. These complaints were repeated over and over again, from the time of Stephen Langton who was not the first to do so, to Dante who was not the last.[8]

Another consequence of the new study of law was perhaps more decisive. In former days, law was a matter dealt with by kings, grandees, and wise old men—by *witan* of every pattern—and it was administered by noblemen, clerics, and others enjoying the king's confidence. Beginning with the twelfth century, however, law became a matter to be treated with scientific accuracy, and justice was administered (the later, the more exclusively) by judges trained in the laws and in legal thinking. This evolution resulted in a remarkable change of the earlier medieval social stratification. As the number of Doctors of Law increased (wrote, around 1180, Ralph Niger), the jurists in their pride demanded to be called not doctors or masters, but *domini*, lords;[9] that is, they assumed a title normally reserved to noblemen and prelates who represented the two ruling classes during the earlier Middle Ages. From the twelfth century onward, the two knighthoods of former days (the *militia armata* of chivalry and the *militia inermis* or *celestis* of the clergy) were comple-mented or supplemented by a third knighthood of jurists, the *militia legum* or knighthood of law, and soon of letters at large (*militia litterata* or *doctoralis*).[10] Roman law stipulated that a *filius familias* could dispose freely of his *peculium castrense*, that is, of everything he had earned as a soldier (*miles*) or as a public official, as a lawyer, or otherwise in the service of the Prince. The medieval jurists interpreted the word *miles*, "soldier," in the medieval sense of "knight"; and since Roman law "equiparated" the lawyer and the *miles* or knight, the glossators began to claim knighthood for the jurist.[11] This claim was put up, at the latest, by the great Placentinus who died in 1192; it was repeated by Azo and the *Glossa ordinaria* on Roman law composed by Accursius around 1230, and by many others as well. And thus it happened that by the second half of the thirteenth century the doctor's hat was generally recognized as an equivalent of the *cingulum militare* of knighthood.[12] By applying the terminology of Roman law to the conditions of the high Middle Ages (in fact, by misinterpreting Justinian's laws) the jurists further arrived at the theory that every Doctor of Laws who had taught at a university for twenty years had the rank of a count.[13] However that may be, the tombs of the great jurists in Bologna display, without an exception, the title *Dominus*, Lord, before the name of the deceased.

The social rise of legal intelligentsia certainly reflected the general importance of the learned jurists and their authority to which eventually all princes, secular and spiritual, paid their respects. Justinian had styled Ulpian his friend (*amicus*) and father (*parens*) just as he styled the jurists Theophilus and Dorotheus his predecessors (*antecessores*) and gave them the title of *viri illustres*.[14] It was natural for the medieval jurists to make the most of Justinian's words. Azo, for example, said quite bluntly that legal science "effects that the professors of law rule solemnly over the *orbis terrarum* and sit in the imperial court judging in a lordly fashion tribes and nations, plaintiffs and defendants."[15] Bracton repeated, and enlarged on, Azo's words, changing, however, "emperor" and "imperial" into "king" and "royal."[16] And Cynus of Pistoia exclaimed: "Thou seest, oh student, how much the [legal] science effects which makes the jurisprudent a father and friend of the Prince."[17] Indeed, the twelfth, thirteenth, and fourteenth centuries were the golden age of the jurisprudents. As the jurists became the chief advisers and councillors of princes, the princes became more and more dependent on them. As early as 1115 we find Irnerius in the entourage of Emperor Henry V where he also served as a judge.[18] Further, no medievalist will have missed the stories about Barbarossa conversing with, and seeking the counsel of, the learned Four Doctors of Bologna. Moreover, the professional jurist became the professional administrator of justice, the professional judge. Gone were the times when the customs and laws of a country were remembered by the wise old men only and when some sort of natural reason, combined with a man's social standing, made a person fit to sit in court as a judge. What counted in the age of the new jurisprudence was that the judge arrived at his sentence in a scientific, rational fashion, which among other things excluded ordeals by fire or water, and that he judged according to his lawbooks or was able—as in England—to expound the common law scientifically as a professional. By gradually monopolizing the administration of justice, the legal profession, however, began to encroach upon the position of the king himself in his capacity of judge. The medieval king could, and would, sit in court if he so pleased and could himself adjudicate the cases before him. This custom died slowly. Frederick II still sat in court; so did Henry III of England as well as Edward I and Edward II.[19] Later something changed. It is true, the king was the fountain of justice; he was supposed to interpret the law in case of obscurity; the courts were still the "king's courts" and the king was still considered the judge ordinary of his realm whereas the judges, who derived their power from him, acted only as delegate judges. For all that, the custom arose that the king should not pass judgment himself: *Rex aut Imperator non cognoscunt in causis eorum*, "king and emperor do not pronounce judicially in their causes," says Andreas of Isernia quite explicitly.[20] Cynus uses approximately the same words ("Imperator causas suas non ipse cognoscit: sed iudices alios facit"), but adds: "Licet quando velit, et ipse possit in re sua iudex esse."[21] Indeed, it was common opinion that in cases pertaining to the fisc the prince could be *iudex in causa propria*, and, as Bracton shows, also in cases of high treason[22]—opinions well prepared by Pope Innocent IV discussing the limitations of a bishop's competency to pass judgment himself.[23] Normally, however, the king was supposed to judge exclusively through his judges who were juristic professionals and who, in lieu of the king, were expected to have all the pertinent laws present to their mind, *in scrinio pectoris*.[24]

Ever since the end of the thirteenth century, the jurists also gave a reason for that custom. The South-Italian Andreas of Isernia, writing around 1300, was hardly the first to make the blunt statement that the king has to rely upon his jurisprudents because *raro princeps iurista invenitur*, "rarely will a prince be found who is a jurist."[25] In similar terms, Sir John Fortescue explained that it was unfit for a king "to investigate precise points of the law ... but these should be left to your judges and advocates ... and others skilled in the law. In fact, you will render judgment better through others than by yourself, for none of the kings of England is seen to give judgment by his own lips, yet all the judgments of the realm are his...." And Fortescue added that the legal experience necessary for judges is scarcely attainable in twenty years of study.[26] It was this doctrine which finally brought about one of the fiercest clashes between Sir Edward Coke and King James I. At a Star Chamber session, the king, taking his seat on the normally empty throne, declared he would ever protect the common law. "No," interjected Sir Edward Coke, "the common law protects the king." The angry king, shaking his fist at Coke, later argued that "he thought the law was founded upon reason, and that he and others had reason as well as the judges." To that Coke replied calmly that indeed the king had excellent gifts by nature, "but his Majesty was not learned in the laws of his realm of England, and causes which concern the life, or inheritance, or goods, or fortunes of his subjects, are not to be decided by natural reason, but by the artificial reason and judgment of law, which... requires long study and experience before that a man can attain to the cognizance of it." [27]

Raro princeps iurista invenitur: the modern idea of a king who no longer is supposed to take causes out of his courts and give judgment upon them himself, originated from the stratum of scientific jurisprudence which emerged in the twelfth century. The new jurisprudence which so often has been claimed (and rightly so) as supporting royal absolutism, in this case put some restrictions on royal arbitrariness by depriving the king from functioning actively on the bench as supreme judge. Roman law, however, had the effect of bridling the king in other respects as well.

During the great strife between Pope Gregory VII and Emperor Henry IV both curialists and imperialists began to make use of the *lex regia* or *lex de imperio* for the purpose of arguing whether or not an emperor could be deposed. The law, transmitted by the *Digest*, the *Code*, and the *Institutes* of Justinian, advanced the doctrine that the *imperium*, originally vested in the *populus Romanus* and its *maiestas*, had been conferred by the Roman people upon the Roman emperor. This act, in itself, was double-edged, as it touched upon two principles diametrically opposed to each other. It could imply (and this was the opinion of the imperial party) that the Romans, once and for all, had renounced the supreme power, which irrevocably they bestowed upon the Prince, or rather upon the Prince's office. On the other hand, the same law allowed the curialists to defend the opposite thesis: that the Prince, individually, had been appointed by the Roman people as the administrator of the empire, and that this appointment was not at all irrevocable. Manegold of Lautenbach (*ca.* 1085) even went so far as to say that a prince who failed as a governor could be chased away just as a farmer could chase away an unfaithful swineherd.[28] The prince thus became an employee of the sovereign people, since the supreme power was supposed to rest always and imprescriptibly with the sovereign people of Rome.

We notice that herewith the principle of popular sovereignty was foreshadowed during the Struggle over Investitures, and may add that it permeated the ideologies of the twelfth century. For one thing, the City-Romans in the days of Arnold of Brescia defended this idea when Barbarossa prepared to come for his coronation to Rome, and the Roman leaders claimed that the citizens of the Eternal City alone were entitled to dispose of the imperial diadem—an argument to which Barbarossa answered that he held his *imperium* from God alone and from God directly.[29] The history of Rome in the thirteenth and fourteenth centuries actually centered upon the theory of Roman popular sovereignty until finally, in 1328, an emperor, Louis of Bavaria, actually received the diadem at the hands of the senators and people of Rome, not in St. Peter's, but on the Capitoline Hill.[30] It is true, of course, that the civilians during the twelfth and thirteenth centuries and beyond were inclined to uphold the origin of the imperial power directly from God; but they also left no doubt that indeed the ancient Roman *populus* acted within its right when it claimed to be the ultimate source of the imperial power, whereas opinion was divided with regard to the claims of the medieval City-Romans or, for that matter, with regard to any medieval *populus*. It was finally as a result of the intransigence of the hierocratic theory, according to which the emperor depended not on God directly but on the pope, that the Roman lawyers, and some moderate canonists as well, recognized the popular origin of the imperial power, and used the idea of popular sovereignty as a means to freeze out the papal claims. Hence the jurists, while always ready to back the direct, divine origin of imperial power, tried to combine the imperial claims to direct divine descent with those to popular origin. The *Glossa ordinaria* of Accursius therefore neatly combined "God" and the "people" as the two sources of imperial authority and thereby came close to the, so to say, final formulation of John of Paris around 1300: *populo faciente et Deo inspirante.*[31]

To the debate on the *lex regia* the twelfth-century jurists contributed after their fashion by glossing on that law: Irnerius and Roger, Pillius, Placentinus, and Azo as well as canonists such as Rufinus, Bazianus, and the authors of anonymous works.[32] The arguments of the *lex regia* in favor of the popular origin of imperial power were used against papal claims by Frederick II, and against papal as well as imperial claims by the Senator Brancaleone and by Cola di Rienzo, and culminated of course in the doctrine of Marsilio of Padua.[33]

On the other hand, the context in which the *lex regia* was quoted in the *Digest* and the *Institutes* seemed to support the budding royal absolutism, for it was quoted in order to substantiate the sentence which for centuries remained the pith of absolutist desires: *Quod principi placuit, legis habet vigorem.* "What has pleased the Prince, has the force of law," for the Prince legally owned the power to legislate after the people had conferred the *imperium* upon him. Roman law, however, also provided the means to check unscrupulousness on the part of the prince. As opposed to the absolutists, the constitutionalists referred to a law in the *Code*, the *Digna vox*, in which the legislator frankly declared himself bound to the law: "It is a word worthy of the majesty of the ruler that the prince professes himself bound to the law: so much does our authority depend upon the authority of the law."[34] Therewith the gates were flung open to the problem of whether the prince be "above the law" or "under the law." It shall not be denied that the problem itself existed before, but it became articulate with the reactivation and the exegesis of Roman law, and gained additional importance by the question whether and to what extent the ruler was bound to local customs.[35] The jurists, of course, were fully aware of the glaring contradiction presented by Roman law itself, of the antinomy between the maxims *princeps legibus solutus* and *princeps legibus alligatus*, and they tried to discuss away the discrepancy by stressing that the prince, though not fettered by the law, should voluntarily bind himself to the law, especially to the laws he himself may have issued. On the basis of this antinomy John of Salisbury felt prompted to interpret the prince as being at once an *imago aequitatis* and a *servus aequitatis*, just as Frederick II claimed to be at once "Father and son, lord and servant of Justice."[36] It was perhaps Thomas Aquinas who, in his orderly fashion, overcame the apparent legal impasse when he explained that indeed the prince was *legibus solutus* with regard to the *vis coactiva*, the coercive power of man-made positive law which received its power from the prince anyhow; on the other hand, Aquinas held that the Prince was bound to the *vis directiva*, the directive power of natural law to which he should submit voluntarily—and for that purpose Aquinas, too, quoted the *Digna vox*.[37] This cleverly phrased opinion, by which Aquinas combined most of the earlier arguments, offered not only for the moment an acceptable way out of the dilemma: it was acceptable to both adversaries and defenders of the more absolutist concepts of kingship, and therefore it was still quoted by Bossuet while Louix XIV himself acknowledged its essence.[38]

We recognize that Roman law had its say in eminently political and ethical matters, sponsoring, as it did, both popular sovereignty and royal absolutism, both a kingship above the law and one bound to the law, and that thereby, to say the least, it kept the discussion moving. To some extent we probably should connect (as A.-J. Carlyle did) the conflict among the jurists about the *lex regia* with the conflict between the new lawbooks and the customs, or the customary law, of the land.[39] There is, however, an ethical substratum in this dispute as well as in the *Digna vox* itself: "It is worthy of the majesty of the ruler that the prince professes himself bound to the law."

Political ethics, to be sure, were influenced by Roman law in very many respects. For one thing, there developed, beginning in the twelfth century, a growing awareness of the transpersonal, or "public," character of the commonwealth, the *res publica*. On the basis of Roman law John of Salisbury styled the prince a *persona publica*, a *potestas publica*;[40] and it did not take long before one began to learn that also the fisc (whose characteristics were broadly discussed in the Tenth Book of Justinian's *Code*) was a public institution which "never died" and therefore survived the individual prince. This was true also of the "Crown" in the abstract and in a suprapersonal sense of the word which began to be used in France and in England as early as the twelfth century: Suger of St. Denis and Henry I of England (under whom the office of "coroner," charged with maintaining judicial and fiscal rights of the crown, came into being) may stand here as the landmarks. Slightly more emotional was the notion of *patria* applied to the kingdom in twelfth-century literature, in France (*Song of Roland*) as well as in England (Geoffrey of Monmouth). Moreover, a few years ago Gaines Post showed how much the two laws, Roman and canon, contributed to giving currency to the idea of *patria* which likewise implied a transpersonal concept of public perpetuity: to fight for the *patria*, to die for the *patria*, even to kill without qualms one's father or brother for the sake of the *patria*, to procreate children for the *patria*, or to pay special taxes *pro necessitate* or *pro defensione patriae*. All those were ideals (no matter whether we like them or not) which were disseminated by the two laws and the new jurisprudence.[41]

Those political or public ethics inevitably influenced also the image of the ruler. The *prooemium* of Justinian's *Institutes* opens with a philosophical remark of general importance: "The imperial majesty must needs be not only decorated with arms, but also armed with laws that it be able to govern rightly in either time, in war and in peace." This opening of the authoritative juristic textbook not only suggested a farewell to the purely military ideal of a kingship relying upon the sword, but also contained a challenge for a king to act as a legislator. The dialectics, however, of the formula *armis decorata—legibus armata* conjured an image of majesty rooted in far deeper layers, and the humanistically well versed jurists of the Renaissance recognized that Justinian's formula was a transformation of Greek ideals and that it reflected that *optimum* of rulership expounded in Plato's *Republic*: kings who philosophize and philosophers who rule as kings. Emblematic drawings rendering the gist of Justinian's formula were not rare in the Renaissance. They showed a king brandishing a sword in one hand and a book in the other, until finally an *impresa* of the sixteenth century, bearing the motto *Ex utroque Caesar* (an allusion to Justinian's *utrumque tempus*), changed the meaning of the book in the prince's left hand, which now no longer was supposed to represent "Laws" specifically, but "Letters," because "by these two, that is, Arms and Letters, Julius Caesar... was made the lord of the whole world." Or else, the book stood for "Arts" in general, as explained by the accompanying verse: "A *Prince's* most ennobling parts/Are skill in *Armes*, and love of *Arts*."[42]

That kind of dialectical tension was, so to speak, daily bread in the twelfth century, in which not only the ideals of "knight" and "cleric" merged, as, for example, in the orders of knighthood as well as in courtly poetry,[43] but in which also the *rex literatus* appeared as another ideal. In a way, John of Salisbury anticipated the Renaissance motto when he declared (and he was not the first to do so) that an illiterate king was nothing but an *asinus coronatus*.[44] John of Salisbury does not refer to the Prologue of the *Institutes*, though he quotes it in another connection. But Glanville, the great English jurisprudent under King Henry II, opened the prologue to his *De legibus* with the very words of the *Institutes*, changing only Justinian's *imperialem maiestatem* into the more modest and appropriate *regiam potestatem*. His paraphrase then wandered to the

Scottish lawbook commonly called the *Regiam maiestatem;* it served the writer of *Fleta* to formulate his prologue, and it is found also in a spurious proem to Bracton's *De legibus,* whereas the genuine Bracton drew directly from the *Institutes* or from Azo's *Summa Institutionum.*[45] If we add the late medieval tractates on the subject of "Knighthood and Jurisprudence," *De militia et iurisprudentia,* we not only recognize the influence of the prologue to the *Institutes,* but also begin to see more clearly the bearings of the "legal knighthood," the *militia legum,* to which, as early as the twelfth century, the jurists aspired.[46]

Scientific jurisprudence gradually began to change the vocabulary of statecraft, and the new vocabulary began to influence statecraft itself. If those concerned continuously read and heard and had discussions about whether the people or the prince should be recognized as the true founder of law; or about the fact that the prince is not only decorated with arms, but also armed with laws; that the prince is *legibus alligatus,* though in some respects he be *legibus solutus,* and that what pleases him has the strength of law, then indeed it should not be surprising to find that the prince accepted and grew into the new role of legislator. Indeed, the law-making king began to eclipse the law-preserving king of earlier centuries, and the *rex legislator* superseded the more religiously tinted *rex iustus.* The image of Justinian and Tribonian began to obscure that of Melchizedek, whose name was translated *rex iustitiae.*[47] That is to say, under the impact of jurisprudence and juristic rationalism the ideal of liturgical kingship began to disintegrate. Its roots had been undercut anyhow by the papacy of the Church Reform. Now it fell to Justinian's lawbooks and their vocabulary to replace and, in a secular sense, restore some of the religious values of kingship, which had determined, as an effluence of the ruler's liturgical consecration (then still considered a sacrament), the image of kingship in the centuries preceding the Struggle over Investitures.

At the height of that struggle, around 1100, the so-called Norman (or York) Anonymous defended more vigorously than any other author the idea of Christ-centered, liturgical kingship, and therewith that of the priestly character of the king who was "not quite a layman," nay, was (as a result of his anointment) a *rex et sacerdos.* Forty years later, in King Roger II's prologue to his Assizes (1140), the shift from liturgy to law becomes manifest in a peculiar way. The position of "king and priest" was claimed, after a fashion, also by Roger II; but he regained his quasi-priestly character not through the Church (this was impossible after the Gregorian Age), but through the high pretensions of Roman legal philosophy, extracted from the prologue to the *Digest*, where the jurisprudents were compared to priests. The ancient liturgical language still reverberated in King Roger's prologue, but its spirit was that of Justinian. Like Justinian, the Sicilian king called his lawbook an oblation to God, an offering of mercy and justice, and then continued: "By this oblation the royal office assumes for itself a certain privilege of priesthood; wherefore some wise man and jurisprudent [in the *Digest*] called the law-interpreters Priests of Justice."[48] That is to say, the point of reference of this new ideal of priest-kingship was no longer the Anointed of God of the *Books of Kings* and the *Psalter*, but the legislator and jurisprudent as depicted in the lawbooks of Justinian.

The metaphorical quasi-priesthood of the jurisprudents, and thereby of the king who was the *iudex iudicum* of his kingdom, was frequently discussed and interpreted by the glossators. In a twelfth-century collection of legal word definitions, the author, drawing from the *Institutes*, expounded under the heading *De sacris et sacratis* the new (or, in fact, very old) dualism: "There is one thing holy which is human, such as the laws; and there is another thing holy which is divine, such as things pertaining to the Church. And among the priests, some are divine priests, such as presbyters; others are human priests, such as magistrates, who are called priest because they dispense things holy, that is laws."[49] That doctrine of bipartition was carried on in the law schools. The *Glossa ordinaria* refers to it, and Baldus, in the fourteenth century, still defended the thesis that *legum professores dicuntur sacerdotes*, for (says he) there is a *sacerdotium spirituale* as well as a *sacerdotium temporale*; just as Bracton distinguished between *res sacrae* pertaining to God and *res quasi sacrae* pertaining to the fisc.[50] This general mood of the glossators was curiously epitomized by Gulielmus Durandus, the great jurist and liturgical expert at the end of the thirteenth century, who referred to the glossators when he declared, not at all disapprovingly, "that the emperor ranked as a presbyter according to the passage [in the *Digest*] where it is said: 'Deservedly we [the jurisprudents] are called priests.'" It is remarkable that here a positive effort was made to derive the prince's nonlaical character not from his anointment with the holy balm and his consecration, but from Ulpian's solemn comparison of judges with priests.[51]

In this connection we may recall also that it was in the days of Barbarossa only, and not before, that the medieval empire began to be styled "the holy empire," *sacrum imperium*—and every medieval historian

should feel uneasy when in his textbook he constantly reads that Charlemagne, in 800, was crowned emperor of the "Holy Roman Empire,"
a statement teeming with mistakes and misconceptions and as anachro-
nistic as talking about the guns of Alexander or the paratroopers of
Caesar. *Sacer*, in the language of Roman law, meant no more than
"imperial," though in medieval Latin it may have had more Christian-
ecclesiastical connotations. It was, at any rate, from Roman law that
Barbarossa borrowed the epithet *sacrum* for his *imperium*, and it would
spoil the specific flavor of both the time of Charlemagne and the age
of Barbarossa with its new jurisprudence by using uncritically the
epithet "sacred" for the events of 800. And one more little warning
should be sounded. We are far too often inclined to talk about "secularization" of ecclesiastical thought and institutions in connection with the
modern state. Secularization certainly there was—when, for example,
the marriage of Christ to the universal Church, or the marriage of the
bishop to his local church, was by analogy transferred to the political
sphere: the jurists pointed out that the king was wedded to his realm
as a "mystical groom." [52] But we find little of that "secularization" in
the twelfth century. What happened then was not a secularization of the
spiritual, but rather a spiritualization and sanctification of the secular.
Sacrum imperium was not a borrowing from the vocabulary of the Church;
it was a para-ecclesiastical designation in its own right, though when
reintroduced it replaced the old antithesis of *sacerdotium* and *regnum* by the
more coördinating and complementary designations of *sancta ecclesia* and
sacrum imperium, holy Church and sacred empire. In other words, the
sacred character of the empire, and of the emperor himself, no longer
drew its strength from the idea of the *christus domini*, from the altar, or
from the Church, but it was a secular sacredness *sui iuris* and *sui generis*
apart from the Church, a concept which eventually found its most
eloquent interpreter in Dante and his vision of two Paradises, one
imperial-terrestrial and the other ecclesiastical-celestial.

It would be wrong to assume that the dualism of sacredness and
holiness was produced by Roman law alone. From Justinian there
derived the vocabulary, the technical term *sacrum imperium;* Roman law,
however, represented but one current within a very complex evolution,
as may be grasped from many examples. The Christ-centered kingship
of the earlier Middle Ages found one expression in the ruler's title of
honor, *vicarius Christi*. In the thirteenth century, however, this title
became rarer, and without disappearing completely it was replaced

by that of *vicarius Dei*, "Vicar of God." What this change implied was again a loosening of the ties with which the medieval prince was linked to the altar, to the sacrificial God-man who was not only the eternal King but also the eternal Priest. What had happened is again a rather complex evolution of which no more than two strands shall be mentioned here. On the one hand, the dogmatic-theological development of the twelfth century towards defining the real presence of Christ in the Sacrament produced a new accentuation of the very ancient idea of the presence of Christ in the person of the vicariously mass-celebrating priest. The *Decretum Gratiani* quoted a number of places in which bishops and priests were styled *vicarii Christi;* but by the end of the twelfth century *vicarius Christi* became next to exclusively the title of honor of the supreme hierarch, the Roman pontiff.[53] On the other hand, the hierocratic terminology found an unexpected ally in Roman law. For, the civilians, relying upon the vocabulary of Justinian's lawbooks and on Roman authors such as Seneca and Vegetius, began to style the emperor *deus in terris*, *deus terrenus*, or *deus praesens*, taking it for granted on the basis of their sources, that the prince was above all "vicar of God" and not "vicar of Christ." In fact, the designation *vicarius Christi* for the emperor would not have been within the range of legal language at all. Thus it happened that the Christocentric ideal of rulership dissolved also under the influence of Roman law, and gave way to a more theocentric concept. Henceforth, a papal *Christus in terris* (to use an expression of Arnald of Villanova) found a counterpart in an imperial *deus in terris*.[54]

Another bifocality may be discerned with regard to the universalism of the Roman Empire and the territorial monarchies, and herein again Roman law plays an important role. It was in the twelfth century only that Roman law, by which (as was commonly imagined) in ancient times the whole *orbis terrarum* had been governed, became the new *Kaiserrecht*, the valid law of the medieval lords of the *sacrum imperium*. The universalistic character of Roman law was taken for granted even before its reactivation in the twelfth century: around 1050, the hope was voiced by Anselm the Peripatetic that the ancient universalism was to be restored not *armis*, but *legibus*: "Legibus antiquis totus reparabitur orbis"—"By the ancient laws, the whole world shall be repaired."[55] It was a hope still shared by Dante, among many others.

Moreover, independently of Roman law, the universality of the Roman Empire appeared throughout the Middle Ages as an established fact, since St. Jerome, and his identification of Daniel's Fourth World Monarchy with the empire of the Romans, held the sway. In the twelfth century the universalistic tendencies inherent in both Roman law and Roman Empire were linked to the Hohenstaufen emperors, and these medieval princes were backed not only by dreams and myths, but also by the reality of law itself. That union was consummated by the time of Barbarossa, at the latest. The landmarks are the Diet of Roncaglia of 1158, the assertion of the Four Doctors that the medieval emperor was the *dominus mundi*, and the decision of Barbarossa to incorporate one of his own laws, the *Authentica Habita* or *Privilegium scholasticum* granting to students universal safety, in Justinian's *Code*, an act emphasizing that Barbarossa considered himself the direct successor of the ancient Roman emperors.[56] The universality of the empire, however, was not only one of space, but also one of time. Daniel's Fourth Empire (that is, in Jerome's interpretation, the Roman Empire) was to last until the end of the world. This was a myth. But the myth now was backed by jurisprudence since the lawbooks of Justinian stated over and over again that "the empire is forever," *Imperium semper est*. And whereas Jerome's mythical sempiternity referred to the Roman Empire alone, the statement of the lawbooks *Imperium semper est* had implications in the sense that every *universitas*, large or small, was juristically "forever." In other words, the juristic (though not the mythical) sempiternity of the empire was transferable to, and easily adopted by, the territorial monarchies, in fact by any *universitas* or *communitas regni*, even though they were lacking the eschatological-mythical background of the eternal Roman Empire. Subsequently, the claims to universalism on the part of the Hohenstaufen emperors and their successors were challenged by the lords of the territorial monarchies; and the best challenge was to claim the same, or at least similar, prerogatives for the territorial states. This, then, was the climate in which, from the twelfth century onward, some fundamental political dogmas began to develop in the individual monarchies, culminating finally in the famous sentence *Rex superiorem non recognoscens est imperator in regno suo*, "A king not recognizing a superior is emperor within his realm." As a result of this maxim, some special imperial prerogatives, as, for example, the right of appointing notaries public or of legitimizing illegitimate children, were passed on to the kings deeming themselves emperorlike within their realms.[57]

In addition to these fairly well defined imperial prerogative rights, however, there was passed on to the kings also the whole compound of legal philosophy contained in the imperial Roman law. For example, the *Lex Iulia maiestatis* concerning the crime of lese majesty was now appropriated by the kings although in the *Digest* and the *Code* it referred only to the emperor and to the *maiestas* of the Roman people.[58] Further, the statement of St. Jerome, embedded in canon law and saying: *Exercitus facit imperatorem*, "The army creates the emperor," was transferred to the king: *exercitus facit regem*.[59] Also, the famous maxim, derived from the *Code* and declaring that "the emperor has all the laws in the shrine of his breast," was transferred not only to the pope, the *verus imperator*, but also to the King of France; for, a French jurist (probably Thomas of Pouilly, *ca.* 1296–97), says in so many words that "of the King of France it may be said, as it is said of the emperor, that all the laws, especially those pertaining to this kingdom, are shut in his breast."[60] That, furthermore, the Roman emperor was *terra marique dominus*, "lord over land and sea" and over the elements as well, was a notion going back to antiquity. It was applied not at all rarely to Frederick II. Then, in a lawsuit concerning the association (*pariage*) of Philip IV of France and a French bishop, one of the royal legists, Guillaume de Plaisian, pointed out that the French king, since he was "emperor in his realm," had command over land and sea, whereupon the bishop mockingly answered: "Whether the king be emperor in his realm, and whether he command over land and sea and the elements, and whether the elements would obey if the king gave orders to them, is irrelevant to the points at stake."[61] How deeply engrained the belief in the king's power of commanding the elements actually was, even as late as the seventeenth century, may be gathered from the *Diary* of Samuel Pepys who, seeing in the summer of 1662 King Charles II riding in his barge in a downpour of rain, made the telling entry: "But methought it lessened my esteem of a king, that he should not be able to command the rain."[62] Finally, there should at least be mentioned a philosophical concept transmitted from Greek philosophy through the agency of Roman law, which was reapplied to the Hohenstaufen emperor and transferred to the pope in the twelfth century, until in the thirteenth it was passed on to the territorial kings: the idea of the prince as the *lex animata*, the "living" or "animate law." The usefulness of this concept for the theory of absolutism is almost self-evident, especially when, under the influence of Aristotle, the *lex animata* was turned into a *iustitia animata*. For not only was the king said to be present in all his law courts, in which finally he was present also vicariously through his image, his state portrait, or his coat of arms, but there was also a good reason for asserting that the king's will, theoretically, had the force of law: being himself the animate law, the king could do no wrong, since "whatever he did would be *ipso facto* just."[63]

To be sure, it is a long and very involved and complicated way that leads from the twelfth century to the absolutist theories of sovereignty. Nor can this rapid survey claim to have done more than barely touch upon a few problems. For all their brevity and skimpiness, however, the present remarks may suffice to demonstrate that in a discussion of "Twelfth-Century Europe and the Foundations of Modern Society" the impact of jurisprudence on government cannot easily be neglected.

NOTES

* Surgery prevented the present author from being a full-time participant of the Symposium on "Twelfth-Century Europe and the Foundations of Modern Society." He was, however, able to prepare this paper which his friend, Professor Gaines Post, was kind enough to deliver for him and even to defend in the discussion—an act of making a colleague's cause his own for which the author remains a grateful debtor.

1   Charles Homer Haskins himself has surveyed brilliantly "The Revival of Jurisprudence" in Chapter VII of his *Renaissance of the Twelfth Century* (Cambridge, 1939), pp. 192–223.

2   The truly important achievement of the so-called "rebirth of Roman law" was the evolution of a scientific jurisprudence and a jurisprudential method; this point has been stressed repeatedly, most emphatically, e.g., by Woldemar Engelmann, *Die Wiedergeburt der Rechtskultur in Italien durch die wissenschaftliche Lehre* (Leipzig, 1938).

3   A succinct and admirably organized survey of sources and history of canon law to roughly 1300 has been offered by Alphons M. Stickler, *Historia Iuris Canonici Latini*, I: *Historia Fontium* (Turin, 1950); a brief general survey, including canon law in England, was given by the Lord Bishop of Exeter, R. C. Mortimer, *Western Canon Law* (Berkeley and Los Angeles, 1953).

4   For some aspects of the interrelations between the Struggle over Investitures and the reactivation of Roman law, see Karl Jordan, "Der Kaisergedanke in Ravenna zur Zeit Heinrichs IV.," *Deutsches Archiv*, II (1938), 85–125. For Gratian and Roman law, see the report of Stephan Kuttner, "New Studies on the Roman Law in Gratian's Decretum," *The Seminar*, XI (1953), 12–50.

5   For the few documents referring to Pepo, see Hermann Kantorowicz and Beryl Smalley, "An English Theologian's View of Roman Law: Pepo, Irnerius, Ralph Niger," *Mediaeval and Renaissance Studies*, I (1941–43), 237–52.

6   For example, Petrus Crassus (cf. Jordan, "Kaisergedanke") bolstered, and Manegold (see below, note 28) undermined the imperial position by means of Roman law.

7   Hermann Kantorowicz, *Studies in the Glossators of the Roman Law* (Cambridge, 1938), pp. 37f., n. 4. Haskins, *Renaissance*, p. 199, ascribes the separation of civil law from rhetoric to Irnerius, and (p. 215) of canon law from theology to Gratian. To Hostiensis, *Summa aurea*, prooem., nos. 9–10 (Venice, 1586), col. 6, canon jurisprudence was a third *scientia* apart from theology and civil law, a *tertium genus, ex ingenio quasi permixtum*, a *scientia permixta*, because it embraces both the spiritual and the temporal. For the method, see Erich Genzmer, "Die justinianische Kodifikation und die Glossatoren," *Atti del Congresso Internazionale di Diritto Romano : Bologna*, I (Pavia, 1934), 380ff.

8   The jingle: "Dat Gallienus opes et sanctio Iustiniana./Ex aliis paleas, ex istis collige grana," quoted by Stephen Langton as well as by the *Glossa ordinaria*, on *Const. omnem*, v. 'ditissimi,' is sure to be much older; cf. H. Kantorowicz, "An English Theologian's View" (above, note 5), p. 246, n. 2; see also Haskins, *Studies in Mediaeval Culture* (Oxford, 1929), p. 47, for the rivalry between law and theology, and p. 25, for the "lucrative branches of knowledge." See Dante, *Paradiso*, IX, 133ff., and Michele Maccarone, "Teologia e diritto canonico nella *Monarchia*, III, 3," *Rivista di Storia della Chiesa in Italia*, V (1951), 23f.

9   Ralph Niger, *Moralia regum*, c. XIX, ed. H. Kantorowicz, "An English Theologian's View," p. 250, lines 31ff.: "Procedente vero tempore, aucto numero legis peritorum inpinguatus est dilectus, et recalcitravit in tantum ut legis doctores appellarentur domini, indigne ferentes appellari doctores vel magistri." Cf. p. 247, n. 2. Later the title *dominus* was an established fact. See, e.g., Lucas de Penna, *Lectura . . . super tribus libris Codicis*, on *Cod.* 12, 15 (Lyon, 1544), fol. 231^{voa}: "[doctores legum] qui etiam sunt ab omnibus honorandi nec debent ab aliis quantumcumque maximis in eorum litteris appellari fratres, sed domini. contrarium facientes puniendi sunt." Lucas de Penna actually refers to Innocent IV, *Apparatus*, on X, 2, 15, n. 5 (Lyon, 1578), fol. 200, who mentioned the *sententia dominorum*.

10   H. Fitting, *Das Castrense peculium in seiner geschichtlichen Entwicklung und heutigen gemeinrechtlichen Geltung* (Halle, 1871), pp. 531ff., has summed up the essential material. For *militia doctoralis*, see Baldus, on *Cod.* 7, 38, 1, n. 1 (Venice, 1586), fol. 28.

11   The relevant places are *Cod.* 2, 7, 4 and 14; see also 2, 6, 7 (*nobilissimos*). These laws refer to *advocati* only, but the medieval jurists expanded the reference to *jurisperiti* in general. See also *Instit.*, prooem. (below, note 42), and *Cod.*, prooem. *Summa rei publicae*, prol.

12   Fitting, *Castrense peculium*, p. 543, n. 1, for Placentinus (*milites literatoria militantes*); Azo, *Summa Institutionum*, on prooem., n. 2 (Lyon, 1530), fol. 268, distinguished three *militiae*: "Est ergo militia alia armata, alia inermis, alia literata." Already Guido Faba, *Summa dictaminis*, I, n. 28, ed. A. Gaudenzi, in *Propugnatore*, III (1890), 309, addresses a *magister* as *litteratorie militiae cingulo redimito*. This may be a figurative expression; however, the later formularies contain a form for the promotion to the doctorate, saying: ". . . celebri militia et militari cingulo [te] decoramus teque consortio, ordini et numero milicie legum doctorum et professorum aggregamus"; cf.

H. Kaiser, *Collectarius perpetuarum formarum Johannis de Geylnhusen* (Innsbruck, 1900), form 49; see, in general, Fitting, *Castrense peculium*, pp. 547ff.

13   *Cod.* 12, 15.

14   *Cod.* 8, 37(38), 4: "Secundum responsum Domitii Ulpiani...iuris consulti amici mei." *Cod.* 4, 65, 4: "... ad Domitium Ulpianum praefectum praetorio et parentem meum ..." *Inst.*, prooem., §3: "...Theophilo et Dorotheo viris illustribus antecessoribus [nostris]." That the word *nostris* was usually omitted has been stressed by François Hotman (Hotomanus, *In quatuor libros Institutionum* [2nd ed.; Venice, 1569], p. 5; on *Inst.*, prooem., 3, v. "Antecessoribus nostris"), who like all the glossators and commentators pointed out that "father" and "predecessor" referred to the jurisprudents to whom Justinian allocated himself.

15   Azo, *Summa Institutionum*, prologue *Quasimodo geniti* (Lyon, 1530), fol. 267vo, ed. F. W. Maitland, *Select Passages from the Works of Bracton and Azo* (Selden Society, VIII; London, 1895), p. 3: "[scientia iuris] velut almifica dominatrix nobilitat addiscentes ... et ut vera per omnia fatear, iuris professores per orbem terrarum fecit solemniter principari et sedere in imperiali aula tribus et nationes, actores et reos ordine dominabili iudicantes." That the Bolognese Master Boncompagno served as a ghost writer of Azo's prologue is of little or no importance in this connection; cf. Hermann Kantorowicz, *Glossators of the Roman Law*, p. 227, n. 3a.

16   Bracton, *De legibus*, fol. 1b, ed. Woodbine, II, 20; ed. Maitland, p. 7 (with his notes on p. 15): "... quia nobilitat addiscentes ... et facit eos principari in regno [Azo: *per orbem terrarum*] et sedere in aula regia [Azo: *imperiali*] et in sede ipsius regis quasi throno Dei, tribus et nationes, actores et reos ordine dominabili iudicantes ...." For Bracton's additions, see Ernst H. Kantorowicz, *The King's Two Bodies* (Princeton, 1957), p. 160; his changes (*orbis terrarum: regnum; imperiali: regia*) are suggestive with regard to the broader subject of *rex est imperator in regno suo* (see below). That the judge, "as judge," is "sitting in the seat of the King (concerning his justice)," was an axiom defended ardently by Sir Edward Coke, in the case of Floyd and Barker, *Twelfth Part of the Reports*, p. 25.

17   Cynus of Pistoia, *In Codicem*, on *C.* 4, 65, 4, n. 2 (Frankfurt, 1578), fol. 276^v: "Notandum quod Imperator vocat Ulpianum parentem suum, sic respectu scientiae et aetatis [cf. *Glossa ordinaria* on *C.* 4, 65, 4], vocat eum amicum, infra de contra. sti. l. secundum [= *C.* 8, 37(38), 4]. Nam sic legitur in Chronicis, Alexander Imperator praecipuum habuit amicum Ulpianum et Paulum etiam, et vides, studiose, quantum potest scientia: quia facit legum peritum patrem praecipuum [principum?], facit etiam amicum, secundum Augustinum est animi custos et secundum Ieronymum est alter ego." The passage from Cynus was occasionally quoted in later times; see e.g., Johannes Oinotomus, *In quattuor Institutionum ... libros*, on *Inst.*, prooem., 3, n. 1 (§ *cumque hoc*), (Venice, 1643), p. 4.

18   Haskins, *Renaissance*, p. 199; Jordan, "Kaisergedanke," p. 126.

19   For Frederick II as judge, see Fedor Schneider, "Toscanische Studien," *Quellen und Forschungen aus italienischen Archiven und Bibliotheken*, XII (1909),

52ff.; cf. 65: "serenissimo imperatore ibidem presentialiter existente." Cf. Julius Ficker, *Forschungen zur Reichs- und Rechtsgeschichte Italiens* (Innsbruck, 1868), I, 296f., § 162; also III, 362f., §§ 612f. The imperial presence seems to have been restricted to cases of high treason (that is, cases in which the ruler could act as *iudex in causa propria* even in early modern times), and although the emperor occasionally might pronounce the judgment *ore proprio* (Ficker, p. 297, n. 2), he would normally remain silent and leave the procedure to the judges or speak through his *logothetes*.

For England, see W. Holdsworth, *A History of English Law* (7th ed.; London, 1956), I, 34 f., 205 ff. (*Coram rege* court). See, for a few later cases, S. B. Chrimes, in his edition of Sir John Fortescue's *De Laudibus Legum Angliae* (Cambridge, 1942), p. 150, on Ch. VIII, line 32: "proprio ore nullus regum Angliae iudicium proferre visus est."

20 Andreas of Isernia, *In usus feudorum commentaria*, on *Feud.*, II, 55 ("De prohibita alienatione feudi"), n. 84 (Naples, 1571), fol. 281ro-vo.

21 Cynus, on *Cod.* 7, 37, 3, n. 1, fol. 445vo.

22 Cf. Lucas de Penna, *Super tribus libris Codicis*, on *Cod.* 11, 58, 7, n. 16 (Lyons, 1544), fol. 185: "Est enim princeps iudex in causa sua" whenever *causae fiscales* are concerned, or when he revokes things alienated *in praeiudicium dignitatis et coronae*." Bracton, fol. 119b, ed. Woodbine, II, 337, concerning treason or lese majesty, judged by "court and peers" with the king, too, acting as judge, but "debent pares associari, ne ipse rex per seipsum vel iustitiarios suos sine paribus actor sit et iudex."

23 Innocent IV, *In quinque libros Decretalium apparatus*, on X, 5, 40, 23, n. 3 (Lyon, 1578), fol. 369vo.

24 Cynus, on *Cod.* 6, 23, 19, n. 1, fol. 367: "Nota hoc ad quod haec lex quotidie allegatur, quod princeps habet omnia iura in scrinio sui pectoris. quod non intellegas ad literam, quia multi imperatores ignoraverunt iura, *et maxime hodie ignorant*, sed intelligi debet in scrinio sui pectoris, id est, in curia sua, quae debet egregiis abundare Doctoribus, per quorum ora loquatur iuris religiosissimus princeps [cf. *Inst., prooem.*]."

25 Andreas of Isernia, on *Feud.* I, 3, n. 16 ('Qui success. ten.'), fol. 21v: "Potest dici, quod quia princeps multos habet in suo consilio peritos ... [allegation of *Cod.* 6, 23, 19; above, n. 24] et ideo dicitur Philosophiae plenus ... raro enim invenitur princeps Iurista." Cf. *ibid., praeludia*, n. 25, fol. 3vo: "...et maxime Iurisperiti, et qui cum eis [imperatoribus] erant, per quos dicuntur [imperatores] habere omnia Iura in pectore ... [alleg. *Cod.* 6, 23, 19] et Philosophiae legalis plenitudinem ... cum Principes rari sciant iura .... Item Imperator non facit leges, sed Iurisperiti approbati per eum, ut Tribonianus et alii." Matthaeus de Afflictis (d. 1523), *In Utriusque Siciliae ... Constitutiones*, on *Liber augustalis*, I, 37, n. 12, and II, 30, n. 1 (Venice, 1562), I, fol. 157, and II, fol. 65v, repeats Andreas of Isernia almost verbatim.

26 Fortescue, *De Laudibus*, ed. Chrimes (above, note 19), c. VIII, 22f.

27 Coke, *Twelfth Part of the Reports*, pp. 63–65; for the other sources see Catherine Drinker Bowen, *The Lion and the Throne* (Boston and Toronto, 1956),

pp. 304f., 622; Roland G. Usher, "James I and Sir Edward Coke," *English Historical Review*, XVIII (1903), 664ff., esp. 667ff.

28 Eugenio Dupré Theseider, *L'Idea imperiale di Roma nella tradizione del medioevo* (Milan, 1942), pp. 255ff., offers a useful collection of extracts from legal texts concerning the *lex regia;* see, for a discussion of the *lex regia*, Fritz Kern, *Gottesgnadentum und Widerstandsrecht im früheren Mittelalter* (Leipzig, 1914), pp. 251ff. (p. 256, n. 471, the passage from Manegold of Lautenbach, *Mon. Germ. Hist., Libelli de lite*, I, 365, 18ff.); E. Schoenian, *Die Idee der Volkssouveränität im mittelalterlichen Rom* (Leipzig, 1919), esp. pp. 58ff.; for the older literature, see Kantorowicz, *Kaiser Friedrich der Zweite, Ergänzungsband* (Berlin, 1931), pp. 85ff., to which there should be added Karl Jordan, "Der Kaisergedanke in Ravenna," *Deutsches Archiv*, II (1938), 110ff.; Fritz Schulz, "Bracton on Kingship," *English Historical Review*, LX (1945), 153ff.; Walter Ullmann, *The Medieval Idea of Law as Represented by Lucas de Penna* (London, 1946), pp. 48ff.

29 Dupré Theseider, *L'Idea imperiale*, pp. 153–60.

30 In general, see Paul Schmitthenner, *Die Ansprüche des Adels und Volks der Stadt Rom auf Vergebung der Kaiserkrone während des Interregnums* (Historische Studien, 155; Berlin, 1923); see Dupré Theseider, *L'Idea imperiale*, pp. 237ff., for the coronation of Louis of Bavaria.

31 See my remarks in *The King's Two Bodies* (Princeton, 1957), pp. 296ff.

32 See Dupré Theseider, *L'Idea imperiale*, pp. 257ff., and, for the canonists, Friedrich Kempf, *Papsttum und Kaisertum bei Innocenz III.* (Miscellanea Historiae Pontificiae, XIX; Rome, 1954), p. 214, n. 52.

33 See, for Frederick II, Brancaleone, and Rienzo, Dupré Theseider, *L'Idea imperiale*, pp. 173ff., 197ff., 307ff.

34 *Cod.* 1, 14, 4.

35 For the place accorded to customs by Roman law, see *Dig.* 1, 3, 32–40.

36 *Policraticus*, IV, 2, ed. Webb, I, 238, lines 15f.; *Liber augustalis*, I, 31, ed. Huillard-Bréholles, *Historia diplomatica Friderici Secundi* (Paris, 1852ff.), IV, 33; also Dupré Theseider, *L'Idea imperiale*, p. 179.

37 Aquinas, *Summa theologica*, I–IIae, qu. XCVI, a. 5, ad 3; cf. R. W. and A.-J. Carlyle, *A History of Mediaeval Political Theory in the West* (London, 1928), V, 475f.; Jean-Marie Aubert, *Le droit romain dans l'œuvre de Saint Thomas* (Bibliothèque thomiste, XXX; Paris, 1955), pp. 83f.

38 Kantorowicz, *The King's Two Bodies*, p. 136, n. 154.

39 A.-J. Carlyle, "The Theory of the Source of Political Authority in the Mediaeval Civilians to the Time of Accursius," *Mélanges Fitting* (Montpellier, 1907), I, 181–94.

40 *Policraticus*, IV, 2; Gaines Post, "The Theory of Public Law and the State in the Thirteenth Century," *Seminar*, VI (1948), 42–59.

41 See Kantorowicz, *The King's Two Bodies*, pp. 173ff., for the fisc, and pp. 232ff., for *patria;* Gaines Post, "Two Notes on Nationalism in the Middle Ages: 1. *Pugna pro patria*," *Traditio*, IX (1953), 281ff.

42 The decisive places are *Institutes*, prooem., and *Cod.*, Constitution *Summa rei publicae*. For the problem, see Ernst H. Kantorowicz, "On Transforma-

tions of Apolline Ethics," *Charites: Studien zur Altertumswissenschaft*, ed. Konrad Schauenburg (Bonn, 1957), pp. 265–74.

43 This is more or less the theme of the valuable study of Reto R. Bezzola, *Les origines et la formation de la littérature courtoise en Occident (500–1200)* (Bibliothèque de l'École des Hautes Études, fasc. 286; Paris, 1944).

44 *Policraticus*, IV, 6, ed. Webb, I, 254, line 25.

45 See, on these prologues, Kantorowicz, "The Prologue to *Fleta* and the School of Petrus de Vinea," *Speculum*, XXXII (1957), 231–49, and, for the earlier times, P. E. Schramm, *Kaiser, Rom und Renovatio* (Leipzig and Berlin, 1929), I, 282f.

46 See, e.g., Flavio Biondo, *Borsus, sive de militia et iurisprudentia*, ed. B. Nogara, *Scritti inediti e rari di Biondo Flavio* (Rome, 1927), pp. 130ff. See also above, note 10.

47 See Andreas of Isernia, *In usus feudorum*, praeludia, n. 25, fol. 3^{vob}, on the legislating prince: "Item, imperator non facit leges, sed iurisperiti approbati per eum, ut Tribunianus et alii...." For, the prince *est raro iurista*.

48 F. Brandileone, *Il diritto Romano nelle leggi Normanne e Sveve del regno di Sicilia* (Turin, 1884), p. 94. See, for the whole problem, Kantorowicz, *The King's Two Bodies*, pp. 117–23.

49 *Petri Exceptionum appendices*, I, 95, ed. H. Fitting, *Juristische Schriften des früheren Mittelalters* (Halle, 1876), p. 164.

50 Bracton, fol. 14, ed. Woodbine, II, 57f.

51 Durandus, *Rationale divinorum officiorum*, II, 8, 6 (Lyons, 1565), fol. 55vo: "Quidam etiam dicunt ut not. ff. de rerum divis. l. sancta [*Dig*. 1, 8, 9: the prince dedicates *sacra loca*] quod fit presbyter, iuxta illud: 'Cuius merito quis nos sacerdotes appellat' [*Dig*. 1, 1, 1]."

52 See, on the marriage of the prince to his realm, Kantorowicz, *The King's Two Bodies*, pp. 212–23, and, for *Reipublicae mysticus coniunx*, René Choppin, *De domanio Franciae*, III, tit. 5, n. 6 (Paris, 1605), p. 449.

53 See, for those changes, Kantorowicz, *The King's Two Bodies*, pp. 89–93.

54 *Ibid.*, p. 92, nos. 16f.

55 See F. Dümmler, "Gedichte aus dem XI. Jahrhundert," *Neues Archiv*, I (1876), 177, line 25. For the problem, see P. E. Schramm, *Kaiser, Rom und Renovatio*, I, 279ff., and the recent study by Hermann Krause, *Kaiserrecht und Rezeption* (Abh. d. Heidelberger Akad., 1952, N. 1; Heidelberg, 1952).

56 The Fourth (Roman) Empire was eventually fused with a Fifth Empire, that of Christ; cf. Aquinas [Tolomeo of Lucca], *De regimine principum*, III, 12f., ed. Joseph Mathis (2nd ed.; Turin and Rome, 1948), pp. 53ff.; also C. N. S. Woolf, *Bartolus of Sassoferrato* (Cambridge, 1913), pp. 318ff. For the *Authentica Habita*, see *Cod*. 4, 13, 5 post; *Monumenta Germaniae Historica, Constitutiones*, I, 249, no. 176.

57 For the *Rex imperator* theory, see Post, in *Traditio*, IX (1953), 296ff., with a critical discussion of some recent studies on the subject (Calasso, Ercole, Mochi Onory); for the imperial prerogatives, see W. Ullmann, "The Development of the Medieval Idea of Sovereignty," *English Historical Review* LXIV (1949), 1ff.

58 *Dig.* 48, 4; *Cod.* 9, 8. For example, Andreas of Isernia, *In usus feudorum*, on *Feud.* I, 5, n. 13, fol. 32vo–33ro, applies the *lex Julia maiestatis* perpetually to the king of Sicily, and so do the other Neapolitan jurists.

59 *Decretum*, c. 24, D. 93: *exercitus imperatorem faciat.* John of Paris, *De potestate regia et papali*, c. XV, ed. Dom Jean Leclercq, *Jean de Paris* (Paris, 1942), p. 222, line 8, still makes a distinction: *nam populus facit regem et exercitus imperatorem.* Jean de Terre Rouge, *Tractatus de iure futuri successoris legitimi*, I, art. 1, conclusio 24, in François Hotman, *Consilia* (Arras, 1586), Appendix, p. 34: *exercitus populi facit regem sive imperatorem.* Cf. E. E. Stengel, *Den Kaiser macht das Heer* (Weimar, 1910), also in *Historische Aufsätze Karl Zeumer gewidmet* (1910), pp. 262–75.

60 Fritz Kern, *Acta Imperii Angliae et Franciae ab a. 1267 ad a. 1313* (Tübingen, 1911), No. 271, p. 200, lines 12ff.: "et de eo (rege Franciae) potest dici, sicut de imperatore dicitur, videlicet quod omnia iura, precipue competentia regno suo, in eius pectore sunt inclusa." The whole legal opinion discusses imperial rights appropriated by the French king.

61 For the rule over land and sea as a rhetorical commonplace applied to Hellenistic kings, see A. Momigliano, "Terra Marique," *Journal of Roman Studies*, XXXII (1942), 53–64, and, for its application to the *dea Roma*, C. M. Bowra, "Melinno's Hymn to Rome," *ibid.*, XLVII (1957), 25. For Frederick II, see Kantorowicz, *Kaiser Friedrich der Zweite, Ergänzungsband*, pp. 204f. For Philip IV, or rather his crown jurist Guillaume de Plaisian, and the Bishop of Gévaudan, see *Mémoire relatif au Paréage de 1307*, ed. A. Maisonobe, in *Bulletin de la société d'agriculture, industrie, sciences et arts du Département de la Lozère* (Mendo, 1896), pp. 521, 532; Plaisian asserted "quod dominus Rex sit imperator in regno suo et imperare possit terre et mari," to which the bishop replied: "Porro utrum dominus Rex sit imperator in regno suo et utrum possit imperare terre et mari et elementis et, si obtemperarent ipsa elementa, si eisdem imperaret, ... nichil ad propositum nec contra Episcopum facit."

62 See Samuel Pepys' entry on July 19, 1662.

63 For the *lex animata* theory, see Kantorowicz, *The King's Two Bodies*, pp. 127ff.; Krause, *Kaiserrecht* (above, note 55), pp. 37ff.; and, for the age of absolutism, William Farr Church, *Constitutional Thought in Sixteenth-Century France* (Cambridge, 1941), p. 251, also pp. 47 (n. 10), 58, 70, 97, and *passim*.

Part III   EASTERN INFLUENCES ON
EUROPEAN CULTURE

Leo Spitzer

The Influence of Hebrew
and Vernacular Poetry on
the Judeo-Italian Elegy

La ienti de Sion plange e lutta;
dice: "Taupina, male so condutta

em manu de lo nemicu ke m'ao
    strutta."
La notti e la die sta plorando,   4
li soi grandezi remembrando,
e mo pe lo mundu vao gattivandu.

Sopre onni ienti foi 'nalzata,
e d'onni emperio adornata,   8
da Deo santo k'era amata.
E li signori da onni canto
gianu ad offeriri a lo templo santo,
de lo granti onori k'avea tanto.   12

Li figlie de Israel erano adornati,
de sicerdoti e liviti avantati,
e d'onni iente foro mmediati.
Li nostri patri male pinzaru,   16
ke contra Deo revillaru;
lu beni ke li fici no remembraro.

Pi quisto Deu li foi adirato,
e d'emperiu loro foi caczato,   20
ka lo soi nome abbero scordatu.
Sopre isse mandao sì granni osti,
ki foi sì dura e ssì forti,
ke roppe mura e 'nfranzi porti.   24
Guai, quanta ienti foi meciata,
ke tutta la terra ia ensanguinentata!

The people of Zion weep and mourn,
saying: 'Woe is me, sorrowful one, I have been
    given over
into the hands of the enemy who has
    destroyed me.'
Night and day they spend weeping,
remembering their past grandeur
as they now go wandering (captive) over
    the world.
Above all peoples had they been exalted
and endowed with all sovereignty (dominion),
they who were loved by God the Holy one.
And the lords from every corner (of the earth)
would go to make offering in the holy temple
because of the great honors that had accrued
    to it.
The sons of Israel were honored,
they could boast of priests and levites
and were the envy of all peoples.
Our fathers fell into evil thoughts
in that they rebelled against God
forgetful of the benefits he had given unto
    them.
Therefore was the wrath of God provoked
and they were cast out of their dominion,
for they had forgotten His name.
Against them He did send so great an army,
Which was so cruel and so strong
that it broke through the walls and the gates.
Alas, how many folk were murdered
that all the earth ran blood.

ohi, Sion, ke si' desfigliata!

    Oh, Zion, how art thou bereft of thy sons
                            ('unsonned')!

    Lo templo santo abbero desirtato,   28   The holy temple was laid low
ke 'n granti onori foi deficato,   that had been raised in greatest honor,
e foco da celo l'abbe afflammato.   and fire from heaven did consume it.

    Sprecaro torri e grandi palaza,   And towers fell and great palaces
e lo bando gia pe onni plaza: 32   and the ban was cried in every market-place
"Fi a fonnamento si desfacza!"   'Let it be razed to its foundations!'

    Vidisi donni là desfare   And one could see the destruction of women
e ientili omeni de granni affari,   and of noble men of great affairs—
ke 'n nulla guisa si no poi recitare.   36   so that in no way can it be described.

    E ttri navi misero pi mare,   And three ships were launched upon the sea
çença rimo (entenda ki sa iutare!)   having no oars (may He help them who has
                    the power to help them!)

e tutti em mare se prisero iettare.   and all did throw themselves into the sea.
Altri ne vinnéro d'onne canto,   40   Others were sold into slavery on every corner
tutti çença bandire per quanto;   sold cheaply at any man's price.
oi, ke farai, popolo santo?   Woe to thee, what wilt thou do, oh holy
                      people?

    E li leviti e li sacerdoti   And the levites and the priests
como bestiaglia foro venduti,   44   were sold like cattle
enfra l'altra iente poi sperduti.   and then scattered among all peoples.

    Tanto era dura loro signoria,   And so grievous was the foreign yoke
la notte prega dDio ke forsi dia,   that night brought the prayer that God make
                      day

la dia la notti, tanto scuria.   48   and day the prayer for night, so dark was day.

    Ki bole aodire crudeletate   Who wishes to hear of a cruel thing
ke addevenni de sore e frate,   that befell a sister and a brother
ki 'n quilla ora foro gattivati?   who were made captive at that time?

    Ne la prisa foro devisati: 52   In their captivity were they separated,
ki abbe la soro e cki lo frate,   the sister fell to one, the brother to another
e'n gattivanza foro menati.   and the captives were led their separate ways.

    Lo signore de la soro, meciaro,   The master of the sister, the foul creature,
l'abbe venduta ad uno tavernaro,   56   then sold her to one who kept an inn
ke de lo vino là l'embriaro.   and there with wine was she made drunk.

    E lo frate fue tradato   And the brother was given over
ad una puttana pi peccato;   to a whore for sin's sake.
oi, popolo santo, male si' guidato!   60   O holy people, evil are thy guides!

    Venni una ora ke s'adunaro   Then came an hour when they did meet,
quilla puttana e lo tavernaro,   the whore and he who kept the tavern,
e l'una e l'altro lo recitaro.   and the one and the other spoke of what
                      concerned them.

    "Una donna aiu, bella quanto   64   "I have a maiden, fair as a rose,
                  rosa,
bene crido k'è ienti cosa,   me thinks she is a thing of beauty
da la ienti tristi e dolorosa."   sprung from that sad and dolorous people."

    Quilla respundi k' "Io aio uno   The other answered: "I have a youth
                  'nfanti,
ked è sì ienti ed avvenanti,   68   who is noble and of winsome mien
plo ki la stilla de livanti."   more than the evening star."

    In quisto pinzaro parenteze a fari,   So saying they resolved to mate the two
e li loro figli a sserventari,   whose offspring they would make their slaves
e bennerelli pe guadagnare.   72   to sell for gain.

    Foro coniunti ad una caminata: These were brought together in one room,
la donna da canto è sviata;   the maiden turned and went into a corner,
dece: "Trista, male foi nata!   saying: "Woe is me, evil the day I was born!

    De secerdoti io foi figliola   76   I am the daughter of a priest
signuri de lie e dde scola;   of a man of the Law and of the Temple

e mmo cu uno servo stao sola."

Così lo 'nfanti stava da canto;
facia lamento e grandi planto   80
ka "Foi figlio d'uno omo santo,
  mo so adunato cu' na seriente
né dde mia lie né dde mia iente;
como faraio, tristo, dolente?"   84
  En quillo planto s'abbero
                          aoduti,
e l'uno e l'altro conosciuti:
"Soro e frati, ovi simo venuti?"

E l'uno e l'altro se abbraczaro,   88
e con grandi planto lamentaro,
fi ke moriro e pasmaro.
  Quista crudeli ki aodisse,
ki grandi cordoglio no li prindisse,   92
e grande lamento no ne facisse?
  Ki poe contare l'altri tormenti,
ke spisso spisso so convenenti,
plo dori che flambi ardenti?   96
  Santo Dio nostro signore,
retorna a reto lo too forore,
e no guardari a noi piccadori.
  Pe lo too nomo santo e binditto,   100
lo nostro coro aiusta a dderitto,
ke te sirvamo in fatto e 'n ditto.
  E remembra la prima amanza,
a trai noi de quista gattivanza,   104
de quista tenebri e scuranza.
  E lo nemico k'è tanto avantato,
ne lo too furori sia deiettato,
da canto en canto desirtato.   108
  E cetto facza como ao fatto,

e sia strutto e ddesfatto,
ka fao rumpere la lie e lo patto.

  E deriza stradi 'n onni canto,   112
ad adunare en quillo santo
quillo popolo k'amasti tanto.
  E lo santo templo k'è deguastato
de la toa mano sia defecato,   116
lo too prufeta como ao profetato:
  Leviti e sacerdoti e tutta ienti
entro Sion stare gaoiente,
lo santo toi nome bendicenti.   120

and now I am alone with a slave."
He too standing in a corner
did make lament and weep aloud,
for "I am the son of a holy man" (he said)
  "now I am put together with a slave girl,
neither of my law nor of my people.
What shall I do, woe is me, sorrowful one!"
  In this lamenting they did hear each other

and each knew who the other was:
"Sister and brother, to what point have we
                                    come!"

  And the one embraced the other
lamenting sore and weeping,
until they swooned and died.
  Who could hear this cruel thing
and not suffer heartbreak
and not mourn deeply?
  And who could count all the other afflictions
that over and over continue to arise,
fiercer than burning fire?
  Holy God, our Lord,
turn away Thy wrath
and look not upon our sins.
  By Thy holy blessed name,
set our hearts aright,
so that we may serve Thee in deed and word.
  And bethink Thyself of that first love
and lead us out of this captivity,
this darkness and this shadow.
  And let the enemy in his vain boasting
be confounded by Thy wrath,
destroyed from corner to corner.
  Let it quickly be done unto him as he has
                                    done,
be he destroyed and undone,
for he has caused the law to be broken and the
                                  covenant.
  And send forth roads from every corner
that should bring together into that holy place
this people that Thou lovedst so!
  And the holy temple which is laid waste,
let it be raised again by Thy hand,
as Thy prophet has prophesied;
that Levites and priests and all the people
will be in Zion rejoicing,
blessing Thy holy name!

Our poem in the vernacular continues a tradition of Hebrew elegies or dirges destined for the Day of Fasting, the 9th of the month of Ab, dirges which commemorate the destruction of Jerusalem and the Temple, indeed the destruction both of the First Temple in 586 B.C. by the Babylonian Nebuchadnezar and that of the second temple by the Roman Emperor Titus in 70 A.D., both events having fallen on the same day. The Day of Fasting is for the Jews second in importance only to the Day of Atonement. On both these days the fasting lasts from sunset to sunset, on both days the Palestinian Jews visit the Wailing Wall, the only remnant of the ancient Temple. On the 9th of Ab all pleasant things are forbidden, including the study of the Pentateuch, of the Thora—only such passages of the Bible and the Talmud may be read as invite lamentation. On the eve of the day the synagogues are kept in utter darkness. In orthodox communities many Jews spend all the night in the synagogue lying on the floor or sitting on low stools, a sign of mourning. At the services on the eve and on the morning of the 9th of Ab the Biblical book of the Lamentations of Jeremiah (in which Israel's reminiscences of its glorious past, the destruction of the Temple and the diaspora, and the hope for a better future are treated) is chanted in a mournful tone. In Talmudic Hebrew this book is called *Kinoth* (plural of *kinah* 'dirge, office of the dead') and those motifs (along with the name) are found in *kinoth* composed later during the Middle Ages. The most famous New-Hebrew poets of that period, Ibn Gabirol and Juda Halevy, composed *kinoth* (often beginning with the evocation of the allegorical figure of Zion). Already in the ninth century Eleasar Kalir composed elegies which included motifs of contemporary Jewish history, and this trend was maintained through the Middle Ages. Thus we have *kinoth* that describe persecutions at the time of the first crusade, of the thirteenth century when the Talmud was burnt in Paris, and of 1348–49 when the Jews were accused of having caused the epidemic of the Black Death—an odd way for a literary genre to grow: by the recurrence of the same type of sad outward events. Now our poem is a *kinoth*, written not in Hebrew, but in the vernacular. The poem, whose author is unknown, has been edited and studied with admirable philological accuracy by the Italian Semitist Umberto Cassuto who has proved, by a close analysis of its language and style, that it is written in the Judeo-Italian dialect of Rome (which was the center of Italian Jewish life in the Middle Ages) in a language which shows affinities with the standard Italian epic and lyrical minstrel poetry of the end of the twelfth and beginning of the thirteenth centuries in the same area of Italy. For instance, the epithet *taupina* 'the sorrowful one' (l. 2) the self-description of the feminine allegorical figure of the mourning Zion, serves also as self-description of the mourning Virgin Mary in popular Christian litanies of the time.

If then, on one hand, our text shows that the Jews of that period must have participated in the cultural life of the Gentiles, it shows on the other particular linguistic traits of the Jewish community. For instance, the meaning of the word family *gattivare* 'to be in exile,' *gattivanza* 'exile,' is a feature of the Judeo-Romance dialects exclusively, rendering the Hebrew word *galuth*, while in general Romance this meaning of the derivatives from Latin *captivus* is unknown: for the Jews captivity and exile are one.

Doubtless our elegy, which is one of the oldest Italian poems preserved, is also the most distinguished poetic monument of Judeo-Romance medieval literature, which generally consists only of translations either of the Bible or of prayers, and, at best, as in Spain, of variants of the popular ballads of Christian inspiration. Our dirge is remarkable because it has no one direct Hebrew source but freely combines various Hebrew and, as we shall see, non-Hebrew motifs.

Any reader of our elegy, Jew or Gentile, must be deeply moved, not only by the tragedy of the Jewish people, as grave today (when a new Zion finds no peace in God) as ever before, but also by the direct human appeal that suffering beautifully expressed must have. Precisely because of this direct human appeal the literary critic might perhaps hesitate to subject the poem to analysis. Is not the whole poem meant exclusively to move us to sympathetic grief as this is anticipated in the epilogue to the sad episode of the sister and the brother:

> Quista crudeli ki aodisse,
> ki grandi cordoglio no li prindisse,
> e grande lamento no ne facisse? (ll. 91–93)

But on the other hand, as in all truly great poetry, we may find in our poem, if we look into it more closely, an intellectual structure which, as it were, dams up and restrains the flood of feelings—and it is the interplay between flowing emotion and restraining intellect that in my opinion makes it a great poem.

The elegy is indeed constructed mainly in terms of two dimensions, one spatial, one temporal, to both of which there are continuous references in the poem. Both dimensions are represented by the so often recurrent

word 'Zion,' indeed by the leitmotif "Zion," which is found also in the
first and in the last line. *La gente de Sion* is the name throughout chosen
by the poet for the Jewish people (only once does he mention *li figlie
de Israel* 'the children of Israel'), and the name of the city of Jerusalem
is never mentioned. Zion is, of course, the symbol of the seat of the
spiritual power that once was Israel's and that will be reborn—this
Zion is both a geographical place and a historical moment.

Now let us isolate for an instant the temporal dimension. In the first
lines we are introduced to the allegory of Zion that mourns 'night and
day' (l. 4). The adverb *mo* 'now' (l. 6) insists on the contrast between the
miserable present of Israel and the glorious past of Zion—once it had
grandezza, now it is dispersed through the world (*gattivando*)—and with
this contrast is implicitly given the hope for restoration of that pristine
state of glory by the prayer of the believers. Thus the poem will fall into
three parts:

1) the description of the glorious past that was Zion's (ll. 7–15),
2) the misery of the Jewish people after the destruction of Zion,
    exemplified by the episode of the brother and the sister
    (ll. 16–96),
3) the hope for the restoration of Israel to Zion (ll. 97–120).

This trichotomy reminds us of the similar one that is carried through in
the Biblical book of Lamentations; indeed our elegy as well as other
kinoth are contractions or condensations of that Biblical book.

What is more, they are condensations of the Jewish metaphysics of
history, according to which all injustice in this world is an interlude
between the once perfect state of the world and the final reëstablishment
of justice. Ernest Renan, contrasting in his *History of the Jewish People*
the Jewish prophecies, particularly that of Isaiah, with other creeds, has
written:

Our races have always been satisfied with a rather limp justice in the government of this world. Their assurance about another life always offered ample
reasons for complacency when faced with the iniquities of the actual world.
The Hebrew prophet does not appeal to rewards or punishments beyond death.
He thirsts after justice and immediate justice. According to him it is on this
earth that the justice of Jehovah materializes.... Hence a heroic tension, *a permanent outcry, a perpetual attention to the events of this world seen as acts of a God of
Justice.* Hence particularly an ardent belief in final reparation, on a day of
judgment, when all things will be reëstablished as they should be. That day will
be that of the reversal of all that exists.... The miracle of the radical change

of the world will come to pass at Zion. Zion will be the capital of a regenerated world in which Justice will rule. On that day David will become the spiritual king of the whole of humanity.

Now returning to our poem, it is clear from the dimensions of its three parts (81 lines devoted to the central part, 9 and 24 to the first and third) that the main interest of the poet was directed toward that interlude, the fall of the Jewish people from the grace of God, of that people that had been lifted above the other peoples (l. 7), but because of its rebellion against God had incurred His wrath (l. 16). That rebellion was, as it were, a second fall after that of Adam, the fall of a nation, and, just as in the first case, the fall was an interruption of the timeless, paradisiac joy of the union of man with God, an interruption caused by his historical step of sinning, by the national sin *in time*. Thus the 'now' (*mo*) of our poem marks the period of expiation, the central theme of the threnody that is being recited every 9th of Ab, in order to reopen again and again the wounds from which Israel yearns to recover.

This 'now' of Part II is reflected also in the episode of the sister and the brother which we shall touch now only in passing, in order to indicate that, just as the people of Israel were shown (ll. 4–5) remembering their ancient greatness, now dispersed all over the earth, the sister and the brother in their laments also speak of 'once' and 'now':

> I am the daughter of a priest
> . . . .
> and *now* I am alone with a slave.
>
> I am the son of a holy man. . .
> *now* I am put together with a slave girl. . . .

Both voices converge in a statement in the perfect tense which, as it were, seals their common doom:

> *Soro e frati, ovi simo venuti?*
> Sister and brother, to what point have we come? (l. 87)

Now since this central part about the diaspora is framed by Parts I and III, these latter parts will show certain parallel motifs, which distinguish them from Part II: there was, we are told in line 9, a time when Zion was loved by God (*da Deo santo k'era amata*), which time was interrupted by God's wrath (l. 19, *Deu li foi adirato*), but the time of love will return, and consequently in Part III the concepts 'wrath' and 'love' return in chiastic order (ll. 97–98, *Santo Dio . . . retorna a reto lo too forore*

'God, turn away thy wrath'; l. 103, *e remembra la prima amanza* 'and bethink thyself of that first love'; also l. 114, *quillo popolo k'amasti tanto* 'this people that thou lovedst so much'). The Golden Age evoked by the Jews is, of course, not that of pagan antiquity, idyllic peace in nature; it is a course of action according to the will of God, that is, the full development of the functions of the Jewish theocracy. Our text mentions (l. 8) the *emperio*, the empire or sovereignty that had been given by God to Israel. It is mainly spiritual; it consists in the supremacy of the Temple in which the great of the earth worshipped (l. 11) and was adorned, not by princes and kings as in pagan empires, but by the hierarchy by which priests and levites were placed high above the common worshippers (ll. 13–15). To this description, in the first part of our elegy, of the glorious state of Israel now lost, corresponds the description of the redemption of Israel which will show the Temple and the holy hierarchy again in full operation, that is, in their essential function of praising God:

> Leviti e sacerdoti e tutta ienti
> entro Sion stare gaoiente,
> lo santo toi nome bendicenti (ll. 118–20).

It is to be noted, however, that one parallelism is missing or not followed through by our poet in Part III: no mention is made of a restoration of the Jewish worldly empire (*emperio*). In the last part we hear only of spiritual regeneration (l. 101, 'set our *hearts* aright') and (l. 112) of the reunion of the believers in the sanctuary. Since the Temple then is the true core of the 'empire' we shall see in the three parts of the poem the Temple in its different states according to the different ages. Again absolutely parallel wording obtains: after the first glorious state of the Temple of which we have spoken, we read in Part II, ll. 28 foll.:

> The holy temple was laid low
> That had been raised in greatest honor
> [*deficato* = *edificato* 'built up, raised'],

and in Part III, ll. 115 foll.:

> And the holy temple which is laid waste,
> let it be raised again by Thy hand....
> [again *defecato* = *edificato*].

Another leitmotif that is instrumented in different keys in Parts I and III, but is missing in Part II, is that of the 'enemy of Zion.' The diaspora

which was willed by the wrath of God was brought about by this enemy:
Israel finds herself (l. 3) in the hands of the enemy who has destroyed her,
'*the* enemy' whose identity will never be specified. A pure instrument of
God, he may change his avatars in different ages, but he has no historical
face of his own. In Part II he is described only indirectly, as a great
army that shed blood through the land (l. 26), as an impersonal agent,
as an abstract force (*dura ... signoria*, l. 46). And while the behavior of
the two villains, the prostitute and the tavern-keeper, toward two children
of Israel is, of course, an example of the perversity of the enemy, the
enemy is not outspokenly mentioned in this episode. In the immediacy
of suffering these children of Israel may have lost sight of its ultimate
instigator. But in the third part the 'enemy' reappears because in God's
perspective he was never lost sight of. Now we hear what we have not been
told in the part devoted exclusively to expiation by suffering, that the
enemy himself has committed a sin, that of having, in his insolence,
violated the pact that God had contracted with his elect people. Therefore God's wrath that had before raged against Israel will now turn
back (*retorna a reto*, l. 98) and strike the enemy, following an irrational
logic of Jehovah's. For although the enemy acted as an instrument of
God against Israel who had been the culprit in breaking the pact with
God ("our fathers fell into evil thoughts"), nevertheless the Jewish people
remain the elect people and he who acts against them, even if prodded
by God, makes himself guilty—and it may very well be that the enemy's
action is in itself an evil action. Now the punishment of Israel's enemy
will be described in Part III with words reminiscent of the description
of the punishment of Israel in Part II, ll. 106 foll.:

> And let the enemy in his vain boasting
> be confounded by Thy *wrath* [*furore = ira, adirato*],
> destroyed [*desirtato*] from corner to corner.
>   Let it quickly be done unto him as he has done,
> be he *destroyed and undone* [*strutto e ddesfatto*] ....

The word parallelisms between Parts II and III serve to indicate tne
law of retaliation which is explicitly formulated in line 109, "let it
quickly be done unto him as he has done." The principle of retaliation
used here by God against the enemy of Israel is, of course, mentioned in
the Old Testament: in the book of Joel God announces that the children
of the enemy will be sold to the Jews just as he had sold the children of
Israel to other peoples. There was an excellent opportunity for our poet

to develop this motif of the enemy's children being sold. Let us admire him for his discretion in sparing us the outbursts of wild Jewish *Schadenfreude* to which similar poems treat us (in one elegy by Kalir crucifixes and idolatrous images of the Gentiles are undone like mangy dogs). Another motif that distinguishes Part III from II is that of light and darkness; during the period of exile night and day are confused for the Jews according to lines 46–48 which echo a passage of Deuteronomy 28 : 67: "In the morning thou shalt say, Would God it were even, and at even thou shalt say, Would God it were morning," but in the period of redemption (l. 105) 'darkness and shadow' will recede as Isaiah prophesied: "the people that walked in darkness have seen a great light; they that dwell in the land of the shadow of death, upon them hath the light shined."

Having demonstrated the temporal structure of the poem in its leitmotif technique which either brings together Parts I and III or contrasts II and III, let us turn to the spatial dimension also contained in the concept of Zion. We have already seen that in Part I Zion was the center of an empire, that in Part II the *gattivanza* or diaspora took place and that the restoration of Zion is the goal in Part III. We have read in Part I, ll. 7–11:

> Above all peoples had they been exalted
> and endowed with all sovereignty....
> And the lords from every corner of the earth [*da onni canto*]
> would go to make offering....

With this description ll. 40 foll. in Part II are contrasted:

> Others were sold into slavery on every corner [*da onni canto*]
> and then scattered among all peoples.

I find a Biblical inspiration for this line in Jeremiah when God threatens the inhabitants of Damascus: "I will scatter into all winds them [that are] in the *utmost corners*, and I will bring their calamity from all sides thereof."

The reader will have noticed the contrast in the use of the formula *onni canto* in the different parts of the elegy. First the rulers came 'from all corners' to sacrifice at Zion; later the Jews are sold as slaves 'into all corners.' And this motif will reappear in Part III, line 108, where it will be the enemy who will be destroyed *da canto en canto* 'from corner to corner' and it will culminate in the passage in which God is asked

(l. 112: *deriza stradi 'n onni canto*), to send forth roads 'into all corners' in order to bring the dispersed members of Israel together in Zion. The network of roads from all corners of the world which God should create or improvise for his people is our poet's own beautiful invention.

There exists then in the first part a centripetal movement toward the temple of Zion, in Part II a centrifugal movement of dispersal, and again in Part III a centripetal movement toward Zion. In all these cases the movements involve all the corners of the finite world, *onni canto*—it is as though the poet himself had relived the basic Jewish experience, the contrast between a life in the center which is peace and equilibrium and a life in the corner which is restless striving toward the center—in fact, a generally human experience of contrasts within what Georges Poulet would call *l'espace intérieur*, inward space.

The motif of the corners is not forgotten in the episode of the sister and the brother of which we have already mentioned the temporal aspect and which reflects, as it were microcosmically, the macrocosm of Jewish fate. Let us study now the manner in which the poet has connected the episode with the whole of the poem.

The story is brought in at the moment when the poet had described the humiliation of the priests and the levites sold like cattle to other peoples. And the youthful protagonists of the episode, who belong to the aristocracy of the aristocratic people of God, are described first only slightly detached from the background of the community (l. 50): this is the story *de sore e frate* 'the story of brother and sister,' as if to make them appear without any individual face. The whole story will then be told in strict parallelism: the protagonists are, as it were, sculptured as two symmetric pillars supporting the edifice of Jewish suffering. They experience the same misfortune separately—this too being representative of the destiny of the Jewish people. No wonder then that the exclamation uttered by the poet in our episode (l. 60) is worded in terms of the Jewish people: *oi, popolo santo, male si' guidato* 'O holy people, evil are thy guides,' an exclamation parallel to the one used before in line 42, *oi, ke farai, popolo santo?* 'woe to thee, what wilt thou do, o holy people?' Parallelism obtains also in the speeches of the two owners of the Jewish slaves, who intend to exploit their beauty and consequently are forced to acknowledge it. Both use metaphors which have a ring of popular Italian poetry (*bella quanto rosa,... plo ki la stilla da livanti*); as is the habit of folk poetry, lovely human beings are presented as things of nature in their pristine freshness and autonomy. The two symmetrical pillars of villainy must unwittingly bow to the pillars of beauty and nobility and bow also to the majesty of Jewish suffering (*la iente triste e dolorosa*).

And now again the spatial symbolism of the 'corners' intervenes: put together in one room, the sister and the brother will remain in different corners (l. 74, *la donna da canto è sviata;* l. 79, *Così lo' nfanti stava da canto*). The corners here become symbolic of their inborn chastity, as well as of their isolation in misfortune. They will say the same sad things in their respective corners, the saddest element being their common origin from a family of priests—a detail we learn only now although the story was conceived by the poet from the start as an exemplification of the utmost of humiliation suffered by this Jewish aristocracy. The speeches of the two isolated relatives will again be parallelistic. The contrast pointed out by the maiden, *De secerdoti io foi figliola* and *mmo cu uno servo stao sola*, is repeated by the young man; and the parallel exclamations, *Trista, male foi nata* and *como faraio, tristo, dolente*, do not lose their connection with the general fate of the Jewish people that was described in line 2 in a similar exclamation, *Taupina, male so condutta* 'woe is me.... I have been given over into the hands of the enemy.' We understand that the episode of the two children of a priest serves to prove that Zion is in truth *desfigliata* (l. 27), 'unsonned,' bereft of her sons. But precisely in their isolation and dispersal the Jewish people are able to unite and recognize each other just as that sister and brother did:

Soro e frati, ovi simo venuti? (l. 87)

Now this exclamation is not the text that the two protagonists might have actually spoken (they must have said "Sister, to what point have we come" and "Brother, to what point have we come")—it is a stylization, a contraction of their words, which indicates the coalescence of two separate monologues into one operatic duet of voices that renders the feelings of the whole Jewish people about the diaspora. We stressed before the temporal aspect of *simo venuti;* now we shall point out the spatial aspect of the word *ovi* 'to what point' which directs our eyes towards those two desolate corners of the room destined bor the incestuous mating of brother and sister, the two corners in which up to this moment ţhe brother and the sister had stood like columns of shame, estranged from each other. But now they will *leave their corners*, and embrace, and die united by their grief—which reunion preludes a happier reunion of the whole people in joy and peace, in Zion. The lamentation *Soro e frati, ovi simo venuti?* is the turning point in the poem: from this nadir of despair there can only come the upsurge toward the zenith of Zion.

Up to this point we have interpreted the poem mainly as a phenomenon *per se,* and its aesthetic structure (temporal-spatial) was inferred only from the words of the poem itself. But once the inward form of a poem has been understood we must not fear the impact of the study of its sources. On the contrary such a study will, in the case of great poems, confirm the unique aesthetic values which we have found by the 'immanentistic' study of the poem alone. Cassuto has pointed out the sources of the central episode (as of other passages of the poem): a *midrash* which is a commentary on the Book of Lamentations (*terminus ad quem:* seventh century A.D.) and the Babylonian Talmud (*terminus ad quem:* fifth century A.D.). The Midrash version (*M*) reads as follows:

Two children of the high priest R. Zadok, a son and a daughter, were made prisoners; the one fell into the hands of one soldier, the other into those of another soldier; the first soldier went to a prostitute and paid her by giving her the son; the second went to a tavern-keeper and paid for wine by giving him the daughter, so that what was written in Joel 4,5 was fulfilled: "And they have cast lots for my people, and have given a boy for an harlot and sold a girl for wine, that they might drink." After a certain time the harlot went to the tavern-keeper and said to him: "I have a Hebrew youth who resembles the girl that thou hast; well then, let us unite them in matrimony and their offspring we shall divide between us." And so they did. They shut them in a room and locked the door. The maiden started weeping. He said: "Why dost thou weep?" She answered: "Woe to me, the daughter of a high priest who is to be married to a slave!" He said: "Who is thy father?" She answered "Zadok the high priest." He said: "Where didst thou live?" She answered: "In Jerusalem." He said: "In what street?" She answered: "In the street so and so." He said: "What sign was it that marked thy house?" She answered: "A so and so beneath a so and so." He said: "Didst thou have a brother?" She answered: "Yes." He said: "What sign marked thy brother?" She answered: "A birthmark above one shoulder and when he returned from school [the temple] I bared and kissed the birthmark." He said: "And if someone showed thee the birthmark wouldst thou recognize it?" She answered: "Yes." He bared his shoulder before her and she saw that birthmark. They recognized each other and embraced and kissed and wept on the shoulder one of the other until they died. And the Spirit of God cried out and said (Lamentations): "*For these I weep.*"

The Babylonian Talmud (*B*) has another version:

It happened that the son and the daughter of R. Ishmael ben Elisha became prisoners of two masters. After a certain time the two masters met. The one said: "I have a slave boy whom no one in the world equals in handsomeness." The other said: "I have a slave girl whom no one in the world equals in beauty." They then said: "Well then, let us unite them in matrimony and divide between us their offspring!" They made them enter a room. The one was sitting in one corner, the other in another. The one said [thought]: "I, a priest, son of high priests, am forced to marry a slave girl." And she said [thought]: "I, a priestess, daughter of high priests, am forced to marry a slave man!" And they wept all the night long. When dawn came they recognized each other and fell one upon the other and sighed in tears until they died. And for them Jeremiah mourned when he said: "For these I weep, mine eye, mine eye runneth down with water."

The passages of Joel and of Lamentations quoted in the two versions give us a clue to the genesis of the story: In Joel we read as we saw, "And they have cast lots for my people, and have given a boy for an harlot and sold a girl for wine, that they might drink." And in the book of Lamentations is found the line, "My virgins and my young men are gone into captivity." Our story is nothing but a concrete example for what the prophets had expressed in polar terms ('a boy and a girl' and 'my virgins and my young men' being ways of saying 'all the Jewish young people'): in it there are presented two concrete figures of a certain virgin and a certain young man that are gone into captivity. Cassuto thinks that our poet has had before him the two versions, but that *B* became the basis of the episode while only some details in the beginning are taken from *M*. Cassuto, innocent of aesthetic evaluation, feels *B* to be only a more learned version than *M* and he fails to point out that in choosing *B* as the basis our poet has shown his aesthetic sensitivity. For in *M* the anagnorisis comes about as a result of a series of pedantic questions by the brother, catechism style ('where did you live? in which street? in which house?' etc.) and it is finally achieved by the discovery of the birthmark, a rather melodramatic device of the type known in French romantic melodramas as 'la croix de ma mère.' In addition, in *B* the description of the characters in the story has more psychological depth: here the two masters of the Jewish slaves wish to mate the latter not only because of their own greed, but also because, in a kind of involuntary fascination by the beauty of the captives, they feel that they are made for each other. The author of our elegy went one step further in using metaphors (rose, morning-star) usual in the Christian lyrical poetry of the time.

And from *B* came to our poet the suggestion of the brother and sister mourning in the two corners, which motif he fused with the passage from Jeremiah and wove into the whole structure of the elegy. However, in our poem the recognition of brother and sister comes about acoustically, not visually as in *B*. But the poet goes even further by saying, "*In this lamenting they did hear each other and each knew who the other was.*" In other

words, recognition comes organically from the words they had said in
their separate inner monologues; mourning is what makes one Jew
recognize the other. The introduction of this acoustic element which
brings about the denouement of the episode is entirely our poet's find;
for in *B* the protagonists were not truly speaking aloud, only thinking
(the phrases "he said," "she said" may, in fact, as Cassuto shows by his
translation, mean "he thought," "she thought"). Having not "said
anything" they could neither hear nor recognize each other. It is our
poet who made them speak in monologues out of which the duet develops:
soro e frati, ovi simo venuti?—the last three words rendering the feelings
of the whole Jewish community. Now I have pointed out before that in
this line the verb *simo venuti* indicates time, and the adverb *ovi* space.
We are now able to take one further step in the definition of our episode
by stating that the spatial and temporal reminiscences of the two protagonists are inseparable from, but transcended by, the fact of the
acoustic utterance by the two young people of that nostalgia for Zion, a
place in space and a point in time,—that nostalgia which reflects
microcosmically the nostalgia of Israel that will renew itself at whatever
place and at whatever time it chooses to think about itself, and particularly
on the 9th of Ab on which our elegy is destined to be recited aloud and
heard. To this we may now give a title reminiscent of Tasso: *Sion lamentata*, which suggests three dimensions, one of space, one of time, one
acoustic, all potentially contained in the concept Zion, but of which
the third, the acoustic dimension, is the one that, motivating the poem,
actualizes the other two.

Now loud utterance of grief is a feature characteristic of the Orientals,
Jews and Mohammedans alike, and it is well known that with them the
physical expression of those feelings is not only acoustic, but accompanied
by gestures such as beating one's breast, tearing one's hair and one's
clothes. Now all those various, chaotic and barbarous gestures of Oriental
mourning, so alien to an Anglo-Saxon public wary of self-pity and self-
dramatization, all those touches of crude realism have been abandoned
in our poem, in favor of only the acoustic response to deep grief, nor is
any mention made of immoderately loud demonstration. Only the
acoustic element in its purity, but also in its continuity is emphasized:
the dirge is a lengthy one because Jewish mourning is a continuum,
present in our dirge from its first line (*plange e lutta*) through the various
exclamations of lament (l. 2, *Taupina, male so condutta;* l. 25, *guai;* l. 27,
ohi, Sion, ke si' desfigliata!; l. 42, *oi, ke farai, popolo santo?;* l. 60, *oi, popolo*

santo, male si' guidato; l. 75, *Trista, male foi nata!;* l. 84, *como faraio, tristo, dolente?*) up to the end when the poem closes with the word *bendicenti* which evokes the joyful accents of a hymn of thanks, perhaps accompanied by lute and psalterion, in a Zion redeemed in which not the state of dejection of Jeremiah's lamentation (*stare plorando*) but the state of bloom (*stare gaudenti*) of Isaiah's prophecy prevails.

Rethinking now Renan's description of the prophetic message of the latter ("a permanent *outcry*, a *perpetual attention* to the events of this world seen as acts of a God of Justice"), we realize that our liturgical-existential lamentation is another Jewish protest and outcry against the world-that-is-not-Zion. This protest must be *uttered aloud* and periodically reiterated lest the world go limp in its fight against evil and so that the rebirth of the Kingdom of David might come true some day on this earth. It is not mainly Oriental emotionalism, but the desire to call up the regenerative forces, in himself and in other people, the dissatisfaction with the *now* and *here*, that makes the Jew lament. It is therefore that the spatial-temporal references to Zion are embedded in the acoustic texture of our poem, in the *hic et nunc* of sound which constitute our elegy. And this structure, intellectual after all, is what gives our Jewish threnody an almost Dantean orderliness, clarity, and harmony—features which, to a great degree, were made possible by the choice of the Romance vernacular in which stylistic levels could be really separated, whereas the sacred language, Hebrew, would have encouraged the invasion of the divine on all levels and the predominance of unstructured emotional elements. If this be so, we would be justified in putting strong emphasis, in our Judeo-Italian elegy, on the Italian element: this elegy is indeed an Italian poem about Jewish subject matter: *Sion lamentata.*

Milton V. Anastos

Some Aspects of Byzantine
Influence on Latin Thought[1]

After the disaster of 1071 at Bari, as a result of which Byzantine forces were expelled from Italy,[2] it might have been expected that the influence of Byzantium on the West would have waned and diminished, especially since the victory of the Normans in this fateful year had been preceded by the rupture between the Byzantine and Roman churches, which had taken place on July 18, 1054,[3] when Cardinal Humbert deposited the bull of excommunication on the high altar of the Church of Hagia Sophia. National and ecclesiastical antagonisms, it might have been thought, would have combined to drive out all memory of the hated Greeks from the Latin world.

Actually, this animosity found expression in a number of diatribes entitled *Contra errores Graecorum*,[4] or the like, in which the Latins attacked the Byzantines for a number of reasons, but not least because of the refusal of the Byzantine Church to accept the Latin doctrine of the double procession of the Holy Spirit. Nevertheless, not even those who despised the Greeks, or disagreed with them, could avoid succumbing to the allurement of Greek learning, to which the intellectual currents of the period subsequent to 1071 proved, as it turned out, to be exceedingly favorable. Indeed, so numerous and widespread were the manifestations of the penetration of Hellenic ideas into the life and thought of the West in this era that the twelfth century must be considered a turning point in the history of civilization on this account. The present essay provides only a brief introduction to this vast and complicated, but fascinating subject.

ROBERT OF MELUN ON THE GREEK LANGUAGE

Among those who looked with suspicion and disfavor upon the study of Greek was Robert of Melun (Robertus de Meleduno or Meledunensis), a distinguished theologian, born in England near the end of the eleventh century, who succeeded Abelard at the *Schola artium* of Mount Ste. Geneviève (*ca.* 1137), and then became successively magister at the school of Melun near Paris, magister of theology at St. Victor in Paris, and finally bishop of Hereford in England from *ca.* 1160 until his death in 1167.[5]

His position with regard to Byzantine theology and Greek philology in general is contradictory and inconsistent, but probably reflects an attitude that was not uncommon in his day. Before going on, therefore, it may be instructive to consider briefly what Robert has to say on this head. He felt so strongly about the sinister consequences of instruction in Greek that he devoted nine pages in the *Prefatio* of his *Sententie* (written *ca.* 1152–60)[6] to an assault upon its advocates. He admitted that it was unsuitable (*culpabile*) to apply the unpolished idiom and style of children (*inani puerorum concinnitate*) to the exposition of the Catholic faith. It was, however, much more reprehensible, he felt, to go to the other extreme, as many of his contemporaries were then doing with great aplomb, and sprinkle quotations in Greek throughout their writings so as to cover their Latin with a shining mantle of Greek[7] and thus win fame for esoteric lore.

He denounces those who used Greek as suffering from one of two complaints. Either, he charges, their minds are so blinded by the tumor of idle pride, that they judge that what is not is, and solemnly assert that what is is not, deeming the good to be useless and deformed, and the ugly beautiful and desirable. Or else, Robert continues in words that reflect the anguish and torment he suffered in the course of his lessons in Greek, they look down upon their hearers as so inept as to consider nothing clear except what is obscure and nothing sweet except "what is compounded of the bitterness of gall."[8]

In attempting to teach theology by way of the Greek language, Robert objects, the professor of Greek not only does not lead the mind of his students to understanding, but creates uncertainty and ambiguity. Although the theologian should concern himself with showing what theological concepts mean, he wastes his time and that of his classes with foreign grammar and vocabulary, thus reducing his pupils to the level of children learning their letters for the first time.[9] Instead of helping him with the understanding of ideas, Robert charges, his teacher compelled him to struggle with Greek words, which could never be adequately translated into Latin anyway, and did not at all promote his comprehension of theology. "Our little Greek master (*greculus preceptor*)," he says, does not seem to have the progress of the pupil very much in mind, but appears instead to be looking for nothing but an opportunity for an ostentatious display of the knowledge of Greek.[10]

"By what principle of faith," Robert asks, "by what fitness of discipline, when a professor intends to expound the unity of the divine substance and explain the distinction of the persons, does he resort to a mixture of languages, and not confine himself to Latin? Why does he say that there are three *hypostases* and one *usia*, and not express this in Latin, or else altogether in Greek?"[11] The adoption of Greek theological terminology, especially of this Trinitarian formula, one *usia* in three *hypostases*, was just about universal in the twelfth century, but Robert stubbornly professes to regard the introduction of Greek terms as an affectation or even as a device deliberately intended to serve as camouflage for error.

He claims that "the lamentable experience of the present time" clearly proves that his attack on Greek studies is well-founded, but it is difficult to tell from this cryptic remark whether Robert was alluding here to his theological opponents, like Gilbert de la Porrée (or, perhaps more properly, Porreta),[12] who drew heavily upon Greek materials in translation, or whether he merely meant that the professors of Greek were more concerned for rhetorical and philological subtleties than for the substance of theology. At any rate, he compared them to the foolish virgins of Matthew 25, since, he says, "they have lamps but no oil," that is, they have "melodious words, full of deceptive color, which vainly caress the ears, but do not illumine the mind. Because [these teachers] lack oil, that is, are empty of meaning, those who listen to them will be excluded from the granary of the Lord of the Harvest, and will be cast like empty, crackling stalks into the fire" (Matt. 13 : 30; Luke 3 : 17). Spurning what he calls the "vain embellishment of words" that gains nothing for the faith but "a damnable contempt," Robert condemns "this method of teaching, which consists of the mixing together of Greek and Latin words, feeds the ears, and delights by sound, but does not penetrate to the soul to inform it by faith."[13]

Robert was not the only one who protested against Greek theology. Hugh of Fouilloy (*ca.* 1160) refused to use "Greek, barbarian, or other unusual terms which confuse simple folk," [14] and Eberhard of Bamberg (sometime before 1169) rejected the Greek authorities to which Gerhoh of Reichersberg had appealed on a point of Christology as *minus authenticum*.[15] An adversary of Abelard (Pseudo-William of St. Thierry) branded Maximus the Confessor (d. 662) as the source of heresy in John Scotus Erigena, and Walter of St. Victor (*ca.* 1178) denounced what he called the "errors and heresies of John of Damascus," to whom he refers disparagingly as *nescio quis Iohannes Damascenus*.[16] Many others expressed dissatisfaction with the introduction of Greek phraseology and methods of analysis, but these voices of dissent and disapproval were soon silenced.

Even the seemingly irreconcilable Robert of Melun was by no means so inflexibly hostile to Greek scholarship as his strictures on this subject in the *Prefatio* to his *Sententie* might have led us to believe. For at the beginning of his career (*ca.* 1137–40), while teaching at the *Schola artium* of Mount Ste. Geneviève, as we learn from his pupil, John of Salisbury, he expounded the *Topica* of Aristotle in his lectures.[17] Later on, he quoted Origen, Eusebius of Caesarea, and John Chrysostom in his *Questiones de epistolis Pauli* (written between 1145 and 1155) and the last named also in his *Questiones de divina pagina* (of *ca.* 1143–47), while a few words from the Pseudo-Dionysius are invoked by him in the first book of his *Sententie*.[18] Furthermore, he not only cites John of Damascus with approval in the second book of the abridged edition of his *Sententie*, but also takes over from John the very word, *hypostasis*, the adoption of which by Latin theologians he had ridiculed in the passage summarized above (n. 11). He even reproduces the word in the Greek form of the genitive plural, *hypostaseon*, which he apparently copied from Peter the Lombard.[19] This abridgment of the *Sententie* seems to have been prepared by his disciples, rather than by Robert himself, but it probably represents his own ideas. It is not likely that the abbreviators interpolated a quotation from John of Damascus which was lacking in the manuscript of the work they were epitomizing.

To judge from the texts he cites, Robert depended exclusively upon Latin translations from the Greek, and had no direct contact with the original. This fact possibly explains in part the apparent inconsistency of his attitude towards Greek: he had no objection to Greek authors if suitably clad in Latin dress, but he would have nothing to do with the language itself.

BYZANTINE INFLUENCE ON LATIN ART

The anti-Hellenic tirades found in the *Prefatio* of Robert's *Sententie* reflect the bitterness engendered by the remorseless conflicts between the Byzantines and the Crusaders. This animosity was, of course, warmly reciprocated by the Greeks, who, as we learn from Anna Comnena and other sources, frequently regarded the Latins as a crude and particularly loathsome breed of barbarians. On the Byzantine side, this resentment of the Latins led, in 1182, to a massacre of the Latin community of Constantinople; and the hatred of the Latins for the Greeks culminated, apart from the outrages perpetrated upon Constantinople in 1204, in the Norman sack of Thessalonike, the second city of the Empire in 1185,[20] in which a great part of the population was put to the sword. "Thus," as Nicetas Choniates, a contemporary Byzantine historian, put it, "between us and them (the Latins) yawns a vast chasm of discord. We have no meeting of minds and stand diametrically opposed, even though we keep up our external contacts and often share the same habitations."[21]

Despite all this friction and rancor, however, the splendor and beauty of the city of Constantinople, with its magnificent palaces, incomparable churches, scintillating mosaics, sparkling marbles, and seemingly boundless treasures of fine stuffs and precious stones of every description, dazzled the Latins[22] and filled them both with envy and with the desire to imitate the works of art they beheld. Merchants and travellers usually carried souvenirs from Constantinople, which they had either bought or stolen, and the Crusaders soon acquired a passion for Byzantine jewelry, richly adorned reliquaries, gold, silver, ivories, enamels, silks, and textiles, which led, in a dark hour, to the wanton looting of Constantinople in 1204.

In the first Crusade, the Latins had pillaged the Greek cities on their line of march;[23] and, during the second Crusade (but, of course, not as a part of it), in 1147, King Roger II of Sicily (1101–54) made off with a treasure of such dimensions, including precious metals and valuable stuffs, from Thebes, then a wealthy city, that the ships on which he loaded his booty rode heavy in the water. He also plundered Corinth and Athens, and carried off from Thebes a number of women skilled in weaving, in order to stimulate the silk industry in Sicily. At the same time, he took with him, it would seem, Byzantine craftsmen who had had experience in designing and producing mosaics. Roger's Admiral, George of Antioch, in all likelihood made a special point of assembling Byzantine mosaicists in these raids, and the Normans must have taken advantage of other similar opportunities to round up the experts they needed to decorate the cathedral of Cefalù (*ca.* 1131–75), the Cappella Palatina (*ca.* 1140–89), and the Martorana (*ca.* 1143–51) in Palermo, and the Cathedral of Monreale (*ca.* 1172–92). They may well have been enabled to do so by the marriage negotiations with the Constantinopolitan court in 1143 and 1171–72, by the conclusion of peace between William I and Manuel II in 1158, the embassies exchanged in the years 1181–82, or during William II's expedition to the East in 1185, which was marked by the bloody attack on Thessalonike.[24]

Whenever or however the mosaicists were obtained, it is clear that the mosaic decoration of these four great Sicilian monuments is Byzantine in craftsmanship, iconography, and style. Western and Arabic traits can be detected at various points, but the mosaics were indubitably planned by Byzantine artists and set up under their close supervision. The very idea of producing monumental mosaics of this type is also Byzantine in origin, and its adoption by Roger and his successors indicates that they were consciously imitating Byzantine absolutistic rule. For there can be little doubt that Roger connected the great mosaics of Byzantium with Byzantine political theory, and used his own mosaics as symbols of his autocratic power in both state and church. This point is illustrated by the mosaic in the Martorana in Palermo, which represents Roger II arrayed in the royal robes of the Byzantine emperor, receiving his crown from Christ in a typical Byzantine iconographical scheme. Roger used Byzantine law codes, and in negotiating with the Byzantine emperor demanded that he be recognized as the latter's equal in all respects.[25]

In Sicily, as well as in southern Italy, the Greek language and the Byzantine liturgy continued to flourish even after the Byzantine defeat at Bari in 1071. A large number of south Italian churches and Basilian monasteries, many of them in crypts and caves, were decorated in the Byzantine manner, and many illuminations in twelfth-century codices of the Exultet-rolls of South Italy are marked by Byzantine characteristics, as are a number of Latin illuminated manuscripts which were prepared by artists who had had direct contact with Byzantine art either in the Near East or in the West.[26]

Other notable examples of Byzantine influence can be seen in the mosaics of the twelfth century in the Church of San Marco in Venice, in the mosaics of the Basilica Ursiana at Ravenna (1112), possibly in the apsidal mosaics of Santa Maria in Trastevere (*ca.* 1140), in some of the famous bronze doors of Venice, Southern Italy, and Sicily, in the architectural design of a series of churches in the environs of Perigord, notable for domes resting on pendentives, and in the technique of ornamentation found in many Romanesque churches, especially in Languedoc and Provence. It is of some interest to note that the bronze doors and romanesque patterns of decoration often reproduce motifs such as palmettes, stylized acanthus leaves arranged in rinceaux and intricate designs of interlace, and animals framed in medallions, with which the Latins became acquainted through portable objects like textiles, ivory boxes, and illuminated manuscripts.[27]

LITERATURE, PHILOSOPHY, AND THEOLOGY

Less obvious but perhaps more profound and far-reaching was the Byzantine influence on literature, philosophy, and theology. The publication of new texts and studies relating to our period, which in recent years has been accelerating at an extraordinary rate, is not only demonstrating anew that the so-called "Renaissance of the twelfth century," to use the title of Haskins' famous book, was in every sense a great era in the history of thought, but is also proving in a very substantial manner that the use of Greek materials, in Latin dress at least, was far more prevalent than once had been supposed.[28] Actually, apart from the bits of Plato and Aristotle that had been current in Latin since the early centuries, several Byzantine classics had been known in Latin for a long time. Porphyry's *Eisagoge* to the *Categories* of Aristotle, written at the beginning of the Byzantine period, had been translated into Latin not only by Marius Victorinus in the fourth century but also by Boethius (with commentaries) in the sixth, and left its mark on the whole of medieval philosophy. In the ninth century, the same service had been performed for the Pseudo-Dionysius by Hilduin and John Scotus Erigena, the latter of whom discharged a similar function for Maximus the Confessor and Gregory of Nyssa.[29]

These and many more had been accessible in Latin before the beginning of the twelfth century, during which the increased contact with the Greek world through the Crusades and the humanistic court of the Normans in Sicily, to say nothing of other factors, created a new and practically insatiable demand for Greek authors, ancient and medieval. The number of Latins in this period who were competent to make satisfactory translations from the Greek was not great, but a few notable experts achieved considerable success in this field. Henricus Aristippus, who undertook a hazardous study of the eruptions of Etna and, after a distinguished career, died in prison in Palermo (1162), not only rendered into Latin Plato's *Meno* and *Phaedo*, and the fourth book of Aristotle's *Meteorologica*, but also appears at least to have planned to go on to do Diogenes Laertius and Gregory of Nazianz.[30] James of Venice produced a Latin version of Aristotle's so-called *Logica nova*, which comprised the *Analytica Priora* and *Posteriora*, the *Topica*, and the *Sophistici Elenchi*.[31] Admiral Eugenius of Sicily (d. 1202) aided an unknown scholar in making Ptolemy's *Almagest* (or more correctly, *Syntaxis Mathematike*) available in Latin, and seems himself to have been responsible for a revision in Latin of the Greek original of the so-called *Prophecy of the Erythraean Sibyl*.[32]

Another noted linguist, Moses of Bergamo by name, is associated with a Latin paraphrase of the grammar of Theodosius of Alexandria.[33] In addition, Euclid's *Dedomena* (*Data*), *Optica*, and *Catoptrica*, Proclus' so-called *Elementatio philosophica* (or *physica*), and the *Pneumatica* of Hero were turned from Greek into Latin by anonymous hands, as were also the *Kiranides*, a curious collection of materials bearing on the occult powers of animals, plants, and stones.[34]

These translators were concerned primarily with pagan lore. But others, like Burgundio of Pisa, who was one of the most prolific writers and distinguished diplomats of the twelfth century, devoted themselves both to ancient science and to medieval theology. He translated ten works of Galen, some Hippocrates, an extract from the *Geoponica*, and a great number of theological texts, including the *De fide orthodoxa* of John of Damascus, three long treatises of John Chrysostom, the *De natura hominis* of Nemesius (which circulated then under the name of Gregory of Nyssa and had been done into Latin by Bishop Alfano of Salerno in the latter part of the eleventh century), Basil's commentary on Isaiah, and apparently many more.[35] Less productive than he was Hugo Eterianus' brother, Leo Tuscus, who had a career resembling that of Burgundio in diplomacy and Greek scholarship, and left a Latin rendering of the *Liturgy of St. Chrysostom* and of the ninth-century dream book (*Oneirocriticon*) by Achmet.[36] Mention should be made also of the activities of Cerbanus of Hungary, who put some of John of Damascus (*De fide orthodoxa*) and Maximus the Confessor into Latin.[37]

Though many Latins like Robert of Melun resisted the penetration of Byzantine ideas, at least ostensibly, the majority enthusiastically welcomed "the light from the East"—*orientale lumen*, as it was termed by William of St. Thierry, a Cistercian monk (d. 1147), who was attracted to the *De hominis opificio* of Gregory of Nyssa *via* the version made by John Scotus Erigena *ca.* 862-64, which he followed closely in his *De natura corporis et animae*. William was influenced also by Gregory's brother, Basil, by Origen, and by the Pseudo-Dionysius.[38] Even the obdurate and anti-intellectual St. Bernard of Clairvaux succumbed to the same forces and drew heavily upon Origen, Gregory of Nyssa, and Maximus the Confessor.[39] Cyril of Alexandria was often cited in the twelfth century,[40] and the great interest in the theology of Pseudo-Dionysius led John Sarrazin not only to write a commentary on that author's *Celestial Hierarchy* but also, at the instance of John of Salisbury, to revise Erigena's translation of this same work because it was all but unintelligible.[41]

These are only a very few of the large number of writers in the twelfth century who were affected in one way or another by Greek authorities. It was once believed that the appeal to Greek sources, pagan and Christian, on the part of some authors like Peter Abelard, Gilbert de la Porrée, and Joachim of Flore, was an important factor in the heretical teaching of which these men were deemed guilty. But recent studies have thrown doubt upon this once widely held generalization, and it is now being denied that it was Greek theology or learning which had led these men astray, and even that they ever were heretics at all.[42]

The new approach to medieval theology involved in this judgment merits careful investigation for its own sake as well as for its bearing upon the transmission and reception of Greek scholarship, both secular and theological, in the West during the Middle Ages. As a small contribution to the study of this problem, I offer the following analysis of two theological treatises, one of which stresses opposition to Byzantine theology, and the other indebtedness thereto.

In exploring the relationship of Byzantine thought to that of the West, it should be remembered that Byzantine theology constitutes the most striking and most contemporaneously relevant of the Byzantine contributions to civilization. The basic doctrines of the Trinity and the Incarnation, as these were understood not only in the twelfth century but also in all ages from early times until the present day, were formulated and codified by Byzantine theologians at the Seven Oecumenical Councils (325-787) in technical language that still commands all but universal assent in the entire Christian Church. The Roman Church participated in these decisions, it is true, but only through the presence of a very few delegates, and the councils were dominated by the Byzantine emperors, who convoked them and invested their dogmatic decrees with the force of law.[43]

The Byzantine insistence (see the next section) that the Holy Spirit proceeds from the Father alone stems from the so-called Niceno-Constantinopolitan Creed of 381 (now usually, but unfortunately, designated in the Churches as the Nicene Creed, from which it differs markedly). According to the *symbolum fidei* of 381, the Holy Spirit "proceeds from the Father, and is worshipped and glorified together with the Father and the Son." Apparently in 589 the Church of Toledo in Spain added *Filioque* to this Creed and meant to assert thereby that the Holy Spirit "proceeds from the *Father and the Son*." This addition, which sanctions the "double procession" of the Holy Spirit, was officially endorsed by Rome under Pope Benedict VIII (1012–24), but is rejected by the Byzantine Church because it does not occur in any of the oecu-menical formularies.

In the theological discussions which follow in the next two sections, it should be noted carefully that the Trinitarian problem is concerned with the Father, Son, and Holy Spirit, and their relation to the Godhead and to each other, whereas the Christological problem has to do with the relation between the two natures, the human and the divine, within the person of Jesus Christ. After much confusion and misunderstanding, the Greek and Latin terms for the Godhead (the divine substance, essence, or nature common to the three persons) and for the individual, distinct person became standardized in orthodox circles. The former was designated as οὐσία (*substantia* or *essentia* in Latin) or φύσις (*natura*), the latter as πρόσωπον or ὑπόστασις (*persona, hypostasis,* and *subsistentia* in Latin); and it became customary to speak of the Trinity as consisting of one substance in three persons. Peter Lombard and Peter of Poitiers usually referred to the divine substance as *essentia*, but they by no means spurned the synonyms, *substantia* and *natura* or *usia*, the transliteration of οὐσία. To avoid confusion, therefore, in my analysis of Latin theological terminology (pp. 159 ff. and 168 ff. below), I follow the usage of the sources closely, using *essence* for *essentia, substance* for *substantia, nature* for *natura,* etc.

HUGO ETERIANUS ON THE DOUBLE PROCESSION OF THE HOLY SPIRIT

Let us look first at the treatise, *De sancto et immortali Deo*, written between 1176 and 1177 by Hugo Eterianus (otherwise known as Hugo of Pisa), which deals exhaustively with the Byzantine critique of the Roman doctrine of the double procession of the Holy Spirit. Hugo lived approximately fifteen years at Constantinople, from about 1166, if not so early as 1161 or before, until perhaps as late as the beginning of 1182, the year of his death, which took place in Italy sometime between the middle of July and the seventh of December, only a few days or weeks after he had been named cardinal deacon of Sant' Angelo by Pope Lucius III (1181–85). During their sojourn in Constantinople, Hugo and his brother, Leo the Tuscan, who served the Byzantine Emperor Manuel I (1143–80) as interpreter, acquired not only a thorough command of the Greek language, but also a wide acquaintance with the writings of the Byzantine theologians of their own day and of previous times, which they read with great avidity in the libraries of the capital city.[44]

Manuel, as is well known, sought to establish friendly relations with the West, and in his eagerness to restore the unity of the Roman Empire and secure for himself recognition as emperor in the West as well as in the East, was attempting to secure the union of the Greek and Roman churches.[45] In furtherance of this ambition he asked Hugo to prepare a list of patristic authorities that would sanction the Latin doctrine of the double procession.[46] Hugo was pleased to comply with this request, which had been supported also by a similar demand on the part of the three Roman clerics who journeyed to Constantinople about 1168 in order to negotiate with Manuel for the union of the Churches.[47] The Pope (Alexander III, 1159–81) was delighted, and urged Hugo to persuade Manuel to show reverence to Rome and bring about unity in the Church by recognizing the supremacy of the Roman pope.

Hugo set about this task with great enthusiasm and even went so far, he tells us himself,[48] as to prepare a Greek version of his treatise, in order, no doubt, to win converts among the Byzantines to the Latin point of view. Aiming at two targets, he intended both to fortify his co-religionists in their defense of Latin dogma, and to convince the Byzantines that the double procession was consistent with Byzantine theological tradition and could be demonstrated out of the works of impeccable Byzantine theologians like Athanasius, Basil, John Chrysostom, and Cyril. For this reason, he took great pains to ransack Byzantine patrology for evidence proving that distinguished Byzantine authorities taught the procession of the Holy Spirit from the Father and Son. His detailed summaries and his meticulous refutations of the Byzantine objections to the double procession also indicate that he was seriously hoping to be able to persuade the Greeks that they could embrace this Latin doctrine without apprehension, and thus lay the foundation for the reconciliation with Rome toward which the Emperor Manuel aspired.

In spite of his great erudition, however, Hugo does not present an argument that can be reduced to a logical outline. Except for the first part of the third book, he did not attempt to organize his material systematically, nor did he seek to construct a case based upon points which succeed each other in order of importance according to the requirements of logic. Instead, in the manner of compilers of *catenae* and *excerpta*, Hugo piles topic on topic without attempting to subordinate or link one to another. The first and second books and the end of the third are built around the Byzantine syllogisms hostile to the Latin dogma. But in his refutation of each one of these, considered individually, he proceeds in a coherent, orderly manner. In what follows, emphasis will be laid on this part of Hugo's work. The third book, which was devoted to the affirmative defense of the double procession by metaphysical argumentation and the recitation of Biblical and patristic *testimonia*, will be left out of account, except for a summary of the section on the papacy and the oecumenical councils, and a critique of Hugo's citation of the Greek fathers.

After dedicatory epistles to Pope Alexander III and the Latin Patriarch Aimericus of Antioch, and quotations from Plato and Plotinus on the triadic division of the incorporeal universe, not without a reference to Aristotle,[49] Hugo begins by saying that the three persons, Father, Son, and Holy Spirit, are one (*unum, una unitas, una substantia, unum principium*),[50] that the Father begets (*gignit*) the Son and sends forth (*emittit*) the Holy Spirit, and that, since the Father does not differ from the Son, the Holy Spirit proceeds from the Son as well as from the Father. For, he explains, if the Spirit proceeded from only one of these two, it could not belong equally (*commune*) and without difference to both, but only to the one from which it proceeded. Since the Spirit does belong equally and without difference to both, however, it belongs no less to the Son than to the Father, and proceeds from them both.[51]

To this general definition of the Latin doctrine of the double procession, Hugo admits, the Greeks objected that, if the Holy Spirit proceeded from the Father and the Son, the Holy Spirit, being one, would have two causes (*principia*), and duality (or the number two) would be the cause of unity (or the number one). This was manifestly absurd, the Byzantine theologians, Archbishop Nicetas of Nicomedia (fl. 1135) and Bishop

Nicholas of Methone (d. 1165), had protested, since the contrary is true, unity being the constituent element or cause of duality and of all numbers.

Hugo replied first by stating, on the authority of Aristotle, that all terms in syllogisms should be of the same genus. Secondly, he declared it inaccurate of them to designate the Father and the Son as two principles, for they are not two things, substances, principles, or Gods, but, though two persons or hypostases, make up together only one principle as the source of the Holy Spirit.[52] That is, he distinguishes the divinity or the godhead—the essence, *substantia, usia,* or nature, which is one and is shared by Father, Son, and Holy Spirit alike—from the three hypostases or persons, who are one in essence, but nevertheless three members of the same Trinity.

Hugo himself might perhaps seem to be guilty of the very logical error he reprehends, since he is content to designate the Holy Spirit as one, that is, one person, but insists that the Father and the Son, two distinct persons (i.e., two in the same sense that the Holy Spirit is one), constitute only one nature. He attempts to extricate himself from this difficulty by comparing the unity of the Father and the Son as sources of the Holy Spirit to the distance from Thebes to Athens. The *ascensio* here is not the *descensio,* he says, or *vice versa;* nevertheless both together form one distance, not two. Similarly, he argues, the Father is not the Son, nor the Son the Father, but both of them form one *principium,* not two, just as both the Father and the Son are creators of the universe, but in the work of creation operate as one cause, creator, and principle, not two.[53]

Hugo's comparison of the Father and the Son to the distance between Athens and Thebes is perhaps ingenious, if somewhat peculiar. In other contexts, however, he imitates the Nicene theologians of the fourth century, in comparing them, more felicitously, to the sun, its rays of light, and its heat, three individualized but inseparable phenomena, which were in medieval times believed to be the same in substance, and therefore affording an excellent example of how three distinct hypostases could be regarded as consubstantial or *homousioi.*

Next, Hugo considers the contention of Nicetas of Byzantium, a disciple of Photius in the second half of the ninth century, that, if the Spirit proceeds from the Son as from the Father, the Spirit must be the son of a son (thus a grandson), and so on *ad infinitum.* For Nicetas took it to be the logical consequence of the Latin doctrine of the double procession, that that out of which the Spirit proceeds has a Son.[54] This is not only impossible and indemonstrable, Hugo objects, but is based upon the erroneous assumption that the Father as *genitor* is the *emissor* of the Spirit, that is, that the Spirit proceeds from the Father in the Father's capacity as Father of Jesus Christ, whereas, in point of fact, it is *qua cause* or *principium* that he sends forth the Spirit. According to Hugo, the Spirit is not the son of the Father, since the latter has only one son, not two. The Father does not emit the Spirit insofar as he differs from the Son, but insofar as he does not differ from the Son; and the Father differs from the Son only in those functions by which he does not project the Spirit. Or, as we should say, the Father differs from the Son only in that he begets the Son, but emits the Spirit by virtue of those qualities which he and the Son jointly possess.[55] Moreover, he adds, the attributes pertaining to all three persons together indistinguishably because of their being one in nature are far more numerous than those which uniquely and specifically characterize each one of them individually as distinct members of the Trinity.[56]

At another point, Hugo faces the objection raised by Nicetas of Nicomedia on the basis of the principle that the characteristics which are not distinctive of one of the three persons belong to all three alike. This being so, Nicetas maintained, if the procession of the Spirit is not attributed solely to the Father but also to the Son, the projection of the Spirit will be the joint property of all the three persons, so that the Spirit will then be both the projected and the projector (*emissor simul et emissus*).[57] Here Hugo rejects the major premise (i.e., that the qualities not peculiar to one member of the Trinity are common to all three), and contends that the Father and the Son share some qualities in which the Spirit does not participate.[58]

Following somewhat the same lines as Nicetas of Nicomedia in the last syllogism, Nicholas of Methone attacked the Latins for assuming that, since the Father and the Son are one in nature, the Spirit must proceed from the Son as well as from the Father. If this reasoning be sound, Nicholas had countered, it would be equally true to say that the Son is generated by the Spirit no less than by the Father, since the Father and the Spirit are also of the same nature. Otherwise, Nicholas ironically concluded, the Spirit would not be one in nature with the Father, and the Macedonian view of the inferiority of the Spirit to the Father would be vindicated.[59]

Here again, as in the example previously noted, Hugo in effect repudiates the major premise in Nicholas' syllogism, and argues that the

Latins defend the double procession, not because the Father and the Son are one God, but because the Son is equal to the Father and to the person of the Father. He realizes that his opponents will rejoin that the Spirit is also equal to the person of the Father, and therefore should, like the Father, be regarded as the Father of the Son. This conclusion is untenable, however, in his judgment because "it is nowhere stated that the Son belongs equally to the Father and the Spirit, although all confess that the Spirit belongs equally to the Father and the Son." The Son is always mentioned alongside the Father, he avers, in all gifts of the Spirit, but it is impious to speak of the Spirit as Father or the Son as the son of the Spirit. Hugo then reiterates in several different ways his conviction that the Father's projection is not connected with his character (*proprietas*) as Father.[60]

In the Second Book, after some introductory remarks on the nature of God and the universe, in which he quotes from Aristotle and Pseudo-Dionysius, Hugo turns to grapple with a series of propositions advanced by Nicetas of Byzantium. If, Nicetas had written, the Spirit proceeds from the Son, as from the Father, the procession from the Son must be either the same as that from the Father or different. If it is different, it must be either better or worse. If it is better, the Son will necessarily be proved better than the Father. But if it is worse, the Son could not be of the same nature as the Father. On the other hand, if the procession from the Son is equal to that of the Father, it will be the same as the Father's. Then, the question arises as to whether the procession from the Son completes the existence of the Spirit or not. If it does not, it is pointless, and would violate the principle that nothing about God is in vain (*nihil autem circa Deum frustra*). But if it does actually complete the existence of the Spirit, the procession from the Father would be imperfect.[61]

Scorning all of these alternatives, Hugo insists that neither the Father nor the Son projects the Spirit *ex parte* but both project it completely, perfectly, and equally (*ex toto et perfecte uterque pariter*), for the Son, as the image of the Father, who alone derives his being directly from the Father without any intermediary (*solus enim Filius existit de Patre absque medio*), emits the Spirit as the Father does.[62]

Some Byzantine theologians (note 74 below) who refused to countenance the double procession were, however, inclined to accept a compromise, according to which the Spirit was said to proceed from the Father *through* the Son (*per Filium*, διὰ τοῦ υἱοῦ). But the most irreconcilable, like Nicetas of Nicomedia, refused to make this concession. If, Nicetas said, we hold that the Spirit proceeds from the Father *through* the Son (*ex Patre per Filium*), while the Son issues directly from the Father without intermediary (*sine medio*), the Spirit is inferior to the Son, because that which participates in something through an intermediary is inferior to that which participates in it directly. Hugo overturns Nicetas' major premise (that that which participates in something through an intermediary is inferior to that which participates in it directly) by citing the example of the Word of God, which participates in the human race through the medium of a rational soul, although no one would conclude that the Word of God is on this account inferior to the rational soul or to his Virgin Mother.[63] (See note 144, below.)

Rejecting the double procession because, among other things, it seemed to him to deny the Spirit equality with the Father and the Son, Nicholas of Methone had protested that, if we admit that the Son receives from the Father the power of producing the Spirit, we are bound to conclude that the Spirit lacks this honor since he is not enabled by the Father to be the cause of the Son or of any being like himself.[64] Hugo attacks this difficulty by quoting John 16 : 7: "Unless I go, the Paraclete will not come to you, but if I go I will send him to you," which he takes as proof that the Son produces the Spirit. Then he explains that the Spirit is not the cause of any being similar to himself, lest there be the addition of a fourth member to the Trinity. Moreover, he says, the Son is assigned the function of judging, in which the Spirit does not participate, as in John 5 : 22f.: "The Father judgeth no man but hath committed all judgment unto the Son. That all men should honor the Son, even as they honor the Father." Similarly, the Son receives the function of transmitting the Spirit from the Father, just as he receives life and judgment from the same source. Hugo apparently means, though he does not say so, that the bestowal of the function of judgment on the Son, and not on the Spirit, does not affect the honor or standing of the Spirit. But he does add that, just as the *nascibilitas* of the Son does not prevent him from having the same nature as the Father, so the procession from the Father and the Son does not prevent the Spirit from having the same nature as the Father and the Son.[65]

Hugo comes at length, near the end of the second book, to the great Patriarch Photius (858–67, 877–86), who was the chief author of the Byzantine panoply of arguments against the double procession, and the principal source of subsequent Byzantine writings on this theme. In addition to having fashioned the most devastating of the Byzantine syllogisms on the inadmissibility of *Filioque* to the Creed, Photius specifically raised the question of the juridical validity of the Latin case. Which of our fathers or priests or what oecumenical council, Photius asked, ever taught that the Spirit proceeded from the Son? The Second Council (which met in Constantinople in 381), he argued, declared that the Spirit proceeded from the Father, and this doctrine, as confirmed by five subsequent oecumenical councils, was no longer subject to revision.[66]

Hugo's reply is threefold. In the first place, he asks rhetorically, what synod sanctioned the use of leavened bread (which the Byzantine Church used in the Eucharist) or prescribed that it be cut by a lance? For he interpreted the Last Supper, celebrated by Christ before his Crucifixion, to be the paschal meal of the Jews, which necessarily involved the use of azyma (i.e., of unleavened bread). This he proves by reference to the New Testament (Luke 22 : 15: "With desire have I desired to eat this pascha with you before I suffer," and Matthew 26 : 17: "Where dost thou wish us to prepare the pascha for thee?"), and to John Chrysostom, Cyril, and Epiphanius. He defends the Latins against the charge that, in clinging to unleavened bread, they are judaizers, by pointing out that the Orthodox Church had institutionalized many practices of Jewish origin (such as the use of "temple, altar, oil, water, light, incense, images of the angels," and the custom of not shaving).[67] Then he asks what council authorized the Greeks to prescribe oil in connection with baptism, or hot water in the Eucharist, or the frequent chanting of Κύριε ἐλέησον instead of *Christe eleison*.[68]

Secondly, he admits that the Councils had taught that the Spirit proceeds from the Father and had not mentioned the Son in this connection. But, he adds, "although the Father alone is named, the Son is clearly to be understood also, both because the [Spirit] did not come forth from the Father without an intermediary,"[69] and because the Father never said that he *alone* produced the Spirit, nor did any of the prophets or fathers ever say so. In other words, he insists, John 15. 26 merely indicates that "the Spirit proceeds from the Father," and does not specifically state that the Spirit proceeds "from the Father alone."[70]

Thirdly, he argues in Book III that, just as the Second Oecumenical Council in 381 added the clause on the procession of the Holy Spirit to the Nicene Creed of 325, and just as the Council of Chalcedon put out a supplement to the Creed of 381 (i.e., to the Symbol today designated in the Churches as the Creed of Nicea) to combat Nestorius and Eutyches, the Pope of Rome was justified in introducing the phrase *Filioque*. For the Pope had, and always will have, the right to "confirm the brethren, issue decrees, and set forth interpretations" when need arises. Furthermore, he urges, the Chalcedonian prohibition of additions and changes in the Creed was not affected by the insertion of *Filioque* because the latter did not alter the meaning of the Creed.[71] Thus, in the last analysis, here and in the succeeding paragraphs, Hugo vindicates *Filioque* by reason of the primacy of Rome and of the authority of the Pope as the head of all of the churches in Christendom.[72]

Hugo then refutes the criticism that the procession of the Spirit from the Son could not be eternal since the apostles and prophets received the Spirit from Christ in historical time, by alleging that this procession did not begin in time but must be understood as from all eternity, like the generation of the Son.[73] He next rejects the proposal of Nicetas of Maronea, who became archbishop of Thessalonike (fl. 1133), that the Latins give up the addition of *Filioque* to the Creed, and hearken to the teaching of Athanasius, Cyril, and John of Damascus that the Spirit proceeds from the Father *through* (*per*), rather than out of (*ex*), the Son, because he took the preposition *per* (through) with the accusative to be the equivalent of *ex* (from) with the ablative. Hence, he concludes, the Greeks who tolerate the procession *per Filium* must also accept the Latin doctrine of the procession *ex Filio*.[74]

Hugo's chief contribution to Latin theology lay in his conscientious study of Byzantine patristic literature. In the first place, he quoted or summarized the leading Byzantine arguments, and answered them as well as he could. Secondly, he was able to cite Greek authors in behalf of the double procession much more fully than previous Latin writers, like Alcuin (d. 804), Theodulph (d. 821), Aeneas of Paris (d. 870), Ratramnus (d. 868), and Anselm of Aosta (d. 1109), who had dealt with the problem far less thoroughly, and had been able to muster only a few Greek authorities on their side.[75] Having had the advantage of a long sojourn in Constantinople and free access to the great theological libraries of the capital city, Hugo succeeded in finding five Byzantine props for the Latin cause that had been unknown in the West hitherto.

Three were from the *Ancoratus* of Epiphanius (d. 403), according to which God the Spirit belongs to the Father and to the Son, is from the Father and the Son, and is from both.[76] Two others Hugo discovered in Cyril of Alexandria (d. 444), who asserts in one that the Spirit is of the Father and the Son, and proceeds in substance from both, "or rather, from the Father through the Son." But, it should be noted, Hugo disingenuously suppressed the last part of this sentence, which contradicts the point he was trying to make. Nevertheless, he was able to unearth a phrase from Cyril which represents the Spirit as coming from the Son.[77]

In addition, Hugo claims Basil of Caesarea (d. 379) as a proponent of the view that there would be no order in the Trinity unless the Father were the cause of the Son and the Holy Spirit, the Son came from the Father, and the Holy Spirit were deemed to be of both. But these words cannot be found in the extant works of Basil. Nor can it be proved that Basil's treatise, *Adversus Eunomium* (3,1), really contained the clauses which Hugo records, to the effect that the Holy Spirit derives its being from the Son (*ab ipso esse habens, et ab illo accipiens..., et quod omnino de illa causa exeat*). Even if this passage proved Hugo's point, it apparently does not occur in the earliest Greek MSS of Basil, and was repudiated by Byzantine theologians as an interpolation, notwithstanding its acceptance by the Latins and *Latinophrones* like Bessarion (d. 1472).[78]

Hugo attempts, also, to turn John of Damascus into a proponent of Latin dogma by assuming that the latter's words, "we deny that the Spirit is of the Son (*ex Filio*, ἐκ), but call him the Spirit [of the Son]," can be construed as corroborating the double procession. For, he contends, if the Spirit is the Son's, he must also proceed from the Son. Indeed, he takes this perverse exegesis so seriously that he rejects as a later addition an indubitably authentic passage from John's *Homilia in Sabbatum Sanctum*, which was indisputably and irreconcilably hostile to the Latin theory.[79]

These tactics availed him little among his Greek opponents, but his collection of excerpts from Byzantine patrology proved useful to the Latins in later times, and demonstrate a wide and penetrating knowledge of Greek theology. It must be admitted, however, that only four or five of his quotations from the Greek (notes 76 f. above) could possibly be regarded as confirming the double procession. The rest are either completely irrelevant or only very indirectly pertinent.

JOHN OF DAMASCUS AND THE
LIBRI SENTENTIARUM OF PETER THE LOMBARD

Although Hugo Eterianus stressed as strongly as he could the Byzantine authorities in whom he found, or professed to find, support for the Latin dogma of the double procession of the Holy Spirit, his primary goal was to attack a fundamental article of Byzantine theology. He appealed to Greek sources whenever it served his purposes to do so. But his intention was polemical. Despite his ostensibly eirenic goal of winning the Greeks over to the Latin view, his aim was to subvert a long established position of the Byzantine Church. He quoted the Greek fathers not so much for their own sake or to illustrate and expound a doctrinal point as such, but chiefly in order to refute and confound the Byzantine theologians of his own day out of their own theological tradition.

A very different attitude, as we shall see below, marks the reception of the new Latin translations of the great theological encyclopedia of John of Damascus, the ἔκδοσις ἀκριβὴς τῆς ὀρθοδόξου πίστεως, which the Latins usually designated as *On the orthodox faith* (*De fide orthodoxa*) and Peter the Lombard cited as *De Trinitate*, apparently because he thought that the Trinity was its chief topic. John flourished in the eighth century (d. 749), but his summary of orthodox theology, actually only the third division of a larger work entitled *The Fountain of Knowledge* (πηγὴ γνώσεως), was not rendered into Latin until sometime before 1145, when a Latin version of a portion of the text was produced in Hungary by Cerbanus. A few years later, about 1153–54, the whole of the treatise was translated by Burgundio of Pisa, whose rendition of the Greek not only held the ground until *ca.* 1235–40, when Robert Grosseteste issued it in a revised form, but also continued to be copied even as late as 1500. Grosseteste's recension seems not to have been transcribed after *ca.* 1300, and still remains unpublished. But we now have the good fortune of being able to study the methods and achievements of the two translators of the twelfth century in the admirable edition of Eligius M. Buytaert, which forms the basis for all subsequent research on this subject.[80]

The *De fide orthodoxa* was turned into Latin once again at the end of the medieval period by the Carmelite Johannes Baptista Panetius (d. 1497). But the other two sections of John's *Fountain of Knowledge*, the *Dialectica* (or "chapters on philosophy") and a handbook *On heresies*, were unknown in Latin during the Middle Ages, except for the *Dialectica*, which was made available by Robert Grosseteste.

Considerable energy has been devoted to these Latin translations, and much progress has been made in identifying passages in the writings of Peter the Lombard, Arno and Gerhoh of Reichersberg, and other writers of the twelfth century who show acquaintance with John of Damascus. But the scholars who have investigated this question have satisfied themselves with the selfless task of editing texts and listing parallel passages, without attempting to evalute the substantive theological use that was made of these materials.[81]

Accordingly it may be of interest to examine the quotations from John of Damascus carefully in order to determine the precise role played by him in the twelfth century. Special interest attaches to the references to John made by Peter the Lombard, whose four *Libri Sententiarum* (*ca.* 1155–57), after some vicissitudes in the twelfth century, received the stamp of orthodoxy in the thirteenth, especially with regard to Trinitarian questions, and exerted a truly enormous influence upon Latin thought in the Middle Ages and even subsequently.[82] There is no doubt that the great popularity of Peter's *Sententiae* and the influence of his example were important factors in the great prestige which the views of John of Damascus acquired in the twelfth century and above all in the thirteenth, when Thomas Aquinas, Albertus Magnus, Robert Grosseteste, Alexander of Hales, Bonaventura,[83] and many others, in no small measure affected by the precedent set by Peter in this regard, relied heavily upon John as a major theological authority. In the twelfth century, writers like Peter of Poitiers (d. 1205),[84] Gandulphus of Bologna (d. *ca.* 1185),[85] an anonymous *Summa Sententiarum*,[86] and Stephen Langton (d. 1228),[87] to name only a few,[88] borrowed extensively from Peter the Lombard, and derived at least some of their citations of John of Damascus from him. Others, like Gerhoh (d. 1169)[89] and Arno (d. 1175) of Reichersberg,[90] Simon of Tournai (d. 1201),[91] Alan of Lille (d. 1202),[92] and William of Auxerre (d. 1247),[93] apparently were independent of Peter in their citation of John.

Peter usually refers to John as Ioannes Damascenus, or simply as Ioannes. Like most of his contemporaries, Peter gives no indication of acquaintance with more than the third book of John's great theological encyclopedia. This circumstance led some scholars to infer that Peter had secured a Latin translation limited to the first three books. But it has recently been argued that he had seen the whole of Burgundio's *De fide orthodoxa*, but did not have the opportunity of studying more than a portion of it at the time that he was composing the *Sententiae*. However this may be, it has been shown that Peter originally used Cerbanus' version, and subsequently corrected it at some points after he had seen Burgundio's.[94]

Passages from John of Damascus frequently occupy a key position in Peter's patristic armory,[95] and are cited to reinforce major points of doctrine. In all but one of these, Peter finds John's treatment of the subject in hand extremely congenial as a principal source and justification of his own views. In this one instance, however, Peter disagrees with

John, and rejects an analogy used by the latter in expounding the relation of the divine essence (*substantia, essentia*) of the Godhead to the three persons of the Trinity.[96] The Cappadocian fathers in the fourth century had explained the paradox of how the Father, the Son, and the Holy Spirit, though three in number and all divine, were nevertheless not three Gods but only one. This they had done in part by comparing the relationship between the divine substance and the three members of the Trinity to that which obtains between men and the human race. John, Peter, and Andrew, for example, are three in number, they had maintained, but only one in nature because, as members of the human race, all three have the same nature.[97]

Following in their footsteps, and faithful to his boast that he was in no sense an innovator but only a recorder of patristic tradition, John of Damascus had said that "that which is general or universal is predicated of the particulars that belong to this category. Hence, (in the Godhead) the substance is the universal, and the hypostasis is the particular— particular not as possessing a portion of the nature, but particular in number, like an individual. For the hypostases are said to differ in number, not in nature."[98] As John had said on another occasion, "substance indicates the common category that embraces hypostases of the same nature, like God or man. But the hypostasis designates the individual, like Father, Son, and Holy Spirit, or Peter and Paul."[99]

After quoting these two texts from John, Peter points out that the doctrine they embody (that God is the universal like man or mankind, and that the Father, Son, and Holy Spirit are individuals like Peter and Paul), contradicts Augustine. In this case, he preferred to follow Augustine's conclusion that three men, though of the same nature, are not only one man but three, and that two men are something more than one man, whereas in the Godhead the Father and the Son together are not greater in essence than the Father alone or the Son alone, since the three persons together are equal to each person individually.[100]

Of course, John of Damascus would not have denied the proposition set forth in the last sentence, and in another context Peter depends upon John as his sole authority for maintaining that: "the Father is not greater than the Son, nor is the Father or the Son greater than the Holy Spirit, nor are two persons [of the Trinity] together greater than one, nor are three together greater than two, nor is the essence greater in three than in two, nor in two rather than one, since the whole is in each." This concept Peter borrowed from John, who, as Peter notes, had said, "We confess the whole nature (*naturam*, φύσιν) of the Godhead to be present in its entirety (*perfecte*, τελείως) in each of its hypostases [or persons]: the whole [of it] in the Father, the whole in the Son, the whole in the Holy Spirit. Therefore, God the Father is perfect, God the Son is perfect, God the Holy Spirit is perfect."[101]

Though Peter disavows John's application of the relation between the universal and the particular to that which obtains between the divine substance and the three persons, he introduces John's words on this subject by remarking that he was one of the great Greek authorities (*inter Graecorum doctores magnus*), whose *De Trinitate* had been translated into Latin at the instance of Pope Eugene III. But he then adds that what John really meant was unobjectionable. For, he says, John applied the terms, universal and particular, to the Trinity and its three persons respectively because of the similarity which he descried between eternal and temporal categories, not because he intended to apply philosophical modes of reasoning to God. Augustine, on the other hand, Peter remarks, felt the difference between the eternal and temporal categories more keenly than such similarity as may have appeared between them, and consequently considers these designations unsuitable for the Trinity.[102]

Peter probably found the passages from Augustine on which he relied in Abelard or Hugh of St. Victor.[103] But this philosophical attitude stemmed from John Scotus Erigena's *De divisione naturae*, I,I, according to which God was neither genus, species, nor accident. Erigena, in turn, who had translated the works of the Pseudo-Dionysius the Areopagite from Greek into Latin, derived from the latter and from Augustine's *De Trinitate*, as he specifically states, the notion that none of the ten Aristotelian categories is applicable to God. The concept itself can be traced back to Philo, Clement of Alexandria, and the Neoplatonists.[104]

In the next *capitulum* of the same *Distinctio*, Peter singles out for special treatment the statement of John quoted in the previous section that the hypostases differ in number, not in nature. He agrees that they do not differ in nature. But he is unwilling to accept John's dictum that they differ in number if the difference envisaged denotes a difference of individuals or particulars (in the way that Socrates, e.g., differs from Plato). On the other hand, he recognizes another kind of numerical difference among things which in enumeration or computation are not added to each other (viz., to form a larger whole, unit, or amount) but are distinguished from each other, as one, two, or three in number. In this latter sense, he concedes, it is possible to say that the Father is one, the

Father and Son are two, and the Father, Son, and Holy Spirit are three, and, similarly, that this person is one, this and that person are two, and this, that, and the other person are three. Even so, he concludes, it is more appropriate that these three persons be distinguished by their properties and in no other way.[105]

Like Peter the Lombard, Peter of Poitiers in his *Sententiae* examines John's doctrine that the divine *substantia* could be defined as the universal and the *hypostasis* as the particular. He agrees with the Lombard both in giving the preference to Augustine in this matter, and in granting that there is an analogy between the philosophical terminology and the relation of the divine substance to the three hypostases.[106] But, unlike the Lombard, he adopts without qualification John's definition of the hypostases as differing from each other in number, not in nature. He omits altogether the objections noted above and merely reproduces faithfully what Peter had said about the kind of numerical difference he would accept with regard to the Trinity. Imitating the Lombard, Peter of Poitiers explains that "One thing is said to differ from another because it is not that or anything which the other is, nor is it contained in the other. Thus, the Father is not said to differ from the Son in number because he is what the Son is and is in the Son. But he is said to differ from him in number because he is counted with him, since it can be said that the Father, Son, and Holy Spirit are three, or (in regard to two of them) are two."[107]

Like the majority of Latin theologians, Peter had taken over the Byzantine Trinitarian formula, μία οὐσία ἐν τρισὶν ὑποστάσεσι, which had been translated into Latin in the form, *una substantia, essentia, natura,* or *usia* and *tres personae, hypostases,* or *subsistentiae*—one substance in three persons. This he found not only in John of Damascus,[108] whom he quotes, but also in Jerome's Epistle to Damasus on the Catholic faith. He does not share the antagonism which marked Robert of Melun's attitude to these Byzantine terms; but, like Jerome, he warns that "poison lurks within the honey," and that the word *hypostasis* should be used as an equivalent for *persona,* not for *usia* or *natura,* with which the heretics deliberately equated it, as if there were three divine natures rather than one.[109]

Peter appeals to the authority of John of Damascus in support of a number of basic theological propositions. Thus, in expounding the dogma that the distinguishing features of the three persons determine the *hypostases* (of the three persons) and not the substance or nature of the

Godhead, he repeats John's exposition of this matter.[110] John had explained that the three hypostases differ from each other, not in their substance, but in the qualities which characterize them as distinct persons. That is, as John put it, the hypostasis (or person) of the Word (i.e., Jesus Christ) is consubstantial (*homousios*) with the Father and has all that the Father has, being distinguished from the Father's hypostasis only by having been begotten, but in no way separated (*secedentem*) from the Father's hypostasis.

This was the method of reasoning by which Athanasius and the Cappadocian fathers in the fourth century had proved that the belief in the Trinity did not compromise monotheism. Insisting that the three persons were one in substance, they made a special effort to demonstrate that the ways in which the Trinity could be regarded as made up of three persons did not destroy the divine unity. Their solution of this problem, which has remained authoritative ever since, was incorporated into the theological encyclopedia of John of Damascus, who summarized the teaching of his predecessors on this topic in the passage quoted here by Peter.[111] We recognize the difference of the hypostases, John had said, in the three characteristics of paternity, sonship, and procession, although the three hypostases are inseparable and undivided. Still, they are united without confusion and remain three, each being perfect and retaining its own characteristics and mode of existence. Thus, they are distinguished but unseparated (*divisas... indistanter*), and, by reason of the unity of substance, they are not divided from the hypostasis of the Father.[112]

Peter then directs this same definition against the School of Gilbert de la Porrée, which had accused him of Sabellianism. Peter maintained that the properties or distinctive attributes of the three persons of the Trinity are in the three persons, and are themselves the persons and the divine essence (*fateamur ergo et proprietates* [*personarum*] *esse in tribus personis, et ipsas esse personas atque divinam essentiam*).[113] But the Porretani contended that, if the properties or individual characteristics of the hypostases are in the divine essence or are themselves the divine essence, the three persons of the Trinity would not differ in any respect, since all three are of the same essence. This, they objected, would eliminate the distinction of the persons, and lead to Sabellianism, according to which the Trinity consisted, not of three distinct eternal persons, but only of three temporary manifestations of the divine essence which succeeded each other in time and did not exist simultaneously.[114]

Peter replied by citing John's dictum that the properties of the hypostases determine the hypostases, not the divine nature. According to the Lombard, these words mean that the properties of *Paternitas* (of God the Father) and Sonship (of Jesus Christ), though being in the divine essence, are not present therein to the same extent that they are in the individual hypostases. Hence, he concludes, it is not correct to say that the divine essence both generates (as a Father) and is generated (as a Son). For the property determines the person, so that, by reason of one property, one hypostasis (the Father's) generates, and, by reason of another property, another hypostasis (the Son's) is generated.[115]

Proceeding then in Book III to Christology, Peter Lombard leans upon John of Damascus to demonstrate that what the divine Logos assumed was a complete human nature, including a human body and rational soul, with all their qualities, and that he was perfect God and also perfect man.[116] These citations from John were aimed at the Monophysites, who held that Jesus Christ had only one nature, the divine, after the incarnation, and at the Apollinarians, who taught that the divine Logos at the incarnation assumed only a human body and a human vegetative soul, but not a human rational soul (or mind).

At the end of this *Distinctio*, Peter reproduces from John a famous anti-Apollinarian text, "What was not assumed was not saved." This was derived ultimately from the Cappadocian fathers, who had formulated it in the course of their polemic against the Apollinarian conception that Christ did not have a human rational soul. It summed up admirably the orthodox objection that if the reasoning power in the incarnate Jesus Christ were not truly human, but only the divine Logos which the Son of God had brought down from heaven, redemption would not have been complete, for the human mind, which required salvation as much as human flesh did, would not then have had any part in Christ and therefore could not have been affected by his triumph over sin and death.[117]

In the second *capitulum* of the same *Distinctio*, Peter turns to John for confirmation of the Christological axiom current in the middle of the twelfth century that the Son of God was united to human flesh through the medium of the soul (*mediante anima*). He reproduces only the sentence in which John declared that this union was mediated by the mind (νοῦς). But his analysis shows that he was familiar with the whole paragraph from which this quotation was drawn. He obviously knew that John had declared the mind to be (the loftiest) part of the soul, and he agrees with John that the mediation of the mind was necessary in order to effect a transition between the purity of God and the coarseness of flesh.[118]

Similarly upon John of Damascus Peter bases the doctrine that, before the earthly generation of Jesus Christ, the Holy Spirit purified the Virgin Mary and made her capable both of receiving the deity of the Logos and of conceiving him, so that the Son of God, who was consubstantial with the Father, overshadowed her "like divine semen" (*sicut divinum semen*) and joined to himself of the Virgin real human flesh that had a rational soul. But the incarnation itself involved on the part of the Logos, not an act of insemination, but an act of creation through the Holy Spirit (*non seminans, sed per Spiritum sanctum creans*).[119]

Despite his manhood, which was complete and total in every sense of the word, Lombard demonstrated by quoting from John, Christ remained completely uncircumscribed. Corporeally, he experienced physical limitations, but he continued to be uncircumscribed in his divine nature, since his flesh was not co-extensive with his uncircumscribed divinity. "Thus," as John had said, "Christ was simultaneously in all things, and beyond them, both when he lay in the womb of the Virgin and in the very moment of incarnation."[120]

Peter then addresses himself to the delicate problem of whether it was a person or a nature which, in the human generation of Christ, assumed a person or nature, and whether it was correct to say that the nature of God became incarnate. Peter at the outset pronounces in favor of the proposition that it was not a nature or a person which assumed a person in Jesus Christ, but rather a person who assumed a nature—that is, he means, the person of the divine Logos, who took on human nature in Jesus Christ.[121] But in reviewing the ecclesiastical authorities on this matter (Augustine, the eighth and eleventh councils of Toledo, Hilary of Poitiers, and Jerome), he notes that there is a conflict of opinion, not only, as he says, among the various theologians who had written on this subject, but even within the writings of the same author. In order to eliminate contradictions, he declares himself satisfied with the conclusion that it was both the person of the Son and the divine nature itself which were joined to the human nature in the Son.[122] For, he explains, the fact that the Son alone is said to have taken on the form of a servant excludes the other two persons, the Father and the Holy Spirit, but not the divine nature itself, from the assumption of the form of a servant. Furthermore, he says, the doctrine that the incarnation is associated with what is specifically or characteristically the Son's (*id quod est proprium Filii*), not with what is common to the Trinity (*non quod commune est Trinitati*), must be understood as signifying that it was the divine nature in the hypostasis of the Son (*proprie in hypostasi Filii*), and not as existing in common to the three persons (*non in tribus communiter personis*), which was united with the human nature.[123]

This solution he adopts directly from John of Damascus, who had asserted that "in the incarnation of God the Word, the whole, perfect nature of the divinity became incarnate (i.e., was joined to human nature) in one of its hypostases." In this union, it was not merely a part united with a part, but "the whole nature or substance of the divinity that was joined with the whole of human nature." That is, John says, "it is the same nature which subsists in each of the hypostases, and when we say that the nature of the Word became incarnate, we mean, according to the blessed Athanasius and Cyril, that the divinity was joined to flesh, and we confess one incarnate nature of God the Word. For the Word possesses both that which is common to the (divine) substance and that which is distinctive of the hypostasis or person."[124]

It is of no small significance in the history of the Byzantine influence in the Latin West in the twelfth century that John of Damascus is used to resolve so important a conflict and lead to a conclusion of great significance in Christology. It is somewhat ironical, however, that the ancient Apollinarian trick, which circulated the heretical writings of Apollinarius in the fourth century under the protective mantle of the venerable name of Athanasius, the indefectibly orthodox champion of the Nicene theology, whose authority none would dare to question, not only deceived Cyril of Alexandria in the fifth century, the Emperor Justinian in the sixth, and John of Damascus in the middle of the eighth, but under these distinguished auspices imposed also upon Latin theology, and left its stamp upon both the *Sententiae* of Peter Lombard and the *Summa* of Thomas Aquinas.[125]

Actually, the formula, *una natura Dei Verbi incarnata* (see note 124), one incarnate nature of God the Word, is plainly heretical, and was condemned by the fathers in the fourth century, as well as by the Fourth Oecumenical Council, which met at Chalcedon in 451, because it denied that Christ had two natures—the divine and the human. It was not until the sixth century that the fraud was discovered.[126] But then it was too late, and the orthodox have always defended the formula, explaining that it really implies two natures. Nevertheless, it is from the logical point of view unfortunate that the Apollinarian deception succeeded, both because it enabled the Monophysites to claim the support of Athanasius for their view that Jesus Christ had only one nature, and because it forced Cyril, Justinian, and other defenders of orthodoxy into extremely tortuous paths of argument, which otherwise could have been avoided.

Further on in the third book of the *Sentences*, Peter summarizes at length three different theories of the nature of the "hypostatic union" of God and man in Christ. He marshals excerpts from the fathers in support of each of the three, and notes also what he took to be the weak points of the first and the second, the latter of which was espoused by John of Damascus and represented the position of the Church as a whole. But since he refrains from offering any criticism of the third, it has been conjectured that he himself was one of its advocates, and accordingly believed that the human flesh and soul of Jesus were not combined with the divine nature in order to form a person, but served as the garment (*velut indumento*) of God the Word, so that he might become visible to mortal eyes. The proponents of this view held that God became man *secundum habitum*, i.e., by being clad with the flesh and soul of a man, and were therefore led to deny that Christ, so far as he was a man (*secundum quod homo*), was a substantial reality (*persona* or *aliquid*).[127]

This Christological nihilism, as it has been called, was untenable and was condemned after Peter's death by Pope Alexander III (1159–81). But John of Cornwall in his polemic against it stoutly affirmed that it was only an *opinio* of the school of Abelard put forward by Peter for discussion, not an *assertio* of the latter's own final judgment. Apparently Peter Lombard himself had also disclaimed responsibility for such *opiniones*.[128] Thus we cannot be certain whether Peter favored or opposed the second of these three hypotheses, that of John of Damascus. Whatever Peter's own attitude may have been, he sets forth John's exposition of the hypostatic union in some detail; and the Church, including Thomas Aquinas, has followed John of Damascus on this matter.[129]

John, Peter shows, compensated fully for the ambiguity of the Christological formula (notes 124–26) he had unwittingly taken over from the Apollinarians by his unequivocally dyophysite ("two-natured") description of the two perfect natures—the divinity and the humanity—united in one composite hypostasis (*composita hypostasis*, ὑπόστασις σύνθετος), which had once been the *simplex* (ἁπλῆ) *hypostasis* of the Logos alone but which, after the incarnation, became the vehicle not only for the properties and characteristics of Christ's divine Sonship (*divinae Dei-Verbi filiationis characteristicum et determinativum idioma*, τῆς θείας τοῦ Θεοῦ Λόγου υἱότητος τὸ χαρακτηριστικὸν καὶ ἀφοριστικὸν ἰδίωμα), by which he is distinguished from the Father and the Holy Spirit, but also for the properties and characteristics of the flesh which marked him as an individual man who was different from Mary and other men.

It is regrettable that Peter terminates his quotation here and does not add the next few lines, in which John completes his classical definition of Christ's hypostasis. Still, in his next excerpt from John, Peter makes it clear that John ruled out both Nestorianism and Monophysitism. Nestorianism he eliminates by stressing the fact that the two natures are united without separation or division in one composite hypostasis. He does away with Monophysitism by insisting that, in coming together, the two natures suffer neither confusion, conversion, nor change, and are united in a substantial (οὐσιώδης) union. By this he means that the union is real (ἀληθής), not illusory, and that the two natures do not supplement each other so as to form one composite nature (φύσις σύνθετος), but are truly joined together in one composite hypostasis. Here the difference of the two natures is preserved, the created remaining created, the uncreated uncreated, the mortal mortal, the immortal immortal, the circumscribable circumscribable, and the uncircumscribable uncircumscribable, of which the one, as Leo I (440–61) had said, coruscates with miracles, and the other is subjected to indignities.[130]

The divine continues as it was, John adds in Peter's next selection from the *De fide orthodoxa;* the human is neither transformed into the divine nor eliminated; and the two do not form one composite nature, compounded out of divinity and humanity, since such a nature would be consubstantial (*homousion*) with neither of the natures out of which it was composed, and such a Jesus Christ would be consubstantial neither with God nor with Mary, and could then be called neither God nor man. On the contrary, Christ, John says, is perfect God and perfect man and is confessed to be both of and in two natures.[131] John reinforces this point by attacking the position of the Adoptianists and their followers that Christ was only an ordinary man who by God's grace had been predestined and enabled to become, but had not been eternally, Son of God. Such a Christ, John felt, could not have been truly God from all eternity, as the earliest tradition of the Church declared him to have been. He therefore takes pains to refute Adoptianism with the pronouncement, quoted by Peter, that Jesus Christ was "not a deified man but God, who became man."[132]

It is not clear whether Peter would have agreed with John that this affirmation was essential to safeguard the perfection of Christ's divinity.

But he realized that the corollary of this proposition, which asserted the completeness of Christ's human nature, was altogether indispensable. Christ must have been fully divine, the theologians had taught, in order to make possible the resurrection and redemption of mankind. He had also to have been fully man, in order to guarantee that all mankind might have a share in his redemptive work. If he had not been truly God, he could not have conquered sin and death. Had he not been truly man, mankind could not have benefited from his victory. This reasoning was founded upon the belief that Christ was both the Son of God the Father, as God, and of Mary, as man. Hence, Peter devotes the final *capitulum* of the next *Distinctio* to Christ's double nativity, which affirms this doctrine; and he expounds it on the basis of Augustine and John, according to the latter of whom "we venerate two nativities of Christ: the one [whereby he was begotten] of God before the ages, which is beyond cause, reason, time, and nature; the other, which took place in these latter days, for our sake ... and for our salvation....," when he was born miraculously of the Holy Spirit and the Virgin.[133]

This paragraph from the *De fide orthodoxa*, which was anti-Adoptianist and anti-Monophysite in purpose, is a paraphrase of a part of the Chalcedonian Symbol, as also is the sentence adduced from John on the nature of Christ's humanity, which John had defined (*tradit auctoritas*) as including all human characteristics save sin.[134] Still, Peter says elsewhere, again on the authority of Augustine and John, though the flesh of Christ was perfectly human in all respects, except for sin, it could properly be worshipped, because it was not just ordinary flesh (*nudam carnem*) but flesh in union with deity, since both natures of Christ, the human and the divine, had been brought together in the one hypostasis [i.e., person] of God the Word. Like Cyril of Alexandria, John had compared this relationship of the divine and the human in Christ to a piece of coal (cf. the human nature), which becomes dangerous to touch only when it has been brought into contact with fire (cf. the divine nature).[135]

Finally, it was in the *De fide orthodoxa* that Peter found warrant for interpreting the gender of the adjectives used for the Godhead as a whole and for God and Christ. Following the patristic tradition, John had explained that the neuter adjective (*totum*) applied to the "nature" and the masculine (*totus*) to the hypostasis ("person"). Thus, one could say that "totus Christus est Deus perfectus" and "totus [est] homo perfectus," but not "totum," since Christ is both God and man, not just one or the other. On this account, Peter observes, it is correct to affirm that *totus*

Christus, that is, the whole *person* of Christ, which includes the two natures, the human and divine, is in heaven, in the grave, and everywhere. If the neuter adjective (*totum*) were used, however, the reference would be, not to the person of Jesus Christ, but only to the entirety of *one* of his two natures. For this reason the fathers had believed that *tres unum* [neuter] *sunt* (the three are one *thing*—the divine nature of the Trinity), and hence all equally God, but can be distinguished, *alius* and *alius* [masculine], as distinct persons.[136]

Especially noteworthy is Peter's appeal to John of Damascus as his major authority in elucidating the fundamentals of orthodox Christology, according to which Jesus Christ had two perfect natures, the divine and the human, united in one hypostasis or person, without confusion or change, division or separation. In this respect Peter was followed by Arno of Reichersberg (d. 1175),[137] neither of whom based his analysis of this doctrine upon the dyophysite creed of Chalcedon, which had been promulgated at the Fourth Oecumenical Council in 451, and had remained ever since the orthodox definition of Christology in both the East and the West. Their reliance on John of Damascus rather than on the dogmatic decree of Chalcedon illustrates the exalted position which the name of the former had attained. It is even more significant, perhaps, that the entire twelfth century seems to have been of one mind with them in this respect. For recent researches indicate that the scholars of this era depended heavily upon John of Damascus for an authoritative résumé of the orthodox dyophysite Christology, and usually ignored the symbol of 451.[138]

Equally striking is the somewhat similar neglect of the Nicene Creed, the touchstone of orthodoxy on Trinitarian dogma. It is indeed remarkable that, like the majority of his contemporaries, Peter Lombard refrains from transcribing or summarizing the text of these two important oecumenical formularies. He does, however, reproduce a few words from the article on the Holy Spirit in his defense of the double procession, but he attributes them to the Council of Nicea (325), not realizing that this article did not appear in the Creed until the Council of 381.[139]

The Chalcedonian Creed was quoted in its entirety only once in the twelfth century, by Walter of St. Victor in the *Contra quatuor labyrinthos Franciae*,[140] which he wrote (*ca.* 1178) as an attack upon Peter Abelard, Peter Lombard, Peter of Poitiers, and Gilbert de la Porrée. These four Walter denounces as the four labyrinths, or, by metonymy, the four

Minotaurs, the most abominable monsters of France. Since he condemns John of Damascus along with the "four labyrinths," it is not surprising that he felt obliged to seek out a more congenial authority on Christology. He was probably pleased to be able to refer to the Council of Chalcedon rather than to John of Damascus, whom he repeatedly brands as a heretic. Yet even he was compelled, on occasion, to buttress his argument with theological principles enunciated by John.[141]

John is outranked by Augustine and others in bulk of citation in Peter Lombard's *Libri sententiarum*. But he stands high as a decisive spokesman on basic principles of Christian doctrine; and the Lombard's respectful attitude towards John may be taken as an illustration of the profound indebtedness of the medieval world and of our own era to Byzantine thought. In the twelfth century, the *De fide orthodoxa* was valued both as an authoritative summary of dogmatic theology, and as a key that enabled the Latin West to unlock a great treasury of patristic literature, most of which had been previously unavailable.

IMPORTANCE OF BYZANTIUM IN THE HISTORY OF CIVILIZATION

Even after this brief summary, it should be obvious that the influence of Byzantine art and theology on the West during the twelfth century was extensive, deep, and penetrating. This was only a partial manifestation of the same forces which Byzantium exerted not only upon the Middle Ages and the Renaissance, but also upon the modern world.

This influence extended to many other aspects of life as well. Roman law, for example, as codified by Byzantine jurists under Justinian I, and Byzantine political theory experienced a revival in the twelfth century,[142] and have contemporary relevance—the latter as the prototype of Soviet absolutism, which has its Byzantine aspects, and the former as the foundation of the legal systems of continental Europe, Latin America, and the sovereign state of Louisiana.

Perhaps, in conclusion, it may be of interest to mention one case of the Byzantine transmission of the classics which transformed the whole of modern history and affords an example of the dependence of the empirical sciences on the humanities that may be of some relevance in this age of tragic unawareness on the part of many in high places that the liberal arts are indispensable to our way of life, and must be cultivated intensively if we are to survive.

I refer to the geographical encyclopedia (τὰ Γεωγραφικά) of Strabo, a

Greek who flourished at the end of the first century before Christ. The Latin West knew nothing of Strabo until the Council of Ferrara-Florence (1438–39), when George Gemistus Pletho (*ca.* 1355–1452), a Byzantine philosopher celebrated in both the East and the West as the greatest scholar of his day, made a determined effort to persuade the Latin scientists whom he met to study the Strabonic geography. Strabo, Pletho felt, deserved particular attention because of what he had to say about the circumnavigability of Africa, which Ptolemy had pronounced to be landlocked, and because of his belief in the existence of unknown but habitable lands east of India. Eventually Pletho succeeded, and in 1458 Guarino Guarini completed a Latin translation of the Greek text of τὰ Γεωγραφικά.

This Latin version had an immediate effect upon Renaissance geography and may have affected the Portuguese voyages around Africa. Most important of all, Christopher Columbus frequently cites Strabo, and is said by his son to have counted Strabo among his chief authorities for believing that, by sailing due west along the latitude of Athens, it would be possible to reach new lands lying east of India. Thus, although we should not credit Pletho and Byzantium with a direct share in the discovery of America, we must recognize that, in interesting the scholars of the West in Strabo's *Geography*, Pletho made an important contribution to the development of the geographical theory of the Renaissance, which reached its culmination in the great achievement of Columbus.[143]

NOTES

1   In what follows the word Byzantine has reference to the Greek Medieval Empire, which fringed the Mediterranean and flourished from 284, the year of the accession of the Emperor Diocletian, to May 29, 1453, when the capital city of Constantinople fell to the Ottoman Turks.

I am grateful to my friends, Professors Marshall Clagett, Gaines Post, and Robert L. Reynolds, of the University of Wisconsin for their invitation to write this paper and for the opportunity to visit the vigorous school of medieval and renaissance studies they have established. I am indebted for counsel and friendly encouragement to my colleagues, Professors Harry A. Wolfson, Eberhard F. Bruck, and George H. Williams, and acknowledge with gratitude the assistance of my student, Mr. Robert D. Crouse, who helped me with a number of problems.

This monograph was completed in June, 1958. Additional bibliography is to be found in my study, "The Knowledge of Greek in the West during the Middle Ages and the Renaissance," which forms the last chapter of

my forthcoming book, *The Mind of Byzantium* (New York, Doubleday, 1961);
cf. also, *ibid.*, the chapter "Constantinople and Rome."

2 L. Bréhier, *Vie et mort de Byzance* (*Le monde byzantin*, 1 [Paris, 1947], pp. 278 f.,;
G. Ostrogorsky, *History of the Byzantine State*, tr. J. Hussey (Oxford, 1956),
pp. 305 f.; J. Gay, *L'Italie méridionale et l'empire byzantin* (*Bibliothèque des
écoles françaises d'Athènes et de Rome*, 90 [Paris, 1904]), 535–38; F. Chalandon,
Histoire de la domination normande en Italie et en Sicile, 1 (Paris, 1907), 184–90.
See also P. Lamma, *Comneni e Staufer, ricerche sui rapporti fra Bisanzio e
l'Occidente nel secolo xii* (2 vols.; *Istituto storico italiano per il medio evo, studi
storici*, 14–18, 22–25 [Rome, 1955–57]).

    In the same year, the Byzantine Empire suffered a grievous defeat at
Manzikert, in Armenia, north of Lake Van, which put an end to effective
Byzantine domination in northern Asia Minor.—Bréhier, *op. cit.*, p. 281;
C. Cahen, "La campagne de Manzikert d'après les sources musulmanes,"
Byzantion, 9 (1934), 613–42.

3 S. Runciman, *The Eastern Schism* (Oxford, 1955), maintains that it is
not possible to fix upon a precise date for the break between the two
Churches.

4 J. de Ghellinck, *Le mouvement théologique du xiie siècle* (*Museum Lessianum, section
historique*, 10 [Brussels-Paris, 1948]), pp. 179 n. 1 f., 184 n. 2, 257, 264, 402 f.,
406 n. 4, 467 n. 6. Cf. note 44 below.

5 For biographical sketch, see R. M. Martin, ed., *Œuvres de Robert de Melun*,
Vol. 1 (*Spicilegium sacrum Lovaniense, Études et documents*, 13 [Louvain, 1932]),
vi ff.; Vol. 3, 1, *ibid.*, 21 (1947), 37.14 and note (cf. F. Anders, *Christologie*,
cited, note 19 below, p. xiii).

6 Martin, *Œuvres de Robert de Melun*, Vol. 3.1 (*Spicilegium*, 21), 36.22–44.15.
On the date see *ibid.*, p. vi.

7 *Ibid.*, 36.25 f.: qui greculum sermonem locutioni lingue latine velut pan-
niculum late splendentem interserunt.

8 *Ibid.*, 37.13: nil dulce sapiant nisi quod est amaritudine fellis confectum.

9 *Ibid.*, 37.29 f.

10 *Ibid.*, 41.10 ff.

11 *Ibid.*, 40.33 ff. Cf. on these words, J. de Ghellinck, "L'entrée d'essentia,
substantia, et autres mots apparentés, dans le latin médiéval," *Bulletin du
Cange, Archivum latinitatis medii aevi*, 16 (1942), 77–112; *idem*, "L'histoire de
'persona' et d' 'hypostasis' dans un écrit anonyme porrétain du xiie siècle,"
Revue néoscolastique de philosophie, 36 (2nd series, 41, 1934), 111–27; cf. Heinrich
Dörrie, "'Ὑπόστασις. Wort- und Bedeutungsgeschichte," *Nachrichten der
Akademie der Wissenschaften, Philol.-Hist. Kl.*, Nr. 3 (Göttingen, 1955), 35–92.
Somewhat before 1148, the anonymous author of "A Short Treatise on
the Trinity from the School of Thierry of Chartres," ed. N. M. Haring,
Mediaeval Studies, 18 (1956), 125–34, discusses four Greek synonyms for the
Latin *substantia* (pp. 126 f., 129 f.).

12 Martin, *Œuvres de Robert de Melun*, Vol. 1 (*Spicilegium*, 13), viii f. Cf. note 42
below.

13 *Ibid.*, Vol. 3.1 (*Spicilegium*, 21), 43.6 ff.

14   Migne, *Patrologia Latina*, 176, 1131A. On notes 14–16 see M. D. Chenu, *La théologie au douzième siècle* (Paris, 1957), pp. 287 f.

15   Epistle 16, Migne, *P.L.*, 193, 555A.

16   Migne, *P.L.*, 180, 288A; M. D. Chenu, "*Involucrum*, le mythe selon les théologiens médiévaux," *Archives d'histoire doctrinale et littéraire du moyen âge*, 22 (1955), 78; "Le *Contra quatuor labyrinthos Franciae* de Gauthier de Saint-Victor," ed. P. Glorieux, *ibid.*, 19 (1952), 187–335; see p. 335 for list of references to John of Damascus and n. 100 below; cf. *ibid.*, p. 319, in which John's opinion is accepted as authoritative (note 115 below); *idem*, "Mauvaise action et mauvais travail. Le 'Contra quatuor labyrinthos Franciae,'" *Recherches de théologie ancienne et médiévale*, 21 (1954), 179–93.

17   Martin, *Œuvres de Robert de Melun*, Vol. 1 (1932), vii.

18   *Idem, ibid.*, Vol. 2 (*Spicilegium*, 18 [1938]), lvii f., 6.1–4, 8.7–9, 13.7 f., 197.19 f., 227.9 f., 257.12 f., 305.1–3, cf. 127.21; *ibid.*, Vol. 1 (1932), li f., 48.6 f., 53.17–20, cf. 18.1 f.

19   *Sententie*, 2, 25, ed. F. Anders, *Die Christologie des Robert von Melun* (*Forschungen zur christlichen Literatur- und Dogmengeschichte*, 15.5 [Paderborn, 1927]), 56.15–17, cf. vi–xv; *De fide orthodoxa*, 3, 6 (Migne, *P.G.*, 94, 1004B); *Petri Lombardi Libri iv Sententiarum studio et cura PP. Collegii S. Bonaventurae*, Vol. 2 (2nd ed.; Ad Claras Aquas, 1916), 3, 5, 1, p. 570 n. 30. Anders' text is taken from the shorter recension of the *Sententie*, which Martin, *Œuvres de Robert de Melun* (Vol. 1 [1932], xiii; *idem, Revue d'histoire ecclésiastique*, 28 [1932], 313–29), deems to be an abridgment of Robert's work prepared by his disciples and not by his own hand. The second volume of the *Sententie*, Martin, *Œuvres de Robert de Melun*, Vol. 3.2 (*Spicilegium*, 25 [1952]), edited for publication after Martin's death by R. M. Gallet, has reached only Book 1, part 6.

20   On the Byzantine contempt for the Latins, see the references to sources collected by G. Buckler, *Anna Comnena* (Oxford, 1929), pp. 440–43, 449–52, 458–61, 469–72, 476–78, 539 (*s.v. Crusaders*), and *passim;* and Φ. Κουκουλές, Θεσσαλονίκης Εὐσταθίου τὰ λαογραφικά, 2 ('Εταιρεία Μακεδονικῶν Σπουδῶν. 'Επιστημονικαὶ πραγματεῖαι, σειρὰ φιλολογικὴ καὶ θεολογική, 6 (Athens, 1950), 375–79.

On the massacres of 1182 and 1185, see Bréhier, *Vie et mort de Byzance*, pp. 346 f., 348 f., who gives the necessary bibliographical indications. Cf. H. Hunger, *Die Normannen in Thessalonike, die Eroberung von Th. durch die Normannen in der Augenzeugenschilderung des Bischofs Eustathios* (*Byzantinische Geschichtsschreiber*, ed. Endre v. Ivánka, 3 [Graz, 1955]); O. Tafrali, *Thessalonique des origines au xive siècle* (Paris, 1919), pp. 182–91.

21   *Historia, Corpus scriptorum historiae byzantinae* (Bonn, 1835), pp. 391 f.

22   Cf. J. Ebersolt, *Constantinople byzantine et les voyageurs du Levant* (Paris, 1918), pp. 27 ff.; A. A. Vasiliev, "Quelques remarques sur les voyageurs du moyen âge à Constantinople," *Mélanges Charles Diehl*, 1 (1930), 293–98. See also S. G. Mercati, "Santuari e reliquie Costantinopolitane secondo il codice Ottoboniano Latino 169 prima della conquista Latina (1204)," *Rendiconti della Pontificia Accademia Romana di Archeologia*, 12 (1936), 133–56. On the

booty carried off in 1204, see Comte Riant, *Exuviae sacrae Constantinopolitanae* (2 vols.; Geneva, 1877–78); Vol. 3 by F. de Mély, *La croix des premiers croisés* (Paris, 1904).

23   S. Runciman, *A History of the Crusades*, 1 (Cambridge, Eng., 1951), 122–33, 149–71; cf. F. Duncalf in K. M. Setton, M. H. Baldwin, *A History of the Crusades*, 1 (Philadelphia, 1955), 269, 271 f., 274 f., 279. Cf. P. Rassow, "Zum byzantinisch-normannischen Krieg 1147–1149," *Mitteilungen des Instituts für oesterreichische Geschichtsforschung*, 62 (1954), 213–18.

24   O. Demus, *The Mosaics of Norman Sicily* (London, 1950), pp. 5 ff., 18, 25 ff., 82, 123–48, 372; F. Chalandon, *Histoire de la domination normande en Italie et en Sicile*, 2 (Paris, 1907), 135–37; E. Caspar, *Roger II* (Innsbruck, 1904), pp. 376–84. Cf. U. Monneret de Villard, "La tessitura Palermitana sotto i Normanni e i suoi rapporti con l'arte bizantina," *Miscellanea Giovanni Mercati*, 3 (*Studi e Testi*, 123 [Vatican City, 1946]), 464–89.

25   P. E. Schramm, *Herrschaftszeichen und Staatssymbolik*, 1 (*Schriften der Monumenta Germaniae historica*, 13, 1 [Stuttgart, 1954]), 34 f., 77–80, 85; A. Marongiu, "Lo spirito della monarchia normanna nell' allocuzione di Ruggero II ai suoi grandi," *Atti del congresso...*, Verona, 4 (see note 142 below), 313–27; J. Deér, *Der Kaiserornat Friedrichs II.* (*Dissertationes Bernenses*, Ser. 2, 2 [Bern, 1952]), 13–19; Demus, *Mosaics*, pl. 58A; E. Kitzinger, "On the Portrait of Roger II in the Martorana in Palermo," *Proporzioni*, 3 (1950), 30–35; W. Ohnsorge, *Das Zweikaiserproblem im früheren Mittelalter, die Bedeutung des byzantinischen Reiches für die Entwicklung der Staatsidee in Europa* (Hildesheim, 1947), pp. 83–121, 139–41; E. Kantorowicz, *Laudes regiae* (Berkeley-Los Angeles, 1946), pp. 158–60; Sigfried H. Steinberg, "I ritratti dei re normanni di Sicilia," *La Bibliofilia*, 39 (1937), 29–57. Cf. P. K. Enepekides, "Byzantinische Prinzessinen im Hause der Babenberger und die byzantinischen Einflüsse in den österreichischen Ländern des 12. und 13. Jahrhunderts," Πεπραγμένα τοῦ θ' διεθνοῦς βυζαντινολογικοῦ συνεδρίου, 2 ('Ελληνικά, παράρτημα 9 [Athens, 1956]), 368–74.

In a provocative article, "L'institution monarchique dans les états normands d'Italie," *Cahiers de civilisation médiévale, x^e–λii^e siècles*, 2 (1959), 303–31, 445–68, L. R. Ménager argues that the Norman kings were not absolute rulers like the emperors of Byzantium, and did not adopt Byzantine political theory. In another valuable paper, "Notes sur les codifications byzantines et l'occident," *Varia, études de droit romain*, 3 (*Institut de droit romain de l'Université de Paris*, 16 [Paris, 1958]), 239–303, he expresses doubt that the copies of the Byzantine law codes (in Greek) which were produced in the West had any real application in Sicily during the twelfth century, and concludes that they served the requirements of scholars rather than of lawyers. These monographs form part of Ménager's eagerly awaited book, *Études sur le royaume normand d'Italie*, and make an important contribution. At the moment, however, I am sceptical about his conclusions, both of which are directed against the authorities noted in the previous paragraph. Perhaps his book will provide evidence to dispel scepticism.

26   A large number of periodicals published by various Italian cities and com-

munities are crammed with material of interest to students of the influence of Byzantium on Italy during the twelfth century. Among these, in addition to the well-known series put out by the learned academies of Venice, Rome, and Naples, mention should be made of the following: *Archivio storico della Calabria* (5 vols., 1912–17); *Archivio storico per la Calabria e la Lucania* (1931—); *Archivio storico Pugliese* (1948—); *Archivio storico per la Sicilia* (1935—); *Archivio storico per la Sicilia orientale* (1904—); *Archivio storico Siciliano* (1876—); *Bessarione* (36 vols., 1896–1920); *Bollettino della Badia greca di Grottaferrata* (1947—); *Brutium* (1922—); *Calabria nobilissima* (1947—); *Iapygia* (17 vols., 1930–46); *Rivista storica Calabrese* (14 vols., 1893–1906); *Roma e l'Oriente* (21 vols., 1910–21); *Siculorum Gymnasium* (1948—). I will refrain from giving the entire bibliography in this paper, but hope that I may be able to return to the subject at another time.

Linguistic matters are discussed in these publications, and especially in three books by G. Rohlfs: *Historische Grammatik der unteritalienischen Gräzität* (*Sitzungsberichte der bayerischen Akademie der Wissenschaften, Philos.-hist. Klasse*, 1949, Heft 4 [Munich, 1950]); *Scavi linguistici nella Magna Grecia* (Halle a. S.-Rome, 1933); and *Etymologisches Wörterbuch der unteritalienischen Gräzität* (Halle a. S., 1930), which contain useful bibliographies. Note also G. Alessio, "L'elemento greco nella toponomastica della Sicilia," *Centro di Studi filologici e linguistici siciliani, Bollettino*, 1 (1953), 65–106; 3 (1955), 223–61; 4 (1956), 310–56; S. G. Kapsomenos, "Beiträge zur historischen Grammatik der griechischen Dialekte Unteritaliens," *Byzantinische Zeitschrift*, 46 (1953), 320–48. See also note 145 below.

Inter alia see L. R. Ménager, "Notes et documents sur quelques monastères de Calabre à l'époque normande," *Byzantinische Zeitschrift*, 50 (1957), 7–30, 321–61; *Atti del primo Congresso storico Calabrese* (1954; published Rome, 1956); F. Russo, "Relazioni culturali tra la Calabria e l'Oriente bizantino nel M.E.," πεπραγμένα (cited, note 25 above), pp. 592–607; K. M. Setton, "The Byzantine Background to the Italian Renaissance," *Proceedings of the American Philosophical Society*, 100 (1956), 1–76; F. Grillo, "Italia antica e medioevale," *Calabria nobilissima*, 5 (1951), 131–44; 6 (1952), 179–86; 7 (1953), 1–8, 57–65, 165–84; 8 (1954), 1–10; M. Scaduto, *Il monachismo basiliano nella Sicilia medievale, rinascita e decadenza, secoli xi-xiv* (Rome, 1947); L. T. White, Jr., *Latin Monasticism in Norman Sicily* (Cambridge, Mass., 1938); A. de Stefano, *La cultura in Sicilia nel periodo normanno* (Palermo, 1938), which is too brief, but has a good bibliography; C. Korolevskij, "Basiliens italo-grecs et espagnols," *Dictionnaire d'histoire et de géographie ecclésiastiques*, 6 (1932), 1180–1236; G. Robinson, *History and Cartulary of the Greek Monastery of St. Elias and St. Anastasius of Carbone* (*Orientalia Cristiana*, XI, 5 [No. 44], XV, 2 [No. 53], XIX, 1 [No. 62], 1928–30); D. L. Raschellà, *Saggio storico sul monachismo italo-greco in Calabria* (Messina, 1925); A. Vaccari, *La Grecia nell'Italia meridionale* (*Orientalia Christiana*, III, 3, No. 13 [Rome, 1925]); G. Minasi, *Le chiese di Calabria dal quinto al duodecimo secolo* (Naples, 1896); P. Batiffol, *L'abbaye de Rossano* (Paris, 1891); P. Rodotà, *Dell' origine, progresso e stato presente del rito greco in Italia* (3 vols.; Rome, 1758–63).

Note the numerous Greek documents issued in Sicily and southern Italy during the twelfth century in S. Cusa, *I diplomi greci ed arabi di Sicilia* (2 vols.; Palermo, 1868–82); F. Trinchera, *Syllabus graecarum membranarum* (Naples, 1865); G. Spata, *Le pergamene greche esistenti nel grande archivio di Palermo* (Palermo, 1862). See the three papers by A. Guillou summarized by F. Dölger, *Byzantinische Zeitschrift*, 49 (1956), 461. Cf. A. Strittmatter, "Liturgical Latinisms in a Twelfth Century Greek Euchology," *Miscellanea G. Mercati*, 3 (note 24 above), 41–64; E. Pontieri, *Tra i Normanni nell' Italia meridionale* (Naples, 1954); S. la Sorsa, *Storia di Puglia*, Vols. 2–3 (Bari, 1953-54). N. D. Evola, *Bibliografia Siciliana* (1938–1953) (Palermo, 1954); and D. Zangari, *Catalogo ragionato della "Collezione Calabra Morano": opere di storia regionale* (Naples, 1922), give long but unclassified bibliographies.

For the latest data, see P. Collura, "Appendice al regesto dei diplomi di Re Ruggero compilato da Erich Caspar," *Atti del convegno internazionale di studi Ruggeriani*, 2 (Palermo, 1955), 545–625; A. Guillou, "Le corpus des actes grecs de Sicile," *ibid.*, 1, 147–53; A. de Stefano and F. Bartolini, *I documenti originali dei re normanni di Sicilia*, 2 fascs., *Archivio paleografico italiano*, 14, 60–61 (Rome-Palermo, 1954). See also note 146 below.

The literature on Byzantine influence in Germany is set forth in Lamma, *Comneni e Staufer*, and Classen, "Konzil von Konstantinopel" (notes 2 and 36; cf. notes 25 and 28, above.) Cf. also the collected papers of W. Ohnsorge, *Abendland und Byzanz* (Darmstadt, 1958); K. J. Heilig, *Ostrom und das deutsche Reich um die Mitte des 12. Jahrhunderts, Kaisertum und Herzogsgewalt im Zeitalter Friedrichs I.* (*Schriften des Reichsinstituts für ältere deutsche Geschichtskunde* [*Monumenta Germanicae historica*], 9 [Leipzig, 1944]), 1–271; and the additional bibliography in my *The Mind of Byzantium*, last chapter.

27   On the arts I note here only a few of the major authorities. Besides O. Demus' monumental forthcoming two-volume study of the Church of San Marco in Venice, see H. Buchthal, *Miniature Painting in the Latin Kingdom of Jerusalem, with Liturgical and Palaeographical Chapters by Francis Wormald* (Oxford, 1957); G. Martelli, "Chiese monumentali di Calabria," *Calabria nobilissima*, 10 (1956), 33–40, a bibliographical summary; B. Cappelli, "Chiese rupestri del Materano," *ibid.*, pp. 45–59; G. Galassi, *Roma o Bisanzio* (2 vols., 2nd ed.; Rome, 1953); G. Agnello, *L'architettura bizantina in Sicilia* (Florence, 1952); E. Kitzinger, "The Mosaics of the Cappella Palatina in Palermo," *Art Bulletin*, 31 (1949), 269–92; C. A. Willemsen, *Apulien* (Leipzig, 1944), useful for excellent plates and a bibliography; H. M. Schwarz, "Die Baukunst Kalabriens und Siziliens im Zeitalter der Normannen," *Römisches Jahrbuch für Kunstgeschichte*, 6 (1942–44), 1–112; P. Orsi, *Sicilia bizantina*, 1 (Rome, 1942); *idem*, *Le chiese basiliane della Calabria* (Florence, 1929); A. Medea, *Gli affreschi delle cripte eremitiche pugliesi* (2 vols.; Rome, 1939); A. Frangipane, *Elenco degli edifici monumentali d'Italia*, Vols. 58–60 (Rome, 1938); *idem*, *Inventario degli oggetti d'arte d'Italia*, Vol. 2 (Rome, 1933), both of which are devoted to Calabria and were reviewed by B. Cappelli, *Archivio storico per la Calabria e la Lucania*, 4 (1934), 104–72; *ibid.*, 10. (1940), 146–82; G. Gabrieli, *Inventario topografico e bibliografico delle cripte eremitiche*

basiliane di Puglia (Rome, 1936); M. Avery, *The Exultet Rolls of South Italy* (plates but no text; Princeton, 1936); A. Colasanti, *L'art byzantin en Italie* (2 vols.; Paris, 1926); O. M. Dalton, *Byzantine Art and Archaeology* (Oxford, 1911); C. Diehl, *L'art byzantin dans l'Italie méridionale* (Paris, 1894). Note, e.g., É. Bertaux, *L'art dans l'Italie méridionale* (Paris, 1903), pp. 401–508 and *passim;* C. Diehl, *Manuel d'art byzantin*, 2 (2nd ed.; Paris, 1926), 713–34; Demus, *Mosaics*, pp. 371, 388 f.

For the bronze doors, see H. Leisinger, *Romanische Bronzen, Kirchentüren im mittelalterlichen Europa* (Zürich, 1956), with superb plates; A. Boeckler, *Die Bronzetüren des Bonanus von Pisa und des Barisanus von Trani*, ed. R. Hamann, *Die frühmittelalterlichen Bronzetüren*, 4 (Marburg-Lahn-Berlin, 1953); C. Angelillis, *Le porte di bronzo bizantine nelle chiese d'Italia, Le imposte della Basilica di Monte S. Angelo* (Arezzo, 1924); A. K. Porter, "Wreckage from a Tour in Apulia," *Mélanges offerts à M. Gustave Schlumberger*, 2 (Paris, 1924), 408–15. C. A. Willemsen's *Apulien* has come out in a new edition as *Apulia*, ed. D. Odenthal, with English translation by Daphne Woodward (New York, 1959).

One of the most striking examples of Byzantine influence on Latin manuscript illumination is to be found in the *Hortus deliciarum* (an encyclopaedia devoted to the doctrine of salvation), of which at least 344 miniatures were known. The codex itself was destroyed by fire in 1870, but a photographic record, based largely on previous publications, has been issued by Joseph Walter, *Herrade de Landsberg, Abbesse du Mont Sainte-Odile, 1167–1195, Hortus deliciarum* (Strasbourg-Paris, 1952).

28   On the knowledge of Greek in the West during the later Middle Ages, see the following (with bibliographies): B. Bischoff, "Das griechische Element in der abendländischen Bildung des Mittelalters," *Byzantinische Zeitschrift*, 44 (1951), 27–55 (excluding Italy); L. Brou, "Les chants en langue grecque dans les liturgies latines," *Sacris Erudiri*, 1 (1948), 165–80; *ibid.*, 4 (1952), 226–38; E. Wellesz, *Eastern Elements in Western Chant* (*Monumenta musicae byzantinae*, Subsidia, Vol. 2, No. 1, American series [Oxford, 1947]); A. Allgeier, "Exegetische Beiträge zur Geschichte des Griechischen vor dem Humanismus," *Biblica*, 24 (1943), 261–88; B. Altaner, "Die Kenntnis des Griechischen in den Missionsorden während des 13. und 14. Jahrhunderts," *Zeitschrift für Kirchengeschichte*, 3. Folge, 4, 53 (1934), 436–93, with important bibliography for the earlier period; M. Manitius, *Geschichte der lateinischen Literatur des Mittelalters*, 2, 3 (*Handbuch der Altertumswissenschaft*, 9, 2, 3, ed. W. Otto [Munich, 1931]), *s.v. Griechisch*, etc.; P. Duhem, *Le système du monde*, 3 (Paris, 1915), 163–230; J. E. Sandys, *A History of Classical Scholarship*, 1 (2nd ed.; Cambridge, Eng., 1906), 524–58. See notes 25–27 above, 29 ff. below. Cf. G. Moravcsik's study of the Byzantine origin of the name Katapán, summarized in *Byzantinische Zeitschrift*, 49 (1956), 464 f.

29   See J. T. Muckle, "Greek Works Translated Directly into Latin before 1350," *Mediaeval Studies*, 4 (1942), 33–42; 5 (1943), 102–14; H. D. Saffrey, "Versions latines d'auteurs grecs," *Bulletin Thomiste*, 8 (1947–53), 221–32; M. Cappuyns, *Jean Scot Érigène, sa vie, son œuvre, sa pensée* (*Universitas Catholica*

Lovaniensis, Dissertationes ad gradum magistri in Facultate Theologica, 2nd series, 26 [Louvain-Paris, 1933]), 128–79; H. F. Dondaine, ed., "Les 'Expositiones super Ierarchiam caelestem' de Jean Scot Érigène," *Archives d'histoire doctrinale et littéraire du moyen âge*, 18 (1950–51), 245–302 (an *editio princeps* of the full text of Erigena's commentary on the work of the Pseudo-Dionysius, based upon a manuscript of the twelfth century); M. Grabmann, *Die Geschichte der scholastischen Methode*, 1 (Freiburg im Breisgau, 1909), 151 ff.; 2 (1911), 59 ff., and *passim*. See also note 147 below.

Cf. also A. Malet, *Personne et amour dans la théologie trinitaire de Saint Thomas d'Aquin* (*Bibliothèque Thomiste*, 32 [Paris, 1956], pp. 161–80, who lists medieval Latin translations of the Greek fathers; and my *The Mind of Byzantium* (New York, 1961), last chapter. For Hilduin and his version of the Pseudo-Dionysius, see P. G. Théry, *Études dionysiennes*, 1–2 (*Études de philosophie médiévale*, ed. É. Gilson, 16 and 19 [Paris, 1932–37], which includes the Latin text.

30   For texts and studies on Aristippus see R. Klibansky, V. Kordeuter, C. Labowsky, L. Minio-Paluello, *Corpus philosophorum medii aevi, Corpus Platonicum, Plato Latinus*, 1–3 (London, 1940–53); M. T. Mandalari, "Enrico Aristippo Arcidiacono di Catania nella vita culturale e politica del sec. XII," *Bollettino storico Catanese* (*R. Deputazione di storia patria per la Sicilia, sezione di Catania*), 4 (1939), 87–123 f. Cf. R. Klibansky, *The Continuity of the Platonic Tradition During the Middle Ages* (London, 1939), p. 27; L. Metelli, "Sulle due redazioni del Fedone latino di Aristippo," *Atti del Reale Istituto Veneto di scienze, lettere ed arti*, 97, 2 (1937–38), Classe di scienze morali e lettere (Venice, 1938), 113-40; G. B. Siragusa, *Il regno di Guglielmo I in Sicilia* (2nd ed.; Palermo, 1929), pp. 297 ff.

Recent researches show that Aristippus had never been a monk in Southern Italy, as some have supposed.—E. Jamison, *Admiral Eugenius*, cited in note 32 below, pp. xvii–xxi; L. Minio-Paluello, "Henri Aristippe, Guillaume de Moerbeke et les traductions latines médiévales des *Météorologiques* et du *De generatione et corruptione* d'Aristote," *Revue philosophique de Louvain*, 45 (1947), 206–35.

31   On Aristotle in the twelfth century, see G. Lacombe, *Corpus philosophorum medii aevi, Aristoteles Latinus*, 1 (Rome, 1939); 2 (Cambridge, Eng., 1955), who gives exhaustive bibliographies; M. Grabmann, "Aristoteles im zwölften Jahrhundert," *Mediaeval Studies*, 12 (1950), 123–62; H. J. D. Lulofs, ed., *Aristotelis de insomniis et de divinatione per somnum* (2 vols.; Leiden, 1947), with a Latin version of the twelfth century; E. Franceschini, "Aristotele nel medioevo latino," *Atti del ix congresso nazionale di filosofia*, Padova, 20–23 Settembre, 1934 (Padua, 1935), 189–207; B. Geyer, *Patristische und scholastische Philosophie*, F. *Ueberwegs Grundriss der Geschichte der Philosophie*, 2 (Basel, 1927), 343–50, lists works of Aristotle available in Latin in the twelfth century; *idem*, "Die alten lateinischen Uebersetzungen der aristotelischen Analytik, Topik und Elenchik," *Philosophisches Jahrbuch der Görres-Gesellschaft*, 30 (1917), 25–43.

On James, see L. Minio-Paluello, "Iacobus Veneticus Grecus, Canonist and Translator of Aristotle," *Traditio*, 8 (1952), 265–304; *idem*, "Note sull' Aristotele Latino medievale, 7. Manoscritti aristotelici latini del xii secolo con note contemporanee: scolii greci alla 'Metafisica' tradotti in latino da Giacomo Veneto," *Rivista di filosofia neo-scolastica*, 44 (1952), 485–95; E. Franceschini, "Il contributo dell' Italia alla trasmissione del pensiero greco in Occidente nei secoli xii-xiii e la questione di Giacomo Chierico di Venezia," *Atti della xxvi riunione della Società Italiana per il progresso delle scienze, Venezia*, 1937, 3, 2 (Rome, 1938), 287–310.

See also the papers and monographs in M. Grabmann, *Mittelalterliches Geistesleben*, 3 vols. (Munich, 1926–56), with bibliography of Grabmann's numerous publications on this subject, *ibid.*, 3, 10–35; F. Pelster, "Neuere Forschungen über die Aristotelesübersetzungen des 12. und 13. Jahrhunderts. Eine kritische Übersicht," *Gregorianum*, 30 (1949), 46–77; R. Herval, "Ecléctisme intellectuel," *Atti*, cited in note 26 above, Vol. 1, 73–104; J. Storost, "La leggenda di Aristotele in Sicilia e in Normandia," *ibid.*, Vol. 1, 155–66.

32   E. Jamison, *Admiral Eugenius of Sicily, His Life and Work* (Oxford, 1957), pp. 3–5, 21 ff., 302 f. Jamison, perhaps wisely, takes no notice of the conjecture of F. Bliemetzrieder, *Adelhard von Bath* (Munich, 1935), pp. 149–274, that the unknown translator of the Almagest was Adelhard of Bath, *ca.* 1153–60.

33   C. H. Haskins, *Studies in the History of Mediaeval Science* (2nd ed.; Cambridge, Mass., 1927), pp. 150, 202 ff.; cf. pp. 144, 145, 297 ff.

34   *Ibid.*, pp. 143, 178–82, 219 f. The text of a Latin translation of the twelfth century has been edited by L. Delatte, *Textes latins et vieux français relatifs aux Cyranides* (*Bibliothèque de la Faculté de Philosophie et Lettres de l'Université de Liège*, 93 [1942]). H. Boese, ed., *Die mittelalterliche Übersetzung der Stoicheiosis physike des Proclus* (*Deutsche Akademie der Wissenschaften, Arbeitsgruppe für hellenistisch-römische Philosophie*, 6 [Berlin, 1958]): ca. 1160.

35   See note 80 below and R. Mols, "Burgundio de Pise," *Dictionnaire d'histoire et de géographie ecclésiastiques*, 10 (Paris, 1938), 1363–69; M. Flecchia, "La traduzione di Burgundio Pisano delle omelie di S. Giovanni Crisostomo sopra Matteo," *Aevum*, 26 (1952), 113–30. For a portion of Burgundio's version of Chrysostom, see H. F. Dondaine, *Recherches de théologie ancienne et médiévale*, 19 (1952), 100–102. On the use of the Greek fathers, cf. Grabmann, *op. cit.*, note 29 above, 1, 76–116; 2, 81–94 and *passim*.

36   A. Dondaine, "Hugues Éthérien et Léon Toscan," *Archives d'histoire doctrinale et littéraire du moyen âge*, 19 (1952), 67–134, with texts and bibliography; cf. P. Classen, "Das Konzil von Konstantinopel 1166 und die Lateiner," *Byzantinische Zeitschrift*, 48 (1955), 339–68; A. Dondaine, "Hugues Éthérien et le concile de Constantinople de 1166," *Historisches Jahrbuch*, 77 (1957), 473–83. See also note 148 below.

37   See the works of E. M. Buytaert, note 80 below, and A. B. Terebessy, *Translatio latina*, cited, note 39 below.

38   Migne, *P.L.*, 184, 309A; J. M. Déchanet, *Guillaume de Saint-Thierry, l'homme et son œuvre* (Bruges-Paris, 1942), pp. 200 ff. and index *s.v.*; *idem, Aux sources de la spiritualité de Guillaume de Saint-Thierry* (Bruges, 1940); pp. 27–59. Cf.

M. M. Davy, *Un traité de la vie solitaire, Lettre aux frères du Mont-Dieu de Guillaume de Saint-Thierry* (Paris, 1946), pp. 191, 211, a translation based on the same author's Latin text (Paris, 1940). A valuable contribution on the impact of Greek thought upon the West has been made by Chenu, *La théologie*, cited, note 14 above, pp. 108–41, 274–308.

On Origen see J. Leclercq, "Nouveaux témoignages sur Origène au xiie siècle," *Mediaeval Studies*, 15 (1953), 104–6; *idem*, "Origène au xiie siècle," *Irénikon*, 24 (1951), 425–39; *idem*, "Saint Bernard et Origène d'après un manuscrit de Madrid," *Revue Bénédictine*, 59 (1949), 183–95. Cf. the anonymous *Ysagoge in Theologiam* (*ca.* 1148–52), ed. A. Landgraf, *Écrits théologiques de l'école d'Abélard* (*Spicilegium sacrum Lovaniense, Études et documents*, 14 [Louvain, 1934]), 270.2 ff.; *idem*, "Zum Werden der Theologie des zwölften Jahrhunderts," *Zeitschrift für katholische Theologie*, 79 (1957), 417–33, n.b. 418 ff.; and note 95 below.

Of the innumerable references to the Pseudo-Dionysius which occur in the twelfth century, cf. *idem*, *Spicilegium*, 14, 233.6 ff., 12 f.; P. Glorieux, "La somme 'Quoniam homines' d'Alain de Lille," *Archives d'histoire doctrinale et littéraire du moyen âge*, 20 (1953), 119, 120, 125, 127, 128, 131, 133, 135, 140, 213, 328; M. T. d'Alverny, "Le cosmos symbolique du xiie siècle," *ibid.*, 20 (1953), 31–81, on the *Clavis physicae* of Honorius of Autun; H. Weisweiler, "Die Ps.-Dionysiuskommentare 'In Coelestem Hierarchiam' des Skotus Eriugena und Hugos von St. Viktor," *Recherches de théologie ancienne et médiévale*, 19 (1952), 26–47; J. M. Parent, "Un nouveau témoin de la théologie dionysienne au xiie siècle" [an anonymous *Summa*], *Aus der Geisteswelt des Mittelalters* (*Beiträge zur Geschichte der Philosophie und Theologie des Mittelalters*, Supplementband 3, 1 [Münster i. W., 1935]), 289–309. Consult W. Völker, *Kontemplation und Ekstase bei Pseudo-Dionysius Areopagita* (Wiesbaden, 1958); and R. Roques, *L'univers dionysien* (Paris, 1954), for bibliography.

39 J. Daniélou, "Saint Bernard et les pères Grecs," *Analecta Sacri Ordinis Cisterciensis*, 9, fasc. 3–4 (1953), 46–55; cf. J. M. Déchanet, "Aux sources de la pensée philosophique de S. Bernard," *ibid.*, pp. 56–77; cf. *ibid.*, fasc. 1–2, 116–24 and *passim*; É. Gilson, "Maxime, Érigène, S. Bernard," *Aus der Geisteswelt des Mittelalters* (volume cited in previous note), pp. 188–95; *idem*, *La théologie mystique de Saint Bernard* (Paris, 1934). I have not seen E. Kleineidam, *Wissen, Wissenschaft, Theologie bei Bernard von Clairvaux* (*Erfurter Theologische Schriften*, 1 [Leipzig, 1955]), but cf. *idem*, *idem*, in *Bernhard von Clairvaux, Mönch und Mystiker* (*Veröffentlichungen des Instituts für Europäische Geschichte Mainz*, 6, ed. J. Lortz [*Wiesbaden*, 1955]), 128–67; E. von Ivánka, "Byzantinische Theologumena und hellenische Philosophumena in Zisterziensisch–Bernhardinischen Denken," *ibid.*, pp. 168–75.

On the translation of Maximus the Confessor by Cerbanus, see A. B. Terebessy, *Translatio latina sancti Maximi Confessoris* (*De caritate ad Elpidium L. i–iv*) *saeculo xii in Hungaria confecta* (Magyar Görög Tanulmányok, ed. G. Moravcsik, 25 [Budapest, 1944]).

40 N. M. Haring, "The Character and Range of the Influence of St. Cyril of

Alexandria on Latin Theology (430–1260)," *Mediaeval Studies*, 12 (1950), 1–19, n.b. 17.

41   G. Théry, "Documents concernant Jean Sarrazin," *Archives d'histoire doctrinale et littéraire du moyen âge*, 18 (1950–51), 45–87.

On genuine Platonism (as opposed to Neoplatonism of the Pseudo-Dionysian variety) see N. M. Haring, "The Creation and Creator of the World According to Thierry of Chartres and Clarenbaldus of Arras," *Archives d'histoire doctrinale et littéraire du moyen âge*, 22 (1955), 137–216, with texts and bibliography; M. D. Chenu, "Platon à Cîteaux," *ibid.*, 21 (1954), 99–106; *idem, La théologie*, note 14 above, pp. 108–41. Cf. R. Baron, *Science et sagesse chez Hugues de Saint-Victor* (Paris, 1957), pp. 73, 168–179.

42   On Abelard see G. Paré, A. Brunet, P. Tremblay, *La renaissance du xiie siècle, Les écoles et l'enseignement* (*Publications de l'Institut d'études médiévales d'Ottawa*, 3 [Paris-Ottawa, 1933]), 275–312; cf. for the method of Abelard and Gilbert, É. Lesne, *Les écoles de la fin du viiie siècle à la fin du xiie* (*Histoire de la propriété ecclésiastique en France*, 5 [Lille, 1940]), *s.v.*; J. Cottiaux, "La conception de la théologie chez Abélard," *Revue d'histoire ecclésiastique*, 28 (1932), 247–95, 533–51, 788–828, who concludes his survey by quoting from Abelard's *Epistola ad Heloissam*: "Nolo sic esse philosophus ut recalcitrem Paulo; non sic esse Aristoteles ut secludar a Christo."—ed. V. Cousin, *Petri Abaelardi opera*, 2 (Paris, 1849), 680; J. de Ghellinck, *Mouvement théologique*, pp. 171 ff., 466, 468, and *passim*, with bibliography.

On Abelard's knowledge of Plato and Aristotle, see the new edition of his *Dialectica*, ed. L. M. de Rijk (Assen, 1956), with list of sources, *ad fin.*; and P. Delhaye, "Un cas de transmission indirecte d'un thème philosophique grec," *Scholastica ratione historico-critica instauranda* (*Bibliotheca Pontificii Athenaei Antoniani*, 7 [Rome, 1951]), pp. 143–67. Cf. J. G. Sikes, *Peter Abailard* (Cambridge, Eng., 1932), 272 ff. An interesting summary of the proceedings of the councils of Soissons (1121) and Sens (1141) by which Abelard was unjustly condemned is to be found in C. J. Hefele and H. Leclercq, *Histoire des conciles*, 5, 1 (Paris, 1912), 593–602, 747–90.

On Gilbert, see the important observations by N. M. Haring, "The Case of Gilbert de la Porrée, Bishop of Poitiers (1142–1154)," *Mediaeval Studies*, 13 (1951), 1–40. Cf. also *idem*, "The Cistercian, Everard of Ypres, and his Appraisal of the Conflict Between St. Bernard and Gilbert of Poitiers," *ibid.*, 17 (1955), 143–72; *idem*, "A Latin Dialogue on the Doctrine of Gilbert of Poitiers," *ibid.*, 15 (1953), 243–89; de Ghellinck, *Mouvement théologique*, pp. 174–79, 230, 242 f., 402 f., 467 f. The rest of the literature can be located through the following: M. A. Schmidt, *Gottheit und Trinität nach dem Kommentar des Gilbert Porreta zu Boethius, De Trinitate* (*Studia philosophica, Jahrbuch der Schweizerischen philosophischen Gesellschaft*, Supplementum 7 [Basel, 1956]); S. V. Rovighi, "La filosofia di Gilberto Porretano," *Miscellanea del centro di studi medievali*, 1 (*Pubbl. dell' Università Cattolica del S. Cuore*, N.S., 58 [Milan, 1956]), 1–64; A. M. Landgraf, "Zur Lehre des Gilbert Porreta," *Zeitschrift für katholische Theologie*, 77 (1955), 331–37; *idem*, "Der Porretanismus der Homilien des Radulphus Ardens," *ibid.*, 64 (1940), 132–48; *idem*,

"Untersuchungen zu den Eigenlehren Gilberts de la Porrée," *ibid.*, 54 (1930), 180–213; *idem*, "Neue Funde zur Porretanerschule," *Collectanea Franciscana*, 6 (1936), 353–65; *idem*, "Mitteilungen zur Schule Gilberts de la Porrée," *ibid.*, 3 (1933), 182–208; V. Miano, "Il commento alle lettere di S. Paolo di Gilberto Porretano," *Scholastica . . . instauranda* (cited above), pp. 169–99. Announcement has been made of a book by H. C. van Elswijk entitled *Gilbert Porreta, sa vie, son œuvre, sa pensée*, which is to be published in the *Spicilegium sacrum Lovaniense*. Among the new editions of Gilbert's works, see, e.g., "The Commentaries of Gilbert, Bishop of Poitiers, . . . on the Two Boethian *opuscula sacra* on the Holy Trinity," ed. Haring in *Nine Mediaeval Thinkers*, ed. J. R. O'Donnell (Toronto, 1955), pp. 23–98; "The Commentary of Gilbert, Bishop of Poitiers, on Boethius' *Contra Eutychen et Nestorium*," ed. Haring, *Archives d'histoire doctrinale et littéraire du moyen âge*, 21 (1954), 241–357; Landgraf, ed. *Commentarius Porretanus in primam Epistolam ad Corinthios (Studi e Testi*, 117 [Vatican City, 1945]).

On Joachim of Flore see F. Foberti, *Gioacchino da Fiore* (Florence, 1934), pp. 75 f. and *passim*, who judges Joachim to have been orthodox; *contra* is P. Fournier, *Études sur Joachim de Flore* (Paris, 1909), pp. 32 f. and *passim*. N.b. the 211-page bibliography by F. Russo, *Bibliografia Gioachimita (Biblioteca di bibliografia italiana*, 28 [Florence, 1954]). Cf. B. Hirsch-Reich, "Eine Bibliographie über Joachim von Fiore und dessen Nachwirkung," *Recherches de théologie ancienne et médiévale*, 24 (1957), 27–44; M. W. Bloomfield and M. E. Reeves, "The Penetration of Joachism into Northern Europe," *Speculum*, 29 (1954), 772–93; Hefele and Leclercq, *Histoire des conciles*, 5, 2 (Paris, 1913), 1327–29. Note that the book of Foberti cited bears the subtitle, *Nuovi studi critici sulla mistica e la religiosità in Calabria*. It is to be distinguished from *idem, Gioacchino da Fiore e il Gioacchinismo antico e moderno* (Padua, 1942), which is devoted to proving that Joachim was not a heretic. To the above add M. W. Bloomfield, "Joachim of Flora, A Critical Survey of His Canon, Teaching, Sources, Biography and Influence," *Traditio*, 13 (1957), 249–311; reviewed by B. Hirsch-Reich, *loc. cit.*, 26 (1959), 128–37.

For hostile criticism of Abelard and Gilbert, see A. Michel, "Trinité," *Dictionnaire de théologie catholique*, 15, 2 (Paris, 1950), 1713–17.

43 This subject will be discussed in detail in my forthcoming book, *The Mind of Byzantium* (Doubleday). On *Filioque*, cf. J. N. D. Kelly, *Early Christian Creeds* (London, 1950), pp. 358–67.

44 Migne erroneously prints Hugo's treatise under the title: "De haeresibus quas Graeci Latinos devolvunt libri tres, sive quod Spiritus Sanctus ex utroque, Patre scilicet et Filio, procedat, contra Graecos."—*P.L.*, 202, 229–396. But A. Dondaine, "Hugues Éthérien," note 36 above, pp. 93 ff., shows that this was the designation of a *Greek* polemic *against* the Latins, and that Hugo's work was entitled *De sancto et immortali Deo*.

For biographical details see *ibid.*, pp. 79 ff., 92; and R. Lechat, "La patristique grecque chez un théologien latin du xiie siècle, Hugues Éthérien," *Mélanges d'histoire offerts à Charles Moeller*, 1 (Université de Louvain, Recueil de Travaux, 40 [Louvain-Paris, 1914]), 485–507, who supplies a list of

references to the passages cited by Hugo from the Greek fathers of the
first eight centuries, but does not analyze what Hugo says or deal with the
later Byzantine theologians like Photius, Nicetas Byzantius, and Nicholas of
Methone, whom Hugo frequently names.

In this section I summarize Hugo's principal arguments. But the subject
deserves more extended treatment, along with the Byzantine doctrine of the
Holy Spirit and the polemics of Latin theologians like Anselm of Aosta
(1033–1109) and Anselm of Havelberg (d. 1158), on the latter of whom
see note 52 below. M. Jugie has written on the Byzantine aspects of this
topic: *Theologia dogmatica Christianorum orientalium ab ecclesia catholica dissiden-
tium*, 1 (Paris, 1926), 154–311; 2 (Paris, 1933), 296–326; and *De processione
Spiritus Sancti ex fontibus revelationis et secundum orientales dissidentes* (*Lateranum,
Nova series*, 2, no. 3–4 [Rome, 1936]), but a fuller and more critical study is
greatly needed. Cf. J. Hergenröther, *Photius, Patriarch von Constantinopel*,
3 (Regensburg, 1869), 175 ff., 791, 814 ff., 833 ff. See also *Tractatus contra
errores Graecorum*, ed. J. Basnage, *Thesaurus monumentorum ecclesiasticorum et
historicorum*, 4 (Amsterdam, 1725), 62–79, cf. 31 f.; Gerhoh's *Tractatus contra
Graecorum errorem negantium Spiritum s. a Filio procedere*, ed. F. Scheibelberger,
op. cit., note 89 below, pp. 341–57; Leo Tuscus, *De haeresibus et praevarica-
tionibus Graecorum*, ed. Dondaine, *loc. cit.*, note 36 above, pp. 116–19, 126 f.

45 P. Lamma, *Comneni e Staufer, ricerche sui rapporti fra Bisanzio e l'Occidente nel
secolo xii*, 1 (see note 2 above), 165 ff. and *passim;* 2, *passim;* L. Bréhier,
"Attempts at Reunion of the Greek and Latin Churches," *Cambridge
Medieval History*, 4 (Cambridge, Eng., 1923), 600–603, 877 ff.; F. Chalandon,
Les Comnène, 2 (Paris, 1912), 161–64, 227, 555–608; *idem, La domination nor-
mande*, Vol. 2, pp. 195 ff., 204 ff., 211–19, 227 ff., 254–61, 299 ff., 356–59,
368–73; W. Norden, *Das Papsttum und Byzanz* (Berlin, 1903), pp. 91–107.
See bibliographical data in the papers cited in note 36 above.

46 Migne, *P.L.*, 202, 232D–233B.

47 *Ibid.*, 233A–B; for the date, see Lechat, "La patristique grecque," pp.
488–92.

48 Migne, *P.L.*, 202, 229 f., 230B ("editum a me utraque lingua librum ac-
cipite"); cf. 231A ("libros ... tam Graece quam Latine scriptos").

49 *Ibid.*, 227 ff., 233C–234D.

50 *Ibid.*, 235A–C.

51 *Ibid.*, 235C–236C.

52 *Ibid.*, 236D–238B. The original text of Nicholas of Methone is printed in
Migne, *P.G.*, 102, 284 n. 33, 291 n. 89; A. K. Demetrakopulos, Ἐκκλησιασ-
τικὴ Βιβλιοθήκη (Leipzig, 1866), 360, c. 1; cf. 366, c. 16. On Nicholas,
cf. V. Grumel, *Dictionnaire de théologie catholique*, 11, 1 (Paris, 1931), 620 f.
What Nicetas had to say on this subject is known to us only through the
Dialogi of Anselm of Havelberg.—Migne, *P.L.*, 188, 1163A–1210B.

On the important role played by Anselm during the controversy on the
procession of the Holy Spirit, see K. Fina, "Anselm von Havelberg, Untersuchungen zur Kirchen- und Geistesgeschichte des 12. Jahrhunderts,"
Analecta Praemonstratensia, 32 (1956), 69–101, 193–227; 33 (1957), 5–39,

268–301 (still being continued), who gives the bibliography of the subject. Note especially G. Schreiber, "Anselm von Havelberg und die Ostkirche," *Zeitschrift für Kirchengeschichte*, 60 (3. Fol., 11, 1941), 354–411; J. Dräseke, "Bischof Anselm von Havelberg und seine Gesandtschaftsreisen nach Byzanz," *ibid.*, 21 (1900–1901), 160–85; E. Dombrowski, *Anselm von Havelberg* (Königsberg i. Pr., 1880).

53   Migne, *P.L.*, 202, 238C–D, 242D.

54   *Ibid.*, 244A–C; Nicetas Byzantius, *Capita syllogistica*, ed. J. Hergenroether, *Monumenta graeca ad Photium eiusque historiam pertinentia* (Ratisbonae [Regensburg], 1869), 92 f., 103.8 f.; cf. Photius, *De Sancti Spiritus mystagogia*, 61, Migne, *P.G.*, 102, 340B and notes. On Nicetas, see M. Gordillo, *Enciclopedia Cattolica*, 8 (1952), 1837.

55   Migne, *P.L.*, 202, 244C–246C.

56   *Ibid.*, 245D–246A.

57   *Ibid.*, 255C–D; Nicetas of Nicomedia *apud* Anselmum, *op. cit.*, Migne, *P.L.*, 188, 1170D. Cf. Nicetas Byzantius, ed. Hergenroether, 89.2 ff., 120.1 ff.; Photius, *op. cit.*, 6, Migne, *P.G.*, 102, 288B and n. 62.

58   Migne, *P.L.*, 202, 255D–256B.

59   *Ibid.*, 268D; Nicholas, ed. Demetrakopulos, 363, c. 6; and Migne, *P.G.*, 102, 281B–284D, with notes, especially n. 28.

60   Migne, *P.L.*, 202, 268D–272B.

61   *Ibid.*, 277 C–D. Nicetas Byzantius, ed. Hergenroether, 108 f., cf. 95; Migne, *P.G.*, 102, 288 f., n. 66.

62   Migne, *P.L.*, 202, 278A–279C.

63   *Ibid.*, 295B–298A. Hugo's statement that Archbishop Nicetas of Nicomedia was opposed to the compromise formula of the procession of the Spirit *ex Patre per filium* seems at first glance to contradict Anselm of Havelberg in *Dialogi*, 2, 27 (Migne, *P.L.*, 188, 1209 B–1210B), according to which Nicetas expressed full accord with Anselm in everything (*assentio etiam omnibus quae dixisti*). But Nicetas added, Anselm goes on to say, that since the Greek people were unfamiliar with the dogma of the procession of the Holy Spirit from the Son, it would be necessary to secure ratification of this doctrine by an oecumenical council of the Church under the authority of the Roman pope and with the sanction of the emperors. As soon as this conciliar definition was obtained, Nicetas promised, the Greeks would gladly join the Romans in proclaiming that the Holy Spirit proceeds from the Son. If we can trust Anselm's account, Nicetas was convinced by the Latin arguments and made what is represented as an unconditional surrender. Actually, however, he was only repeating the traditional Byzantine objection that the double procession was unacceptable since it had never been endorsed by a general council of the whole Church. He pretends that the Greeks would be willing to assent *after* such an oecumenical decision, but he knew very well that no Greek delegation would ever submit to a dogmatic decree authorizing the addition of *Filioque* to the creed. On this analysis, therefore, there is little difficulty in reconciling what Hugo says here with the *Dialogi* of Anselm, as can be seen from the text itself:

Nechites [Nicetas] archiepiscopus Nicomediae dixit: Tuam humilitatem, frater charissime, amplector, et eam devotionem quam habere videris ad veritatem fidei, admiror, et fateor: nequaquam possum non commoveri te loquente; assentio etiam omnibus quae dixisti, et accedo toto animo et toto corpore. Porro verba haec: *Spiritus sanctus procedit a Filio*, quoniam hactenus non sonuerunt publice in Ecclesiis Graecorum, nequaquam subito possunt induci, ut sine aliquo scandalo plebis vel aliquorum minus prudentium publice doceantur, vel scribantur; sed aliquod generale concilium occidentalis et orientalis Ecclesiae auctoritate sancti Romani pontificis, admittentibus piissimis imperatoribus celebrandum esset, ubi haec et nonnulla alia Catholicae Ecclesiae necessaria secundum Deum diffinirentur, ne forte vos vel nos in vacuum curreremus. Extunc omnes nos qui in partibus orientis Christiani sumus, una cum sancta Romana Ecclesia, et cum caeteris Ecclesiis quae sunt in occidente, communi voto et pari consensu sine aliquo nostrorum scandalo verbum hoc, *Spiritus sanctus procedit a Filio*, libenter susciperemus, et praedicaremus, et doceremus, et scriberemus, et in Ecclesiis orientis publice cantandum institueremus.

64   Migne, *P.G.*, 102, 317B and n. 24; ed. Demetrakopulos, 363 f., c. 7 f.
65   Migne, *P.L.*, 202, 302B–303A.
66   *Ibid.*, 317A–318 D; Migne, *P.G.*, 102, 284A–285B.
67   Migne, *P.L.*, 202, 318D–320B.
68   *Ibid.*, 320B–C. Information on these practices of the Greek church can be found in the following: R. Janin, *Les églises orientales et les rites orientaux* (4th ed.; Paris, 1955); F. Mercenier and F. Paris, *La prière des églises de rite byzantin*, 1 (2nd ed.; Amay-sur-Meuse, 1951); S. Salaville, *An Introduction to the Study of Eastern Liturgies*, ed. by J. M. T. Barton (London, 1938); F. Heiler, *Urkirche und Ostkirche* (Munich, 1937); N. Nilles, *Kalendarium manuale utriusque ecclesiae orientalis et occidentalis* (2 vols.; Innsbruck, 1896–97); F. E. Brightman, *Liturgies Eastern and Western*, 1 (Oxford, 1896); J. M. Neale, *A History of the Holy Eastern Church* (2 vols.; London, 1850); J. Goar, Εὐχολόγιον *sive rituale Graecorum* (in the edition of Paris, 1647, or that of Venice, 1730). Consult also the *Dictionnaire d'archéologie chrétienne et de liturgie* (30 vols.; Paris, 1907–53); *Jahrbuch für Liturgiewissenschaft* (15 vols.; 1921–41); *Archiv für Liturgiewissenschaft* (1950—); P. Hofmeister, *Die heiligen Öle in der morgen- und abendländischen Kirche* (*Das östliche Christentum*, N.F., 6–7 [Würzburg, 1948]).
69   Migne, *P.L.*, 202, 320D: "Nam licet solus nominetur Pater, subintelligitur omnino et Filius, eo quod absque medio de Patre non prodeat [*sc.* Spiritus], et cum nusquam Patrem dixisse reperiatur: Ego solus emitto Spiritum...." Cf. 321D.
70   *Ibid.*, 320D–321C.
71   *Ibid.*, 373B–375B.
72   *Ibid.*, 375B–378B.
73   *Ibid.*, 380A–384D.
74   *Ibid.*, 388B–393A. See A. Palmieri, "Niceta di Maronea e i suoi dialoghi

sulla Processione dello Spirito Santo," *Bessarione*, Anno 16, Vol. 28 (1912), 80–88; Nicetas' sixth treatise, which has not yet been published, contains the specific passage to which Hugo alludes, as M. Jugie indicates, "Nicétas de Maronée," *Dictionnaire de théologie catholique*, 11, 1 (1931), 475. But see the fourth treatise, ed. N. Festa, *Bessarione*, 30 (1914), 72.14–16, for Nicetas' view that the Spirit proceeds *from* (ἐκ) the Father alone *through* (διά) the Son.

75   See references given by Lechat, "La patristique grecque," note 44 above, pp. 500 f.

76   Migne, *P.L.*, 202, 394A–B; Migne, *P.G.*, 43, 29B–C: πνεῦμα τοῦ πατρὸς καὶ πνεῦμα τοῦ υἱοῦ . . . : 32C: ἄρα θεὸς ἐκ πατρὸς καὶ υἱοῦ τὸ πνεῦμα . . . .; 118A–B: τὸ δὲ ἅγιον πνεῦμα παρὰ ἀμφοτέρων (i.e., Father and Son), ed. K. Holl, *Epiphanius*, 1 (Leipzig, 1915), 15.12–14, 16.11 f., 88.3–5. The last of these texts was not identified by Lechat; and is accordingly absent from his list.

77   Migne, *P.L.*, 202, 393A–C; Migne, *P.G.*, 68, 148A: εἴπερ ἐστὶ τοῦ θεοῦ καὶ πατρός, καὶ μὴν καὶ τοῦ υἱοῦ, τὸ οὐσιωδῶς ἐξ ἀμφοῖν, ἤγουν ἐκ πατρὸς δι' υἱοῦ προχεόμενον πνεῦμα. Migne, *P.G.*, 71, 377D: ἐξ αὐτοῦ (= τοῦ υἱοῦ).

78   Migne, *P.L.*, 202, 364D (not in Basil); *ibid.*, 328A; Migne, *P.G.*, 29, 656A with n. 79; Lechat, "La patristique grecque," pp. 498 n. 6, 502 f. The Roman Church justifies the addition: L. Lohn, "Doctrina S. Basilii M. de processionibus divinarum personarum," *Gregorianum*, 10 (1929), 329–64, 461–500; but the list of MSS in D. Amand, "Essai d'une histoire critique des éditions générales grecques et gréco-latines de S. Basile de Césarée," *Revue bénédictine*, 56 (1945–46), 135 f., 146 ff., shows that the Migne edition was based on four codices of the eleventh century, which, as the editors remark in Migne, *P.G.*, 29, 656 n. 79, agree in omitting the passage quoted by Hugo. H. Dörries, *De spiritu sancto, der Beitrag des Basilius zum Abschluss des trinitarischen Dogmas (Abhandlungen der Akademie der Wissenschaften in Göttingen, Philol.-Hist. Kl.*, Dritte Folge, Nr. 39 [1956]), 11 n. 1, mentions but does not discuss the problem. See the Acts of the Council of Ferrara-Florence, ed. J. Gill, *Concilium Florentinum, Series B*, 5.2 (Rome, 1953), 262 n. 12, 328 and *passim* (see index *s.v. Eunomius*); L. Mohler, *Kardinal Bessarion als Theologe, Humanist und Staatsmann*, 1 (*Quellen und Forschungen aus dem Gebiete der Geschichte... der Görres-Gesellschaft*, 20 [Paderborn, 1923]), 147 f., 206 f.; H. Vast, *Le Cardinal Bessarion, 1403–72* (Paris, 1878), pp. 80 ff.

79   Migne, *P.L.*, 202, 394B–C; Migne, *P.G.*, 94, 832B–833A (Hugo erroneously omits the words I have bracketed, although they are essential to his interpretation); Migne, *P.L.*, 202, 396A–B; Migne, *P.G.*, 96, 605B. Cf. Lechat, "La patristique grecque," pp. 495 n. 2, 505 f.
      On John's treatment of the procession of the Holy Spirit from the Father alone, see J. Bilz, *Die Trinitätslehre des hl. Johannes von Damaskus (Forschungen zur christlichen Literatur und Dogmengeschichte*, 9, 3 [Paderborn, 1909], 152 ff. Hugo makes two other references to John, but they do not strengthen his case: Migne, *P.L.*, 202, 292D (the Son is the *imago* of the Father, and the Spirit is the *imago* of the Son); 364D (*per Filium datur Spiritus*).
      The literature on John is listed by B. Studer, *Die theologische Arbeitsweise*

*des Johannes von Damaskus (Studia patristica et Byzantina, 2 [Ettal, 1956]).
F. Doelger, Der griechische Barlaam-Roman ein Werk des h. Johannes von
Damaskos (ibid.*, 1 [Ettal, 1953]), maintains that the Greek version of the
famous tale of Barlaam and Joasaph in its present form was actually written
by John of Damascus, as had long been thought. D. M. Lang opposes this
view and derives the Greek text from the Buddhist original by way of successive derivation *via* Manichaean, Arabic, and Georgian recensions: "*The
Life of the Blessed Iodasaph*: a New Oriental Christian Version of the Barlaam
and Ioasaph Romance," *Bulletin of the School of Oriental and African Studies*, University of London, 20 (1957), 389–407; *idem, The Wisdom of Balahvar: A
Christian Legend of the Buddha* (London, 1957). More important for the subject
at hand is the fact that the story circulated widely throughout the West in a
Latin translation, of which a large number of codices were produced during
the twelfth century.—J. Sonet, *Le roman de Barlaam et Josaphat, 1 : Recherches
sur la tradition manuscrite latine et française (Bibliothèque de la faculté de philosophie
et lettres de Namur*, 6 [Namur-Paris, 1949]), 76 ff.

80   Saint *John Damascene, De fide orthodoxa, Versions of Burgundio and Cerbanus
(Franciscan Institute Publications*, Text series, no. 8 [St. Bonaventure, N.Y.,
1955]). The facts and bibliography on the various translations are fully
set out in Buytaert's introduction.* I am greatly indebted to Professor Buytaert for this handsomely printed book and his four valuable articles on
John of Damascus: "Damascenus Latinus on Item 417 of Stegmueller's
Repertorium Commentariorum," *Franciscan Studies*, 13, 2–3 (1953), 37–70; "The
Apologeticus of Arno of Reichersberg," *ibid.*, 11 (1951), Nos. 3–4, Commemo-
rative volume, 1–47; "The Earliest Latin Translation of Damascene's De
orthodoxa fide III 1–8," *ibid.*, pp. 49–67; "St. John Damascene, Peter
Lombard and Gerhoh of Reichersberg," *ibid.*, 10 (1950), 323–43. See also
L. Callari, "Contributo allo studio della versione di Burgundio Pisano del
'De orthodoxa Fide' di Giovanni Damasceno," *Atti del Reale Istituto Veneto
di scienze, lettere ed arti*, 100, 2 (1940–41), Classe di scienze morali e lettere
(Venice, 1941), 197–246; H. Dausend, "Zur Übersetzungsweise Burgundios
von Pisa," *Wiener Studien, Zeitschrift für klassische Philologie*, 35 (1913), 353–69.

81   See Buytaert's papers cited in the previous note and de Ghellinck, *Mouvement théologique*, pp. 368–415.

82   F. Stegmüller, *Repertorium commentariorum in Sententias Petri Lombardi* (2 vols.;
Würzburg, 1947); and V. Doucet, *Commentaires sur les Sentences, Supplément
au Répertoire de M. Frédéric Stegmüller* (Ad Claras Aquas, 1954), reprinted
from the *Archivum Franciscanum historicum*, 47 (1954), provide impressive
testimony to the popularity and esteem which Peter the Lombard enjoyed.
See also J. de Ghellinck, "Pierre Lombard," *Dictionnaire de théologie catholique*,
12, 2 (Paris, 1935), 1941–2019; *idem, Mouvement théologique*, pp. 213–77,
374–86, 400–420.

83   H. Dausend, "Johannes Damascenus in der Chronik des Salimbene,"
Theologische Quartalschrift, 118 (1937), 173–92; I. Backes, *Die Christologie des
hl. Thomas v. Aquin und die griechischen Kirchenväter (Forschungen zur christlichen
Literatur- und Dogmengeschichte*, 17, 3–4 [Paderborn, 1931]), 44 ff.; P. Minges,

* See also note 149 below.

"Zum Gebrauch der Schrift 'De fide orthodoxa' des Joh. Damaszenus in der Scholastik," *Theologische Quartalschrift*, 96 (1914), 225–47; M. Duffo, "St. Jean Damascène, source de Saint Thomas," *Bulletin de littérature ecclésiastique* (1906), pp. 126–30.

84 See notes 106 f. below.

85 Ioannes de Walter, *Magistri Gandulphi Bononiensis Sententiarum libri quatuor* (Vienna and Breslau, 1924), p. lxviii; 1, 93, pp. 62 f.; 3, 35, p. 298; 3, 46, p. 305; 3, 58, p. 315; 3, 71, p. 321; 3, 73, p. 322; 3, 74, p. 324; 3, 92, p. 341; 3, 114, p. 360; see de Ghellinck, *Le mouvement théologique du xiie siècle*, pp. 335–46; A. M. Landgraf, *Dogmengeschichte der Frühscholastik*, 2, 2 (Regensburg, 1954), 153.

86 M. Chossat, *La Somme des Sentences, œuvre de Hugues de Mortagne vers 1155* (*Spicilegium sacrum Lovaniense, Études et documents*, 5 [Louvain-Paris, 1923]), 167 f.

87 A. M. Landgraf, ed., *Der Sentenzenkommentar des Kardinals Stephan Langton* (*Beiträge zur Geschichte der Philosophie und Theologie des Mittelalters*, 37, 1 [Münster i. W., 1952]), 105, 113.

88 Further research will uncover many other examples of this sort. See, e.g., N. M. Haring, ed., "The So-called *Apologia de Verbo Incarnato*," *Franciscan Studies*, 16 (1956), 102–43, n.b. 104, 108, 127.1, 131 n. 372, 134 n. 431; Landgraf, *Dogmengeschichte*, 2, 1, 162, 166; 2, 2, 141, 147 f., 155, 163 f., 171; 3, 2, 43, 45; de Ghellinck, *Mouvement théologique*, pp. 368–415 and *passim*.

89 *Liber contra duas haereses*, Migne, *P.L.*, 194, 1171A–C; *Liber de gloria et honore Filii hominis*, Migne, *P.L.*, 194, 1082D, 1114–15, 1140C; Buytaert, "St. John Damascene, Peter Lombard and Gerhoh of Reichersberg" (cited above, note 80), pp. 330 ff.; D. van den Eynde, *L'œuvre littéraire de Géroch de Reichersberg* (*Spicilegium Pontificii Athenaei Antoniani*, 11 [Rome, 1957]), 58 n. 5, 80 n. 5, 220, 228 n. 3, 297; D. and O. van den Eynde and A. Rijmersdael, *Gerhohi Praepositi Reichersbergensis opera inedita*, 1 (*ibid.*, 8 [Rome, 1955]), 294, 359 f. *Gerhohi Reichersbergensis Praepositi opera hactenus inedita*, ed. F. Scheibelberger, 1 (Linz, 1875), p. 275, contains one rather ambiguous reference to John of Damascus; cf. note 44 above.

90 See Buytaert, "The *Apologeticus* of Arno of Reichersberg" (note 80 above), for the identification of the passages from John of Damascus which he has located on pp. 45, 131, 150, 154 f., 162, 169, in the edition of C. Weichert, *Arnonis Reicherspergensis Apologeticus contra Folmarum* (Leipzig, 1888).

91 J. Warichez, ed., *Les Disputationes de Simon de Tournai* (*Spicilegium sacrum Lovaniense, Études et documents*, 12 [Louvain, 1932]), 38, 59, 140, 221, 237.

92 P. Glorieux, ed., "La somme 'Quoniam homines' d'Alain de Lille," *Archives d'histoire doctrinale et littéraire du moyen âge*, 20 (1953), 142, 143, 176, 192, 214, 249, 251.

93 Landgraf, *Dogmengeschichte*, 3, 2 (Regensburg, 1955), 36, prints a bit from the *Summa aurea* of William of Auxerre which utilizes the fourth book of the *De fide orthodoxa;* see also Landgraf, *ibid.*, 2, 1, 145 f.; 2, 2, 160; 3, 2, 307.

94 Buytaert, *Saint John Damascene, De fide orthodoxa* (see note 80 above), pp. xii f.

95   For Peter Lombard's position on the theological questions treated below, see O. Baltzer, *Die Sentenzen des Petrus Lombardus (Studien zur Geschichte der Theologie und der Kirche*, edd. N. Bonwetsch and R. Seeberg, 8, 3 [Leipzig, 1902]); *idem, Beiträge zur Geschichte des christologischen Dogmas im 11ten und 12ten Jahrhundert, ibid.*, 3, 1 (1898). Baltzer, however, has not attempted to scrutinize or evaluate Peter's dependence upon John of Damascus.

      J. de Ghellinck, *Mouvement théologique*, pp. 242 f., summarizes the statistics: Peter the Lombard cites Augustine nearly a thousand times, Hilary of Poitiers and Ambrose about 80 each. John of Damascus stands highest among the Greeks, with about 30 references. Athanasius, Didymus, and Cyril of Alexandria are used once each, the Pseudo-Dionysius twice, and Origen about a dozen times. For a full list of Peter's authorities, see the Quaracchi edition, cited in note 96 below, Vol. 2, pp. 1047 ff.

96   *Liber I. Sententiarum, Distinctio* 19, c. 9, *Petri Lombardi libri iv Sententiarum studio et cura PP. Collegii S. Bonaventurae*, 1 (2nd ed.; Ad Claras Aquas, 1916, the so-called Quaracchi edition), 132–34.

97   The *locus classicus* is the 38th Epistle of Basil of Caesarea, which was addressed to his brother, Gregory of Nyssa; cf. Epistle 8. For discussion and a collection of later passages, see R. Arnou, "Unité numérique et unité de nature chez les Pères, après le Concile de Nicée," *Gregorianum*, 15 (1934), 242–54; T. de Régnon, *Études de théologie positive sur la Sainte Trinité* (Première série; Paris, 1892), pp. 154–63. Some authorities attribute Epistle 38 to Gregory of Nyssa, and Epistle 8 to Evagrius Ponticus: see B. Altaner, *Patrologie* (5th ed.; Freiburg im Breisgau, 1958), p. 262.

98   *De fide orthodoxa*, 3, 6 (Migne, *P.G.*, 94, 1001C). I have verified all of Peter's references to John in the original, but have based my translations and paraphrases upon the Latin version, with only occasional corrections as required by the Greek text.

99   *Ibid.*, 3, 4 (Migne, *P.G.*, 94, 997A).

100   *Libri Sententiarum*, 1, *Dist.* 19, c. 9, *ed. cit.*, 1, note 96 above, 132 f. Walter of St. Victor, *loc. cit.*, note 16 above, p. 315 f., makes the same objection.

101   *Libri Sententiarum*, 1, 19, 3, *ed. cit.*, 1, 126; *De fid. orth.*, 3, 6 (Migne, *P.G.*, 94, 1004A).

102   1, 19, 9, *ed. cit.*, 1, 133 f.

103   Hugo, *De sacramentis*, 2, 1, 4 (Migne, *P.L.*, 176, 377A); Abelard, *Sic et non*, c. 8; *Theologia Christiana*, 4; *Introductio ad theologiam*, 2, 10 (Migne, *P.L.*, 178, 1360A–D, 1265A–B, 1057 f.).

104   Erigena, *De divisione naturae*, 1, 14 f., Migne, *P.L.*, 122, 461B, 463C. The Pseudo-Dionysius does not quite make this assertion in the same form, but the concept is deducible from his oft-repeated characterization of God as unknowable, supraessential (ὑπερούσιος), and beyond all being, who cannot be included within either the sensible (τὰ αἰσθητά) or the intelligible world (τὰ νοητά). The list of the Aristotelian categories given by Erigena as inapplicable to God roughly corresponds to that which appears in the *Theologia mystica*, pp. 4 f., of the Pseudo-Dionysius: Migne, *P. G.*, 3, 1040D, 1045D–1048B (fourteenth-century paraphrase by Pachy-

meres, *ibid.*, 1044A–1045C, 1057A–1064A). Cf. *De caelesti hierarchia*, 2, 3,
Migne, *P.G.*, 3, 140C–141A (Pachymeres, 156A ff.). See also the de luxe
edition by P. Chevallier, *Dionysiaca*, 1 ([Paris], 1937), 594–602; 2 (n.p.,
n.d.), 753 ff., which contains the Greek text along with nine Latin versions.

The notion that God is not *genus, species,* or any of the categories is usually
traced back to the Neoplatonic exegesis of Plato's *Parmenides*, 141D–142A.—
F. M. Cornford, *Plato and Parmenides* (London, 1939), pp. 129 ff. But it was
first articulated in these words by Clement of Alexandria, *Stromata*, 5, 12
(Migne, *P.G.*, 9, 121A; ed. O. Stählin, *Clemens Alexandrinus*, 2 [Leipzig,
1906], 380.18–20; cf. Plato, *Timaeus*, 27c), apparently on the basis of
Philo. See H. A. Wolfson, *Philo*, 2 (Cambridge, Mass., 1948), 109 f., 113,
153 ff.; *idem*, "The Knowability and Describability of God in Plato and
Aristotle," *Harvard Studies in Classical Philology*, 56–57 (1947), 233–49.

The Neoplatonic affirmations of this principle are of considerable
interest because of their influence upon medieval thought.—Plotinus,
Enneads, 6, 2, 9; 6, 9, 4; Proclus, *In Platonis Parmenidem*, 7, ed. V. Cousin,
Procli philosophi Platonici opera inedita (Paris, 1864), 1181.8–24; cf. 1176.30–40,
1173.7 ff. Cf. L. J. Rosán, *The Philosophy of Proclus* (New York, 1949),
pp. 123 f., n.b. n. 22; note 38 above.

105   Peter Lombard, 1, 19, 10, *ed. cit.*, 1, 135.

106   *Sententiae Petri Pictaviensis*, 1 (*Publications in Mediaeval Studies*, edd. P. S.
Moore and M. Dulong [Notre Dame, 1943]), 282.10–283.46.

107   *Ibid.*, 284.47 ff. Alan of Lille, ed. P. Glorieux, *loc. cit.* in note 92 above,
249–51, discusses this point and concludes that the hypostases differ, not
*numero, sed numero personarum, id est [secundum] pluralitatem personalium proprieta-
tum.* This is what John meant, he says.

108   Peter Lombard, 1, 25, 3, *ed. cit.*, 1, 161–63; *De fid. orth.*, 3, 5 (Migne,
P.G., 94, 1000B).

109   1, 26, 1, *ed. cit.*, 1, 163 f.; cf. 3, 7, 1–2, *ed. cit.*, 2, 583; *De fid. orth.*, 3, 3
(Migne, *P.G.*, 94, 992A–B); Jerome, *Epistula* 15, 3 f. (Migne, *P.L.*, 22,
356 f.); Abelard, *Sic et non*, 9, Migne, *P.L.*, 178, 1366B–C. Cf. note 11 above.

110   1, 27, 3, *ed. cit.*, 1, 173; *De fid. orth.*, 3, 6 (Migne, *P.G.*, 94, 1001C); 3, 7
(Migne, *P.G.*, 94, 1008C).

111   For a good summary of Athanasian, Cappadocian, and other early
Christian theology on this point, see G. Bardy, "Trinité," *Dictionnaire de
théologie catholique*, 15, 2 (Paris, 1950), 1659–1702, with bibliography;
note 97 above.

112   *De fid. orth.*, 3, 5 (Migne, *P.G.*, 94, 1000B–D).

113   1, 33, 1, *ed. cit.*, 1, 207–10, quotation on p. 208. On the arguments of
Gilbert, see Haring, "The Case of Gilbert de la Porrée, Bishop of Poitiers,"
Mediaeval Studies, 13 (1951), 1–40, especially 20 ff.; cf. bibliography in
note 42 above.

114   Argument so summarized: 1, 33, 1, *ed. cit.*, 1, 209. See Haring, *loc. cit.*
in previous note. On Sabellianism, see E. Vagaggini, "Modalismo,"
Enciclopedia Cattolica, 8 (1952), 1162–65.

115   1, 33, 1, *ed. cit.*, 209 f.; *De fid. orth.*, 3, 6 (Migne, *P.G.*, 94, 1001C); cf.

note 110 above. Walter of St. Victor, *loc. cit.*, note 16 above, 319.13 ff., finds this passage from John useful against Sabellianism.

116   3, 2, 1, *ed. cit.*, 2, 554 f.; *De fid. orth.*, 3, 4 (Migne, *P.G.*, 94, 997A); 3, 3 (Migne, *P.G.*, 94, 992A–993A); 3, 6 (Migne, *P.G.*, 94, 1005A–B). The first of these excerpts from John of Damascus was quoted by John of Cornwall in his *Eulogium ad Alexandrum Papam tertium* (written just before the Third Lateran Council, which was held in 1179), ed. Haring, *Mediaeval Studies*, 13 (1951), 277 f. See notes 127 f. and 131 below.

117   For the principal passages on τὸ ἀπρόσληπτον ἀθεράπευτον (what was not assumed could not be cured), see E. Weigl, *Christologie vom Tode des Athanasius bis zum Ausbruch des Nestorianischen Streites (373–429) (Münchener Studien zur historischen Theologie*, 4 [Munich, 1925]), pp. 58–60 ff.; see bibliographies on the Cappadocians, including Amphilochius of Iconium, in Altaner, *Patrologie*, pp. 258–76; on Apollinarius, *ibid.*, pp. 280 f. The latest material on the Monophysites is to be found in A. Grillmeier and H. Bacht, *Das Konzil von Chalkedon* (3 vols.; Würzburg, 1951–54); n.b. the monograph by Joseph Lebon in Vol. 1, pp. 425–580.

118   Peter Lombard, 3, 2, 2, *ed. cit.*, 2, 555; *De fid. orth.*, 3, 6 (Migne, *P.G.*, 94, 1005B). Cf. Landgraf, *Dogmengeschichte*, 2, 1, 160 f.

119   3, 3, 1, *ed. cit.*, 2, 557–59; *De fid. orth.*, 3, 2 (Migne, *P.G.*, 94, 985B–988A).

120   3, 3, 4, *ed. cit.*, 2, 561 f.; *De fid. orth.*, 3, 7 (Migne, *P.G.*, 94, 1012B).

121   3, 5, 1, *ed. cit.*, 2, 566–70. Cf. Landgraf, *Dogmengeschichte*, 2, 1, 124 f., 116–37.

122   3, 5, 1, *ed cit.*, 567, sec. 25; 569 f., sec. 29.

123   *Ibid.*, pp. 569 f., sec. 29.

124   *Ibid.*, p. 570, sec. 30; *De fid. orth.*, 3, 6 (Migne, *P.G.*, 94, 1004B, 1008B–C). Immediately before the last sentence of his quotation from John, Peter interpolates "et unam naturam Dei Verbi incarnatam confitemur," which in the original Greek occurs, not at this point, but in the following chapter (3, 7, Migne, *P.G.*, 94, 1012B: καὶ μίαν δὲ φύσιν τοῦ Θεοῦ Λόγου σεσαρκωμένην ὁμολογοῦμεν). See note 120 above. John was misled by Cyril of Alexandria (Migne, *P.G.*, 76, 1212A; 77, 224D, 245A) into naming Athanasius here. The formula he cites is Apollinarian.—ed. H. Lietzmann, *Apollinaris von Laodicea und seine Schule*, 1 (Tübingen, 1904), 251.1 f. See Buytaert, *Saint John Damascene* (note 80 above), p. 190.

125   On the success of the Apollinarians in concealing the works of Apollinarius under the names of orthodox writers like Gregory Thaumaturgus, Athanasius, and Bishop Julius I of Rome, see H. Lietzmann, *Apollinaris*, pp. 108 ff. On Thomas Aquinas, see Backes, *op. cit.* (note 83 above), pp. 114 f., 150 f., 154, 293. On Justinian, cf. my article "The Immutability of Christ and Justinian's Condemnation of Theodore of Mopsuestia," *Dumbarton Oaks Papers*, 6 (1951), 159.

126   See Lietzmann, *Apollinaris*, pp. 108 ff.; and the author of *Adversus fraudes Apollinaristarum*, Migne, *P.G.*, 86, 2, 1948.

127   3, 6, 1–6; 3, 7, 1 f.; 3, 10, 1; *ed. cit.*, 2, 573–88, 593 f.; de Ghellinck, *Mouvement théologique*, pp. 250 ff., and works there cited; Hefele and Leclercq,

Histoire des conciles, 5, 2, 974–77; E. Portalié, "Adoptianisme," *Dictionnaire de théologie catholique*, 1, 1 (Paris, 1902), 414–18; Baltzer (see note 95 above), *Die Sentenzen*, pp. 84 ff.; *idem, Beiträge*, 65–67; J. Bach, *Die Dogmengeschichte des Mittelalters*, 2 (Vienna, 1875), 200–206, 208; J. A. Dorner, *History of the Development of the Doctrine of the Person of Christ*, 2.1 (Edinburgh, 1869), 313–19.

Note the attack on the third theory in the anonymous *Apologia de Verbo Incarnato* of ca. 1160 (note 88 above) and in John of Cornwall's *Eulogium*, the latter of whom converts two texts (note 116 above, note 131 below) from John of Damascus, *loc. cit.*, pp. 276–79, that had been quoted by his opponents into a buttress for his defense of the first theory. The second of these forms part of Peter's exposition of the second theory.

128   *Loc. cit.*, 116 above, pp. 265, 284; Migne, *P.L.*, 199, 1052C–D, 1053A–B, 1071B–C; n.b. introduction to the *Libri Sententiarum, ed. cit.*, 1, xlviii ff.; de Ghellinck, *Dictionnaire de théologie catholique*, 12, 2, 2003–5.

129   A. Michel, "Hypostatique (union)," *Dictionnaire de théologie catholique*, 7, 1 (Paris, 1921), 512 ff., n.b. 516. A catena of decisive passages from the fathers (n.b. Cyril) on the hypostatic union is to be found in *De incarnatione*, 3, 4, 10–17, *Dogmata theologica Dionysii Petavii*, ed. J. B. Fournials, 5 (Paris, 1866), 391 ff.

130   3, 6, 3, *ed. cit.*, 2, 577 f.; *De fid. orth.*, 3, 4 (Migne, *P.G.*, 94, 997B), 3, 7 (Migne, *P.G.*, 94, 1009A–B), 3, 3 (Migne, *P.G.*, 94, 993B–C). Leo, *Epistola* 28, Migne, *P.L.*, 54, 767B.

131   3, 7, 2, *ed. cit.*, 2, 585; *De fid. orth.*, 3, 3 (Migne, *P.G.*, 94, 988B–989A). Matching the penultimate clause of this sentence ("is perfect God and perfect man"), the Greek has only "perfect God," although "perfect man" is clearly implied by the context, and probably appeared in the Greek texts used by Cerbanus and Burgundio for their translations, which are identical at this point: "Deum perfectum et hominem perfectum eundem" (ed. Buytaert, *op. cit.*, note 80 above, 393.22 f., 174.25 f.). John of Cornwall uses this excerpt from John of Damascus to fortify his case in favor of the first theory, *loc. cit.*, note 116 above, 278.

132   3, 7, 2, *ed. cit.*, 2, 588; *De fid. orth.*, 3, 2 (Migne, *P.G.*, 94, 988A). On Adoptianism, cf. Landgraf, *Dogmengeschichte*, 2, 2, 24 ff.

133   3, 8, 2, *ed. cit.*, 2, 590; *De fid. orth.*, 3, 7 (Migne, *P.G.*, 94, 1009C). On the theological principles involved see, e.g., my "Immutability of Christ" (note 125 above), pp. 144–49.

134   3, 15, 1, *ed. cit.*, 2, 611; *De fid. orth.*, 3, 20 (Migne, *P.G.*, 94, 1081B). John is mentioned here only as *auctoritas*, not by name.

135   3, 9, 1, *ed. cit.*, 2, 591 f.; *De fid. orth.*, 3, 8 (Migne, *P.G.*, 94, 1013B–1016A). On the adoration (*latreia*) of Christ as of God, see the patristic excerpts collected in *De incarnatione*, 15, 3–4, *Dogmata theologica Dionysii Petavii*, ed. J. B. Fournials, 7 (Paris, 1867), 183 ff.; and on the comparison, Cyril, *Scholia de incarnatione unigeniti*, 10 (Migne, *P.G.*, 75, 1380A–B); H. A. Wolfson, *The Philosophy of the Church Fathers*, 1 (Cambridge, Mass., 1956), 384–417 *passim;* cf. Landgraf, *Dogmengeschichte*, 2, 2, 142–44, 147 f.

136   3, 22, 3, *ed. cit.*, 2, 653 f.; *De fid. orth.*, 3, 7 (Migne, *P.G.*, 94, 1012B–C). Cf. Michel, *loc. cit.*, note 129 above, p. 497; Tertullian, *Adversus Praxean,* 22, 10–11.

137   Edition cited in note 90 above, p. 154.

138   My own investigations confirm those of L. Ott, "Das Konzil von Chalkedon in der Frühscholastik," *Das Konzil von Chalkedon, op. cit.,* note 117 above, Vol. 2, pp. 873–922; *idem,* "Gratian und das Konzil von Chalcedon," *Studia Gratiana,* 1 (Bologna, 1953), 31–50. For a reference to the disciplinary canons of Chalcedon, see Landgraf, *Dogmengeschichte,* 2, 1, 18. Hugo, note 71 above, quotes a few words from the Chalcedonian symbol.

139   Peter Lombard, 1, 11, 1, *ed. cit.,* 1, 78 f. Actually, the so-called Niceno-Constantinopolitan Creed of 381, which is now designated as the Nicene Creed in the churches, first appears as an official document in the *Acta* of the Council of Chalcedon in 451.—J. N. D. Kelly, *Early Christian Creeds,* pp. 296 ff.

140   See the text edited by P. Glorieux, *loc. cit.,* note 16 above, p. 255.

141   *Ibid.*

142   On this vast subject I refer to the following, with bibliographical notes: E. F. Bruck, *Kirchenväter und soziales Erbrecht* (Berlin-Göttingen-Heidelberg, 1956), pp. 249–56, and *passim;* F. Calasso, E. Ewig, A. Steinwenter, A. V. Soloviev, "La sopravvivenza delle istituzioni giuridiche romane," *Comitato internazionale di scienze storiche, X congresso internazionale di scienze storiche,* Roma, 4–11 Settembre, 1955, *Relazioni,* 6 (Florence, 1955), 519–650; E. Genzmer, "Il diritto romano come fattore della civiltà europea," *Università degli studi di Trieste, Facoltà di giurisprudenza, Istituto di storia del diritto, Conferenze Romanistiche,* 3 (Trieste, 1954); *idem,* "Die iustinianische Kodifikation und die Glossatoren," *Atti del congresso internazionale di diritto romano, Bologna–Roma, 1933,* Bologna, 1 (Pavia, 1934), 345–430; *idem,* "Quare Glossatorum," *Gedächtnisschrift für Emil Seckel* (Berlin, 1927), pp. 1–69; G. Post, "*Philosophantes* and *Philosophi* in Roman and Canon Law," *Archives d'histoire doctrinale et littéraire du moyen âge,* 21 (1954), 135–38; P. S. Leicht, "Il processo italo-bizantino nell' Italia meridionale," *Atti del congresso internazionale di diritto romano e di storia del diritto,* Verona, 27–29 Settembre, 1948, 4 (Milan, 1953), 329–41; S. Kuttner, "New Studies on the Roman Law in Gratian's Decretum," *Seminar,* 11 (1953), 12–50; cf. *idem, Repertorium der Kanonistik (1140–1234) (Studi e Testi,* 71 [Vatican City, 1937]); *idem, Kanonistische Schuldlehre von Gratian bis auf die Dekretalen Gregors IX. (Studi e Testi,* 64 [Vatican City, 1935]); P. Koschaker, *Europa und das römische Recht* (Munich-Berlin, 1947 [1953 reprint]), pp. 55–76, 354 f., and *passim;* H. Kantorowicz, *Studies in the Glossators of the Roman Law, Newly Discovered Writings of the Twelfth Century* (Cambridge, Eng., 1938); W. Engelmann, *Die Wiedergeburt der Rechtskultur in Italien* (Leipzig, 1939); P. Vinogradoff, *Roman Law in Medieval Europe* (2nd ed.; Oxford, 1929); *Cambridge Medieval History,* 4 (Cambridge, Eng., 1923), 892 f.; H. Niese, *Die Gesetzgebung der normannischen Dynastie im Regnum Siciliae* (Halle a. S., 1910); L. S. Villanueva, *Diritto bizantino* (Milan, 1906), pp. 150 ff. (reprint

from the *Enciclopedia Giuridica Italiana*); E. Seckel, *Beiträge zur Geschichte beider Rechte im Mittelalter* (2 vols.; Tübingen, 1898); F. Brandileone, *Il diritto romano nelle leggi normanne e sveve del regno di Sicilia* (Turin, 1884); F. C. von Savigny, *Geschichte des römischen Rechts im Mittelalter*, 2 (Heidelberg, 1834), 303–18, 494–99 (on Ivo of Chartres); 4 (2nd ed.; Heidelberg, 1850), on the twelfth century, pp. 394–410 on Burgundio. Mention should be made of the collected papers of G. Ferrari dalle Spade, *Scritti giuridici*, 3 vols. (Milan, 1953–56), which include a number of valuable studies on the transmission of Byzantine law to the West; see also F. Calasso, *Medio evo del diritto*, 1 (Milan, 1954).

143 The evidence is set forth in my paper, "Pletho, Strabo, and Columbus," *Annuaire de l'Institut de philologie et d'histoire orientales et slaves*, 12 (1952), 1–18. The best book on Pletho is by F. Masai, *Pléthon et le platonisme de Mistra* (Paris, 1956).

144 Hugo missed the point of Nicetas' argument, which was based on the Neoplatonic theory of a ladder of grades of being, descending from the highest to the lowest. According to this scheme, the One, the highest and most powerful cause in the universe, produced a being (i.e., an individual, whether spiritual or material) which was like it in many respects, but necessarily inferior to it because derived from it. This being, in turn, was the source of others, each of which was superior to that of which it itself was the cause. Thus, the more remote a being was from the One, the less directly it "participated" in the One, and the more inferior it was. That which is produced is said to "participate" in its cause, which is described as "the participated" and always stands higher than that which "participates." These principles were formulated with quasi-mathematical precision by the pagan philosopher Proclus (410–85), but exerted great influence upon the Pseudo-Dionysius and other Christian thinkers. See the critical edition of the Greek text, with English translation and commentary by E. R. Dodds, *Proclus, the Elements of Theology* (Oxford, 1933), propositions 7–9, 23 f., 36 f., 56 f., 126, 128, 130, 132.

ADDITIONAL NOTES

145 Gerhard Rohlfs, *Neue Beiträge zur Kenntnis der unteritalischen Gräzität* (*Sitzungsberichte der bayerischen Akademie der Wissenschaften, Philos.-hist. Klasse*, Heft 5 [Munich, 1962]): see Rohlfs' bibliography on the knowledge of Greek in Italy.

146 André Guillou, *Les actes grecs de S. Maria di Messina, enquête sur les populations grecques d'Italie du sud et de Sicile, XIe–XIVe s.* (*Istituto Siciliano di studi bizantini e neoellenici*, ed. Bruno Lavagnini, *Testi*, 8 [Palermo, 1963]), plus portfolio; *idem*, "Grecs d'Italie du sud et de Sicile au Moyen Âge: les moines," *Mélanges d'archéologie et d'histoire*, 75 (1963), 79–110; *idem* and W. Holtzmann, "Zwei Katepansurkunden aus Tricarico," *Quellen und Forschungen aus italienischen Archiven und Bibliotheken*, 41 (1961), 1–28; Léon-Robert Ménager,

Les actes latins di S. Maria di Messina, 1103–1250 (Testi, 9 [Palermo, 1963]).

147   Albert Siegmund, *Die Überlieferung der griechischen christlichen Literatur in der lateinischen Kirche bis zum zwölften Jahrhundert (Abhandlungen der bayerischen Benediktiner-Akademie,* 5 [Munich-Pasing, 1939]).

148   Cyril Mango, "The conciliar edict of 1166," *Dumbarton Oaks Papers,* 18 (1963), 313–30, with seven plates.

149   Despite a long and persistent search, I was unable to find, until after publication, E. Bertola, "Le citazioni di Giovanni Damasceno nel primo libro delle Sentenze Lombardiane," *Pier Lombardo,* 1 (1957), No. 3, 3–17, whose treatment of the subject is somewhat different from mine.

G. E. von Grunebaum

The World of Islam:
The Face of the Antagonist

If the Muslim historians of Islam were given to systematic self-analysis by means of retrospective evaluation, there would be small inducement in the collective memory for them to fasten on the twelfth century of our era for special attention.

The catastrophe of the Abbasid caliphate incident to the Mongol conquest of Baghdad in 1258 would attract their interest to the thirteenth century all the more as the calamities wrought by the Mongols on the Muslims of Iraq and Iran never did fade from popular consciousness. The intensity of the fears besetting the contemporaries can be gauged by the fact that the Mamluk victory at 'Ain Gâlût which, in 1260, put a stop to the pagan advance to the South has remained an important constituent of Egyptian national pride to this very day. Although perhaps less rich than the thirteenth in events of continuing emotional significance, the eleventh century might exercise a strong fascination on the Muslim student. It is the period in which the social, political, and cultural entity which to the huge majority of the Islamic world of today embodies the orthodox development of the Prophet's message was faced as never before or after, with the acute threat of disintegration which it succeeded in fighting off, emerging from the crisis in a state of spiritual consolidation which enabled it to outsuffer the political miseries that lay ahead.

Our twelfth century, preceding by a little the seventh of the Muslim era, is by no means devoid of interest to the Muslim observer; but its perils and triumphs were, in a sense, local, while the downfall of the caliphate and the recasting of Muslim piety confer on the thirteenth and eleventh centuries an unparalleled importance for the Islamic world as a whole. It is true the "local" problems of Syria (in the geographical sense of the term) were of a rather unprovincial, not to say, international, character in that they were largely conditioned by the Crusades and the Crusader states that, during the twelfth century, in what seems a remarkably short time, almost completed their life cycle. Their initial successes and their continued presence on Muslim soil proved a stimulant to Muslim self-consciousness. They induced a flare-up of religious zeal and caused the lines between the religious communities to be drawn more sharply and fanatically; in fact, the intensification of anti-Christian sentiment reconstituted Sunnite orthodoxy as a political force strong enough to support the rise of the Ayyubids. And the memory of the successful Muslim resistance to the European intruders has not been lost on the modern nationalist who views the history of the Crusades as an encouraging precedent and perhaps as a pattern on which political relations between the Christian West and the Muslim East are necessarily repeating themselves: a sudden and victorious onslaught to be followed by a slow but merciless reconquest. Besides, the expulsion of the Crusaders was the last victory over Westerners won by Arabs.

Yet the effect of the Crusaders' arrival was curiously limited outside the regions directly concerned (which must be defined to include Lower Egypt). A few riots are recorded in which the lower orders of Baghdad attempted to force energetic action on the caliph, and on occasion volunteers would leave the capital for Syria, but on the whole life south and east of the Jezîra pursued its course relatively unaffected by the presence of Christian armies and Christian settlers. The Persian world remained completely untouched. And it needs to be recalled that at the beginning of the century the attitude of the several, mostly short-ruled potentates with whom the Crusader states shared their borders was by no means universally hostile. It would seem that the prevailing particularism could easily come to terms with yet another bevy of small political units in which, as was the case almost universally in those areas, an alien group lorded it over the native Arabic-speaking population and which, therefore, must have appeared to the Muslim princelings as kindred structures which it was entirely licit to make use of in their intricate and shifting political games. The Kingdom of Jerusalem provided a welcome buffer between Egypt—the political center of heterodoxy—and Syria (and Baghdad); the Christian occupation of Antioch and Edessa restored a *status quo* in terms of a desirable regional power balance; the easy relations between Christians and Muslims that obtained in northern Syria after the death of the Fatimid caliph al-Ḥâkim (1021) and as a reaction to his policies made the fact of Christian rule over Muslim territories less painful than it would have been under different circumstances. Within a few decades the Crusaders were, by their very presence and their cultural alienness, to bring about that growth of a psychological and spiritual unity among the Muslims which was the prerequisite of any major counteroffensive. Initially, regionalism and religious dissensions that had, in accordance with an age-old Eastern sociological pattern, led to the formation of social bodies tending nation-like toward independence, were too firmly established to allow a body politic to arise that, in the name of orthodoxy and for the sake of *reconquista*, would bring all of Syria and northern Iraq under its sway.

The caliphate as a Muslim Empire was long defunct even though the contemporaries refused to face the fact and thus compelled their princes to perpetuate the fictitious unity of (eastern and central) Islam by seeking investiture by the caliph of Baghdad with the countries actually under their control. The political and economic decline of the caliphal heart-lands was an accomplished fact; whether the impossibility of maintaining centralized government of large territories with the means of communication at the disposal of contemporary administrators was realised at the time is doubtful; in actual fact the *dâr al-islâm* had become divided among a considerable number of princes whose area of influence was fluctuating ceaselessly. Some of those princes held large territories, such as in the Arabic-speaking world the Egyptian Fatimids (who had entered upon their decline and were to be supplanted by the Ayyubids well before the end of the century) and the caliph at Baghdad who nominally had central and southern Iraq under his direct rule. In the west, the Berber dynasties of the Almohades and the Almoravides gave dwindling Muslim Spain a measure of political stability by uniting it with their North African base. By 1100 the great days of the Seljuks, the political saviors of Sunnite preponderance, were over; a hundred years later, an-Nâṣir (1180–1225) was engaged, with limited success, in rebuilding an independent caliphate as one *Kleinstaat* among others. Thirty-three years after his death the caliphate of Baghdad had been destroyed in consequence perhaps of political entanglements that had been entered into without the necessary power foundation.

We visualize governmental power as fairly evenly spread over a fairly stably delimited territory and as operating through an administrative machinery whose functioning is fairly independent of political vicissitudes at the center; besides, those vicissitudes are not normally assumed to bring about decisive changes in the structure of the body politic; and normalcy, that is to say, predictability of (domestic) obligations is, if not taken for granted, at least considered a yardstick of governmental success. Such would not have been the case among Muslims of the twelfth century. Power was centered (if we except Egypt, the princes of certain towns, and, in a sense, the caliph's court at Baghdad) at the seat of a military ruler; the ruler himself was almost constantly on the move. As a rule, his power declined in proportion to geographical distance from his residence of the moment. Administration was stable insofar as it was independent of him and in the hands of permanently settled local notables. The very moves of the ruler, dictated as they were by the exigencies of the moment, precluded predictability of the subjects' obligations. Normalcy might be found in the conditions that would prevail locally when the prince was too far away or too preoccupied to interfere; his intervention was almost by definition an upset, however salutary.

In town-based principalities such as Damascus and Aleppo political instability and inadequacy on the highest levels led to increased participation of the "bourgeois" element that, for some time, would control a civic militia (aḥdāṯ) which, naturally, was viewed with some reserve by the prince who, more often than not, would be a condottiere of Turkish descent maintained in command by Turkish troops, frequently mercenaries, whose generalship he would usually owe to a predecessor's will or to a suzerain. A measure of civic independence persisted until the Ayyubids succeeded in overcoming particularist resistance and united Syria and Upper Iraq with Egypt. The consolidated power of Saladin had no need for city militias; the improved safety conditions of the unified country made self-help in the towns less of a necessity. The military specialists, Turks, Kurds, some Arabs, safeguarded their position by eliminating any possible rival force. Soldiering and the making of high policy became the prerogative of the military, non-Arabs for the most part; administration and the perpetuation of the religious-cultural tradition remained with the Arabs. The transition from religious teaching to political and even military activity became increasingly rare; but the twelfth (and even the early thirteenth) century still offers some characteristic instances.

Thus, the twelfth century witnessed a reduction of the scope of the average town dweller who from participation in public affairs found himself more and more relegated to a life of political passivity. He could help shape local developments by taking part in guild life and by forcing a measure of conformity with religious injunctions on the government. Whereas only a short while ago he had been able to revolt, he now could do no more than riot.

It is the eleventh and twelfth centuries that saw the final acceptance of misgovernment by the Muslim learned who developed the doctrine that even the bad ruler needs to be obeyed seeing that misrule was preferable to anarchy and that the unbroken continuity of the legal life of the Muslim community was the first and foremost objective of the *umma*. That legal continuity with its concomitant, the ability of the individual to live under the divine will as expressed in the canon law, would be less endangered by an inadequate ruler than by civil disturbance.[1]

In spite of this outlook of the spokesmen of the community the population continued restless and unruly especially in the Syrian towns when under the influence of religious emotion. But the concern with the political shape of things was declining among the classes not directly involved in the business of administration. It is important to realise that the political decay of the Arabic-speaking Muslim world which the Ayyubids managed to redress for a while in no way lessened the efficacy of the Muslim mode of life and the unreflected firmness with which Islam as a basis of social and cultural cohesion, to say nothing of its theological authority, was adhered to. It cannot be emphasized enough that political unity was smoothly replaced (or complemented) by religious-cultural unity, that this religious-cultural unity proved considerably more effective in protecting the stability of the community than political arrangements could ever have done, and that the second great wave of the expansion of Islam set in after the political greatness of the Muslim heartlands had long been a thing of the past.

It was the peculiar achievement of the twelfth century to bring about, by means of the very successes of the Ayyubids, the political conditions in Egypt and Syria which led to the separation of the *salus Islamica* from the *salus* of any or all Islamic states. As concomitants, loyalty to the individual, accidentally existing state decreased, dynastic loyalties unless founded on tribal or more generally ethnic identity tended to weaken, and the Islamic community became the true homeland of the faithful. Its domain needed to be preserved and if possible enlarged for the greater glory of the Lord and as a mercy to the as yet unredeemed; the manner of its distribution among short-lived potentates was somewhat irrelevant. More often than not the government was the indispensable enemy whose existence would have been unbearable but for the learned pious who shielded the people from all too godless demands and for a certain inconsistency of its operations which secured its subjects informally conceded areas of autonomy and periods of respite.

This casualness in matters of high policy was becoming psychologically possible only through the elimination from the Arab-Muslim heartlands of any major body politic dedicated to the support and spread of heterodoxy. This elimination was the greatest accomplishment of the Ayyubids and doubtless the prerequisite of Saladin's *reconquista* of Frankish Syria. The presence of extremist Shiite splinter-groups as state-like communities within the Ayyubid territory was no more than a local irritant even though their activism necessitated by their numerically and geographically precarious position allowed them to assume an importance out of proportion with what must have been their actual resources. The Christian and Jewish communities slid back to the status provided for them by canon law; the correctness of Saladin prepared the ground for the increasingly rigid separation of the denominations that is characteristic for the subsequent age and which is reflected in the unmistakable impoverishment of the Christian and the Jewish intellectual and literary contributions to the Arabic-speaking world as a whole after the twelfth and thirteenth centuries had run their course. Cultural identification with the Muslim appears to have remained a feasible objective in Egypt where the leaders of the so-called Coptic Renaissance of the fourteenth century deliberately cultivated Arabic rather than attempted to rejuvenate their traditional language and patterned their codification of Christian ecclesiastical law on the thinking habits of their Muslim compatriots. In Syria, on the other hand, the emotional tension between Christian and Muslim remained more potent, and the Christian attitude may perhaps be found summed up in the regret voiced by the last important Syro-Christian writer that his coreligionists had at one time rendered possible the efflorescence of an Islamic civilization by transmitting their own classical heritage to the Muslims when they translated Greek scientific and philosophical texts for them into Arabic.[2]

The incessant shifts on the political scene, the countless reports of violent upheavals, the continued inroads of the West, the reorganization of Egypt and Syria by the Mamluks in the thirteenth century—these make it difficult to think of our period in the Near East as an age of consolidation accomplished. Yet such it was. For the consensus of the learned presumably following and verbalizing clearly though not systematically the consensus of a majority of the faithful had reached the decision that the survival of the community depended on what we cannot but consider a cultural retrenchment. More positively put and expressed in terms more adequately reflecting their aspiration: the community must preserve its integrity by reverting to its true base in revelation and tradition; it must concentrate on evolving (or returning to) a thoroughly Islamized mode of existence; it must live within the walls of the Law, eschew the risks of innovation, and curtail the frivolous delights to be derived from bringing Hellenic rationalism and the methods and pronouncements of Hellenic authorities to bear on problems of life and thought that ought to and could be studied and solved with the exclusive help of Muslim materials and the Muslim tradition.

The permanent crisis of the Muslim body politic gave rise to a desire for spiritual unification; and this unification if it could be attained at all presupposed the elimination or at the very least the relegation to a marginal position of such intellectual interests as were likely to prove disruptive. The conflicts of the law schools, however violent, could be tolerated, the conflict of theology and philosophy could not. Characteristically enough, the governments supporting "consolidation" favored the establishment of colleges in which theology, tradition, and especially law (according to one and sometimes all of the four recognized rites) were to be taught for the benefit of the rising class of canonist-administrators; philosophy and the sciences, however, were omitted from the curriculum.

The objective of the community was, to express it in terms of its individual members, the attainment of eternal felicity through obedience to the Lord in His Law; in terms of its resultant social-political task, the preservation of the *umma* as an organization within which the individual could realize his spiritual goal. It is from this central objective that the desirability of any intellectual effort was to be judged. The useful sciences were to be cultivated. Usefulness was determined by serviceableness to the perpetuation of orthodox Islam as a viable social-political entity. Knowledge *per se* is no longer prized; it is, in fact, blameworthy when it endangers the primary aspiration. The old division of the sciences into "Arabic" and "ancient" or "foreign" acquires a new meaning. The Arabic sciences comprise those of direct religious relevance and in addition the auxiliary branches of learning that are indispensable for the cultivation of the major sciences. Thus the science of *tafsir*, or the

Interpretation of the Koran, presupposes the cultivation of Arabic grammar and lexicography and even the study of ancient poetry considering that the sacred text does not yield its secrets unless one is familiar with the linguistic usage of the Prophet's contemporaries and predecessors. The rites of prayer and fasting require for their correct execution a measure of mathematical and astronomical information. The sifting of the spurious from the genuine in tradition justifies the collection of the biographies of the transmitters; the understanding of tradition requires the preservation of precedent through history, and the administration of the community cannot dispense with geography.

Logic, however, though nothing but a method of truth-construction, is suspect because of its pagan Greek origin (and also because of the alien philosophical context within which it first reached the Muslim orbit); the usefulness of medicine is debated in view of the theological implications of the physician's interference with (pre)ordained visitations and in view also of the doubtful legitimacy of its auxiliary, anatomy. The extension of the life-span by godless means is of questionable value. Philosophy was not only "officially" under a cloud but actually obsolescent, which is not to say that it was no longer cherished in the twelfth century but merely that it was no longer socially effective. Not much after the end of our period it did become obsolete in the sense that it failed to address itself to the existential needs of the times. With the possible exception of Ibn Khaldûn (d. 1406) whose message, however, acquired what effectiveness it may have some five hundred years after his death and thanks to the interest taken in him by non-Muslim scholarship, Ibn Rushd (Averroes—d. 1198), the last Arabic-writing Muslim of transcultural significance, was as ineffectual in the Muslim milieu as a whole as were his Spanish contemporaries Ibn Ṭufail (d. 1185) and Ibn Bâjja (Avempace—d. 1138). Averroes' supreme importance for the history of the human mind derives exclusively from the response accorded him after his death by the West.

The significance of Ibn Rushd's role becomes strikingly clear when it is compared with that of Avicenna (d. 1037) whose contribution his Muslim contemporaries and successors were not as yet at liberty to overlook even though it was experienced by many as a disturbing element requiring refutation and neutralization. To the great man whose death almost coincides with the beginning of our period Avicenna symbolized the disintegrative quality of Hellenizing philosophy which, in turn, had come to represent the principal intellectual adversary of Sunnite orthodoxy. Between al-Ghazzâlî (d. 1111) and Averroes (as in the period immediately following) the great men of the community—that is to say, the controversial figures and those whose message had the power to disturb and guide the heart—are organizers of the mystic path such as 'Abdalqâdir Gîlânî (d. 1166), mystic philosophers attempting to overcome the unbridgeable chasm between man and God by monistic speculations bordering on, or perhaps trespassing into, heresy such as Ibn al-'Arabî (d. 1240), and rulers championing Islam against unbelievers such as Saladin. The self-view of the community veers toward the timeless and away from the historical *hic et nunc*. (Yet history was to have another flowering in Egypt before the country fell to the Turks.) The world is divided between belief and unbelief, and the *umma* of the believers has always been fundamentally the same or ought to have been so. No explicitation of divine intentions through history; there is the high point of the beginnings, never to be recaptured, when the Prophet safeguarded the community's direct rapport with the divine; there is the gradual decay inherent in the increasing distance in time from the days when he walked the earth; and there is the ideal community whose maintenance is the task of the learned, with the changeless objective and its reluctantly changing structure, one and indivisible in virtue of a latitudinarian attitude to dissenters (which those but rarely reciprocate) and retaining its stability while time flows by it until the end will envelop it as foretold by prophecy and legend.

The learned are zealous in defense of orthodoxy, the community slow in placing a member outside the pale; the princes incline more and more to the reserve of indifferentism and act only when under pressure of the *'ulamâ'* or when the dissenter appears involved in political machinations. Suhrawardî, whose execution in 1191 was the end of a *cause célèbre*, lost his life because the *'ulamâ'* convinced the authorities of his political dangerousness; his philosophic deviations and his extremely offensive identification of Zoroastrian and Muslim concepts (which, in a sense, denied the uniqueness of the Islamic revelation) would not have sufficed to persuade the government to assent to his removal. The rulers were apt to be more favorably disposed to *Bildung* as such and hence more lenient toward philosophic studies than their lawyer-theologians.[3] It was the *'ulamâ'* who compelled Yûsuf b. Tâshfîn to discipline Ibn Rushd and it was to his sultan's good will that the philosopher owed his early release.

The battle between the Ancients and the Moderns which is bound to accompany any rapid cultural development at certain periods rises into full consciousness and divides the intellectual and artistic world of the day into two parties that face each other in sharp conflict and that, in the last resort, are separated by differing concepts of the potentialities of man. Literature or, more accurately, poetry being the area in which the Arab tradition excelled, it was the field of appreciation and criticism where the contest was waged earliest and where it attracted the widest attention of the educated public. The natural conservatism of a social structure drawing its *raison d'être* from a timelessly valid revelation combined with the pervasive sense of man's creaturely impotence—the corollary of Islam's enthusiastic exaltation of the Lord's unrestrained and majestic arbitrariness—were the powerful allies of those who championed the cause of the ancients. The rapture of creativeness that came over some circles of writers and thinkers in the early centuries of Abbasid rule had to assert itself against that gnawing scepticism with regard to man's worth and ability which made of his intellectual defeats a satisfying confirmation of a state of things one had always been prepared to accept as normatively correct. And yet, the ninth, the tenth, and even the eleventh centuries were animated in influential sections of the élite by a jubilant realization not only of the possibility of progress but of progress as an accomplished fact, at least where literature, philosophy, and the sciences were concerned. Innovation was perceived, admitted, and prized. There was no need to exalt the living over the dead, the moderns over the ancients in regard to their natural endowment; but it was felt and stated that the late-born held the advantage over his predecessors in that he could build on their accomplishments even if it were true that the sons fell short of the gigantic measure of the fathers.

Political misery, economic decline, the disintegration of the cosmopolitan *haute bourgeoisie* of Baghdad and Basra which had constituted a most responsive public for these intellectual combats and had supported the countless conventicles through which the new attitudes and interests expressed themselves, and besides, the barbarization of the actual rulers of Iraq, contributed to the decline of the Moderns' cause. But foremost among the reasons for the victory of the Ancients was the imperious necessity to achieve that consolidation without which, in the view of the leading contemporaries, Muslim society would have broken asunder during the century immediately preceding our period. Intellectual consolidation was inseparable from discrediting the heterodox. In some ways, the "optimism" in regard to man's potentialities was linked up with the ideology of the Fatimid *bāṭiniyya* with its assumption of a perfectible world, recipient of successive revelations through a line of infallible *imām*'s, each one of them the possible inaugurator of a renewed religious structure. The atmosphere in which this ideology would appear plausible and attractive, a frame of mind where intellectual curiosity, the discipline of a hierarchical organization, concern for (the late) classical philosophy and science, reliance on the clair-obscure of cabbalistic methods, fascination with allegory and the secretiveness of a permanent conspiracy were inextricably interlaced, allowed for just that degree of intellectual instability in which the hopefulness of multiple choices will thrive. The attraction of this atmosphere was felt by many who were proof against its theological and political presuppositions. But the fighters for a resurgence of Sunnism as primarily an immutable system of religious law to serve as the stable framework of a self-contained social order found themselves embarrassed as much by this intellectual attitude as by the political threat of the Fatimid counter-caliph.

The literary critics were perhaps most sensitive to the changing needs of the times. By the end of the eleventh century the Moderns had lost. The innovations of the last two or three hundred years were retained and integrated in the *status quo* whose defense was henceforth to be the (fairly easy) task of scholars and critics. Philosophy was rapidly becoming irrelevant (in the sense indicated before); science continued to command the interest of influential circles but it, too, restrained its explanatory zeal. The researchers began to betray a bad conscience when they proved their advancing strength; they were pushed outside the main stream of intellectual development and were at pains to be reconciled with the primary concern of the period—the stabilization of the godly community.

In Persia the reconstitution of a "national" culture created a different outlook. The pride in the progress of poetry and poetical technique since the days of Pahlavi literature was obvious and openly expressed; the weakening of the hold of Arab Islam assisted in the rise of Iran whose language was, in our period, well on its way to becoming the second vehicle of Muslim civilization and whose literature was soon to be recognized in its unique achievements by an Arab observer.[4] In fact, the statement could be defended that the most important development in twelfth-century Islam is precisely that recognition which Persian secured as the second culture language, an evolution that began in the tenth century, gained in strength and scope in the eleventh, but was consummated with immeasurable consequences for the civilizations of India and Central Asia in the twelfth century. The simultaneous decline in the familiarity with Arabic in circles where education was not specifically oriented toward theology, law, and their auxiliaries, is merely what one would expect yet deserves express notice. Did not the translator into Persian of a history of the city of Bukhara which in 933/34 had been written in Arabic by its (Iranian) author, in 1138/39 justify his work on the ground that "most people do not show a desire to read an Arabic book"?[5]

And yet, in the face of an unmistakable and in some ways imposing rise of national creativity and articulateness the optimistic pride in the Iranian achievement which a Gurgânî would voice in the middle of the eleventh century when in his own epic tale of *Vîs u Râmîn* he insists on the progress made by Persian poetry since Pahlavi days,[6] a sense of decline had come to threaten even Iran. The Iranian statesman, Anûsharvân b. Khâlid al-Kâshânî (d. 1138/39), saw fit to publish his memoirs under the title of *Decay of the Times of the Ministers and the Ministers of the Times of Decay*.[7] Kâshânî's mood reflects of course more than anything else the increasingly harassed political condition of Persia proper and in this wise attracts attention to the peculiar fact, not confined to Islam but perhaps more markedly observable in its history than in that of Europe, that the periods of cultural and especially literary flowering are apt to be periods of political decline or despair.

The *Vollender* of the *maqâma* and the greatest literary figure of his day, al-Ḥarîrî (d. 1122), still dared express an optimistic view of contemporary creativeness at the beginning of the twelfth century. "If those present would have a close look at it—do the ancients have anything but well-worn and limited ideas which are transmitted in their name, just because they happen to have been born at an earlier date, and not because of some (kind of natural) precedence such as the person who returns from the watering-place possesses over the person who goes down to it?"[8]

But the fact of stagnation and the threat of decline could not but be reflected in men's appraisal of their intellectual prospects and in the projection of their pessimistic diagnosis into negativistic judgments of themselves and their contemporaries. The superiority of Arab over Greek mathematics, which to him was undeniable, could as late as *ca.* 1160 inspire a Samau'al al-Maghribî with an emphatic assertion that "in every age, knowledge manifests itself in an increasing volume and with greater clarity." "No sage or well-informed historian," Samau'al continues, "will deny the fact that all the various disciplines of knowledge have manifested themselves in a process of gradual increase and ramification. This process stops at no final point and tolerates no irregularities." But in the end even Samau'al becomes afraid of his boldness. He adds a section in which he points out that the superior knowledge of the later-born is not due to any especial originality on his part. It merely so happened that his ideas did not enter someone's brain before. His better understanding solely "implies that he has farther progressed than they (i.e., the Ancients) in the knowledge of just that particular matter." And Samau'al goes out of his way to find excuses to explain why the Ancients failed to hit upon those points where the Moderns succeeded in breaking through to new insights. Generally speaking, the outlook reported by the astronomer Badî' az-Zamân al-Baghdâdî (d. 1139/40) as that of his teacher, 'Abdallâh al-Irbilî, is representative of the times: "He preferred the ancients, just because they lived in ancient times, and he did not try to find out whether they were right or wrong." [9]

Hand in hand with this abdication of intellectual self-assertion goes a softening of the demand for the strictness of rational proof, an increased readiness to accept transrational, or if you wish irrational interference and to break off the search for rational or natural causation sooner than would have appeared permissible to the educated one or two centuries earlier. As the concepts of natural law and of an ineluctable nexus between cause and effect were repugnant to orthodoxy because of the limitation which reliance on "secondary causes" would place on God's omnipotence, it was difficult to develop a theory of cognition which, from an operational point of view, delimited precisely and effectively the border line between science and religion, the realm of the rationally predictable and the domain of ready intervention of superhuman powers. The revival of Muslim theology as an emotionally effective structure inevitably implied a lowering of scholastic stringency in argumentation and greater leniency in the admission of popular ideas and desires.

The miracle as such had always been accepted by orthodox theology— for could not God at any time alter the customary course of nature and had He not done so in many well-authenticated instances? He had allowed miracles to be performed at the hands of His messengers to provide them with an obvious proof of their veracity; and He had, besides, for various reasons, permitted some of His "friends" to act in ways that could not be accounted for in terms of common experience.

Orthodoxy had long fought the idea of the miraculous powers of the saints; in fact, it had been altogether very slow in recognizing sainthood as a preferred position attainable by the pious. Now it turned around and dignified the ineradicable popular belief in human saints by elevating belief in their miracles to an article of faith. Speculations on the structure of the hierarchy of saints and of the different kinds of miracles within their reach were assured of a good deal of interest on the part of the public that precisely in our period witnessed the first systematic attempts to organize the life of the mystic way through the establishment of what most conveniently may be called "orders"—if only it is remembered that the initiates were not cut off from the world by permanent community living and by vows separating them from their families and constituting them as a social class by themselves. The founders of those "orders" (which were to proliferate in the centuries to come and which, in many parts of the Muslim world, have secured a permanent importance in the religious as well as the social life of the community) were typically "saints," and the shaikhs, their successors, would frequently partake of their status at least to the extent of possessing certain miraculous gifts such as healing, telepathic insights, and simultaneous presence in two places.

Consolidation, watchword and triumph of the age, meant more than anything else the reintegration of individual piety into the religious structure. Like any religion of the law, Islam was (and is) in constant danger of seeing the fulfilment of the believer's duty to his God in the punctual and conscientious observation of ritual and precept, in other words, in outward correctness. Personal piety early found refuge with groups of ascetics who, gradually, identified with an ideology that expanded the scope of religious experience beyond the limit that the theologians were willing to legitimize. The bridging of the gap between man and his Lord in the unitive experience of the mystic whose rapture was articulated in terms of varying offensiveness to the orthodox was the declared objective of the many small groups that, as disciples, would cluster informally around a master reputed to have attained the supreme goal of union with the divine. The cleavage between official Islam and personal piety was one of the factors which made disintegration of the *umma* under the impact of organized heresy a real danger (at least in the eyes of the theological as well as the political authorities). The masses were disaffected or uninterested in a religious structure which refused to make room for what was nearest and dearest to their hearts.

The greatness of al-Ghazzâlî (d. 1111), the *mujaddid*, or renewer, of the faith, whose *Revival of the Religious Sciences* was written just before the twelfth century came in, lies exactly in his ability to make a place within "orthodox" Islam for the religiosity of the people without abrogating or even diminishing the importance of the Law. His own development from an authoritative expounder of tradition and law to a lonely seeker after God who found his peace in a very personal mysticism but who resumed his function as a teacher of the faith at the behest of the ruler exemplifies the synthesis for which the period was striving, and it brings out as well the desire of the political authorities for an effective restatement of Sunnite Islam. For it was at the invitation of the caliph that al-Ghazzâlî, before his temporary retirement from the world, composed the outstanding confutation of Ismaili heterodoxy in which the fundamental positions of Sunnism are brought out persuasively in all their intellectual and affective richness.

Retrospectively, the development of Muslim piety can be described as essentially a shift of motivation from the *mysterium tremendum*, God's *jalâl*, to the *mysterium fascinosum*, God's *jamâl*. The shift parallels the reorientation of doctrine where, in the treatment of the key problems of God's essence and righteousness, concern for the relation of finite man with the transcendent God replaces concern for the integrity of the divine transcendence. Simultaneously, the consensus of the learned sanctions both the possibility and admissibility of man's love of God.[10]

The consolidation of orthodoxy in the Seljuq period completes the transfer of emphasis from fear to hope. In chronological terms, al-Ghazzâlî stands almost exactly halfway between the two personalities who may be taken to represent in isolated extremes one of those essentially complementary approaches to the divine: Ḥasan of Basra (d. 728), the warner who deepens the early inspiration of the Prophet through his detachment from the world, who never suffers himself to be free from horror of the Judgment to come nor from sadness over his sinful insufficiency which his asceticism might atone for but never overcome; and 'Abdalkarîm al-Jîlî (d. between 1406 and 1417), the arrogant elect who teaches that God's aspects of majesty, *jalâl*, and wrath are relatively less perfect than those of beauty, *jamâl*, and mercy. In terms of the religious experience, however, Ghazzâlî and his time had already made those choices which were to render possible the extreme position of Jîlî and which had begun to assimilate, to a certain extent, the religious mood of Eastern Islam to that prevailing in the Greek Church after the revival of enthusiastic piety toward the end of the first millennium.

The strengthened confidence in God's willingness to accept of the striving believer expresses itself on a practical level in the integration into "official" religion of the 1,001 formulae which the untaught had always used to induce or compel the Lord's assistance and which are now being recognized as legitimate elements of the devotional life although their presumed efficacy will be derived from the hard-won concentration of the praying heart on its Creator (and not from any magic qualities inherent in the formulae themselves). Simultaneously the religious elite will be increasingly spurred by the feeling that God is inclined to coöperate not only with holiness attained but with the earnest effort at self-sanctification. Steadfastness in self-development will, thanks to God's *lutf*, or loving-kindness, lead to permanent *charisma*. And to attain this *charisma* as a *character indelebilis* becomes the ultimate objective of religious exertion.

For the religious ideal is found incarnated in one human type: from the tenth century onward, in Greek orthodoxy and in Islam, the warrior-defender of the faith is overtaken by the ecstatic saint. Variation diversifies the type but does not transcend it. "Neither deep learning in divinity, nor devotion to good works, nor asceticism, nor moral purity makes the Mohammedan a saint; he may have all or none of these things, but the only indispensable qualification is that ecstasy and rapture which is the outward sign of 'passing-away' from the phenomenal self." [11] In this state of ecstasy the elect attains to, or perhaps this state is, *ma'rifa*, *gnosis*, which the Christian, Isaac of Ninive, had as early as the seventh century defined as "the apperception of immortal life." [12] It eliminates all limitations inherent in ignorance, *agnoia*, i.e., consciousness.

This concept of the saint who is recognized through his power to work miracles revives the Perfect Man of late antiquity and Gnosticism, [13] but it appears now stripped of some of its original exclusivism and esotericism. Like the Christian saint of the "desert" period the Muslim saint is one of a great number of saints; in other words, sainthood is not necessarily out of reach. This is true because the Lord not only collaborates with the saints but very largely effects his purposes on earth through their carefully and elaborately graded hierarchy. This idea of a hierarchy of the elect which mystic writers have taken much pleasure in working out in detail (and which is absent in the Greek Church) rests on the essentially heterodox presupposition which the Persian poet Jâmî (d. 1492) was to express with impressive concision when he said that "God has made perpetual the sign of prophecy." [14]

It is important to realize that the Seljuq government promoted saint-worship as a part of its endeavors to reconstitute orthodoxy by bringing it in line with the religious needs of the lower orders, in other words, as a semipolitical measure. Maqrîzî (d. 1442) describes dramatically the efforts of the Seljuq vizier, Niẓâm al-Mulk (d. 1092), to obtain from the Fatimid government in Cairo the body of ash-Shâfi'î (d. 820) for reburial in the Niẓâmiyya (begun in 1065 and opened in 1067).[15] When the resistance of the Cairines assisted by Shâfi'î's miraculous interference brought the plan to naught, Niẓâm al-Mulk ordered the official Egyptian report publicly read and copies distributed as far as Transoxiana with the result that Shâfi'î's prestige was greatly enhanced—a useful development in the eyes of a government supporting the Shâfi'ite school of canon law.

From the eleventh century on, the mystical ideology with its peculiar emotional atmosphere is popularized in innumerable treatises and collections of *exempla*, those in Arabic mostly in prose, those in Persian mostly in poetical form. It is only natural that to us a few well-known masterpieces of mystical writing overshadow the countless specimens of vulgarisation. Expression tended to become overattenuated or trite. In either guise it succeeded in steeping literature as a whole in the apparatus and the associations of Ṣûfî thought.

The parallel or perhaps converging development of Greek orthodox and Muslim piety in the later Middle Ages does not necessarily suggest direct literary influences. It is true that at least political contact was permanent and intense. It is also true that Asia Minor became in the thirteenth century a stronghold of Ṣûfism and the Ṣûfî orders. And it is interesting to note that there must have existed in the border regions of receding Christianity and advancing Islam for some time a Ṣûfism in Greek garb.[16] But the convergence predates the conquest of Asia Minor and is altogether too profound and at the same time too restricted to certain aspects of the intellectual life to be accounted for by the mere contiguity of the two culture areas. No doubt the fundamental unity of medieval thought as exhibited by Islam and Greek Christendom on the basis of kindred origins and kindred developmental patterns must be considered in this context. But in view of the rather striking similarity of fundamental conditions during the period in which the peculiar form of piety here considered became representative of both religions, a more specific connection would seem to suggest itself.

In Islam as well as in Greek orthodoxy the victory of a confident otherworldliness culminating in ecstatic experiences induced by method-ized practice and administered by organized groups that recognize their human ideal in the "enraptured" saint coincides with, or rather forms an essential part of, religious, intellectual, and political consolidation (or a determined attempt at such a consolidation) which forces even systematic theology to make a place for mysticism.

The threat of disintegration facing Islam under the impact of political catastrophes on the one hand and sectarian criticism combined with Ṣūfī antinomianism on the other was no less severe than the threat facing Greek Christianity after the Latin conquest of Constantinople in 1204. The Empire of the Palaeologi in Nicaea and later (from 1261) again in the ancient capital drew the better part of its strength from the devo-tion of the people to their Church that had for long been the embodiment of the national identity. The government would, for political reasons, work for Latinization but the people resisted. The defeat of Nikephoros Gregoras at the Synod of Constantinople (1341) was a triumph for Greek nationalism as well as for popular piety. By the same token the mystic-izing of Islam, official and unofficial, bespeaks the religious feeling of the people which had to be sanctioned to serve as the rallying point from which to undertake the rebuilding of Islam.[17] It is a kindred stratum of popular piety in Byzantium and in Eastern Islam attaining official admittance under comparable circumstances of extreme stress that explains (to the extent to which phenomena of this order will allow of an explanation) the parallel religious development of those hostile worlds.

From the double vantage point of the Muslim modernist and that of the student of the "golden prime" of Abbasid Islam, the features of cultural retrenchment overshadow anything else the twelfth century brought to the Arabic-speaking world. Consolidation achieved deserves more admiration than the contemporary Muslim and the occidental humanist are inclined to allow. Yet it can hardly be denied that it is during this very period that the relationship of the Islamic to the Western world began to shift to the (at first barely perceptible) disadvantage of the Muslims.

The contemporaries were justifiably unaware of the impending change. They noticed the recession of Muslim power in Spain and Sicily, they had seen the ravages wrought in Muslim Africa by a resurgent nomadism, they were painfully conscious of the decline of Baghdad as a cultural center and even as a town. But at the same time they saw the military virility of the Islamic tradition continue and drew confidence from the victories of Saladin. And what is more, intimate acquaintance with the Frankish settlers confirmed them in their conviction of their superiority—as civilized beings and as guardians of learning, let alone as the repositories of the most perfect of faiths. They were in fact superior in every regard except where it came to political organization; and the superiority of Europe at this point could hardly have been manifest to them who had before their eyes the incessant fratricidal bickerings of the Crusaders as seemingly convincing evidence to the contrary.

The high valuation of Muslim morality which is reflected in the writings of Christian observers and the recurrent notices of apostasy that testify to the continued attraction of Islam as a religion and as a social structure[18] are perhaps more eloquent witnesses in this respect than the amused contempt with which an Usâma b. Munqiḏ (d. 1188) describes Frankish medical procedures and the grossness of the intruders' manners.[19] The contemporary of Saladin could not but view the future of his *umma* with confidence. His cultural self-sufficiency shielded him from any intimate knowledge of the West; the increasing prominence of the religious and cultural elements of his identification, from being unduly disturbed by the political disorders through which he had to live. The fate of the Mediterranean world was in the balance. He could not suspect that contact and recession would turn out to have been two major steps toward the ultimate rise of the defeated antagonist.

NOTES

1   The relationship between individual and state, ruler and law, has been instructively formulated by N. J. Coulson, "The State and the Individual in Islamic Law," *The International and Comparative Law Quarterly*, VI (1957), 49–60. The indifference of the Muslim population to dynastic changes during the later Middle Ages and down to the dissolution of the Ottoman Empire has been discussed by Ṣubḥî Waḥîda, *Fî uṣûl al-mas'ala 'l-miṣriyya* (Cairo, 1950), pp. 43–44. The author points out that only the circles immediately affected by a transfer of power or by the disorders accompanying it exhibited any concern with passing from one set of rulers to another provided only that those in power were capable of defending Islam against the unbelievers.

2   Barhebraeus (d. 1286), *Chronographia*, ed. and trans. Sir E. A. W. Budge (London, 1932), I, 92.

3   One of their late successors well formulated their outlook. "What is decreed in the law of the Muslims is that the branches of knowledge which are

to be sought are the theological sciences and their tools, i.e. the sciences of the Arabic language; other knowledge is not to be sought, indeed it is to be proscribed."—Muḥammad 'Ullaish, Mâlikî muftî, d. 1881; quoted by P. Cachia, *Ṭāhā Ḥusayn* (London, 1956), p. 86. Cf. also Aḥmad Amîn, *Ẕuʿamâ' al-iṣlâḥ fî 'l-ʿaṣr al-ḥadîṭ* (Cairo, 1948), p. 7, who quotes the question put to the Shaikh al-Azhar, Muḥammad al-Inbâbî (in office 1881/82 and 1886/87–1895/96), by the Egyptian Government, whether the mathematical sciences and the natural sciences were permissible topics of instruction for Muslim students, a question which the Shaikh answered affirmatively and on which A. Amîn comments: "as if the Muslims had not been familiar with those sciences, been among their creators and their superior masters!"

4   Ḍiyâ' ad-Dîn Ibn al-Atîr (d. 1239), *al-Maṭal as-sâ'ir* (Cairo, 1312), p. 324.

5   Narshakhî, *The History of Bukhara*, trans. R. N. Frye (Cambridge, Mass., 1954), p. 3.

6   Cf. M. Boyce, "The Parthian *gōsān* and Iranian Minstrel Tradition," *Journal of the Royal Asiatic Society*, 1957, 10–45, at p. 38.

7   *Futûr zamân aṣ-ṣudûr wa-ṣudûr zamân al-futûr;* the work is preserved in the Arabic translation by 'Imâd ad Dîn al-Iṣfahânî, which was prepared in 1183 and brings the narrative down to 1180. Kâshânî's memoirs are discussed in B. Spuler's very illuminating study, "Die historische Literatur Persiens bis zum 13. Jahrhundert als Spiegel seiner geistigen Entwicklung," *Saeculum*, VIII (1957), 267–84, at p. 276.

8   Al-Ḥarîrî (d. 1122), *Sixth maqâma*, trans. F. Rosenthal, "Al-Asṭurlâbî and as-Samau'al on Scientific Progress," *Osiris*, IX (1950), 555–64, at p. 560.

9   Rosenthal, *ibid.*, pp. 562, 563, 559; a passage from al-Asṭurlâbî's affirmation of the modern scholars' creativeness is quoted also in W. Hartner, "Humanismus und technische Präzision," in *Wissenschaft und Wirtschaft* (Frankfurt/M., 1956), pp. 32–33 of reprint. A similar viewpoint was expressed by 'Umar Khayyâm (d. 1132), *Algebra*, ed. K. F. Woepcke (Paris, 1851), p. 2. When Ghazzâlî wrote his *Incoherence of the Philosophers* (*Tahâfut al-falâsifa*) Greek philosophy had apparently already lost that inspirational quality which had induced earlier thinkers such as al-Kindî (d. 873) to submit to its guidance with an almost touching enthusiasm; Ghazzâlî, on the other hand, was able to dispose of it as just another ill-substantiated strain of thought and of the faithfulness of its adherents as an instance of *taqlîd*, blind acceptance of traditional views. The relevant passages from Kindî and Ghazzâlî (among others) are conveniently brought together in A. J. Arberry, *Revelation and Reason in Islam* (London and New York, 1957), esp. pp. 34 ff., 61.

10 The *fuqahâ'* had identified man's duty of *maḥabbat Allâh*, love of God, as his obligation of *ṭâʿa*, obedience; the majority of the *mutakallimûn* rejected the concept as *tashbîh*, or assimilation of God to man. Between A.D. 870 and 888 the Ḥanbalite Ghulâm Khalîl (d. 888) instigated a persecution of Ṣûfîs. He considered *bidʿa* (an illicit innovation) their declaration that "We love our Lord and He loves us. He has made fall off from us the fear of Him by having us overwhelmed by the love of Him." He pointed out

that love was to be directed only to (fellow) creatures and that fear was more excellent and more fundamental in relation to God. Ibn al-A'râbî (Abû Sa'îd Aḥmad b. Muḥammad b. Ziyâd, d. 951/52) speaks of love and fear as of two uṣûl, roots, of faith on the same level, both being equally necessary to the believer even though one or the other may be stronger in the individual devotee (Ḍahabî, d. 1348, as quoted by H. F. Amedroz, *Journal of the Royal Asiatic Society*, 1912, pp. 566–67). The Mu'tazilite, Zamakhsharî (d. 1143), no longer objects to the love of God as such but criticizes sharply the ecstatic practices of the Ṣûfîs which are evoked as its expression. Ibn Tâ'imiyya's (d. 1328) disciple, Ibn Qayyim al-Jauziyya (d. 1350), recognizes love as the aṣl of all religious practice; and he defines this love (with Ghazzâlî) as the longing for the liqâ' Allâh, the meeting with God (cf. I. Goldziher, *Islam*, IX [1919], 157–58, 150).

It is characteristic for the changing attitudes of the times that the theological problem implicit in the concept of the gratitude with which man is expected to respond to God's benefactions was perceived in all its difficulty, discussed at length, and resolved by an appeal to mystical experience by al-Ghazzâlî in the thirty-second book of his Iḥyâ'; his ideas have recently been analyzed for their Greek antecedents by S. van den Bergh, "Ghazali on 'Gratitude Towards God' and Its Greek Sources," *Studia Islamica*, VII (1957), 77–98. In a sense, Ghazzâlî's own development can be interpreted as paradeigmatic for the shift from fear to hope which he experienced in the years between his departure from Baghdad and the resumption of his teaching at Nîshâpûr (1095–1106). That political circumstances contributed to or even necessitated his retreat into Syria (as F. Jabre maintains, "La biographie et l'œuvre de Ghazâlî reconsidérées à la lumière des Ṭabaqât de Sobkî," *Mélanges de l'Institut dominicain d'études orientales du Caire*, I [1954], 73–102, esp. at pp. 89–94) is at least probable; yet the primarily metaphysical character of his fears remains as unmistakable as their catharsis through a mystical apprehension of the divine with its inherent confidence in the ultimate fate of the believer. Cf. also the qualifications expressed with regard to fear as the sole motivation of Ghazzâlî in the great crisis of his life by J.-M. Abd-el-Jalil, "Autour de la sincérité d'al-Gazzâlî," *Mélanges Louis Massignon*, I (Damascus, 1956), 57–72, esp. at pp. 66–70 (apropos of an analysis of Ghazzâlî's al-Munqiḍ min aḍ-ḍalâl).

11   R. A. Nicholson, *The Mystics of Islam* (London, 1914), p. 123. For other conceptions of sainthood cf., e.g., A.-J. Festugière, *La sainteté* (Paris, 1949). On p. 68, Festugière finds for the Christian saint the brief formula: un juste qui souffre; un juste qui rend témoignage (a statement elaborated and greatly enriched on pp. 98 ff.). In this connection the contrast between the original Muslim concept of the martyr, shahîd, lit. 'witness', as one losing his life in active battle for the furtherance of the Islamic cause in this world, a casualty of victorious advance, and the Christian concept of one who wins the heavenly crown through a this-worldly defeat is of some significance. This contrast has been well formulated by W. C. Smith, *Islam in Modern History* (Princeton, 1957), p. 30, n. 27, whose terminology has influenced our own phrasing.

12   A. J. Wensinck, "Mystic Treatises by Isaac of Niniveh," *Verhandelingen der koninklijke Akademie van Wetenschappen te Amsterdam*, Afd. Letterkunde, n.r., XXIII/1 (1923), p. 289.

13   Cf. this writer, "Islam and Hellenism," *Scientia*, XLIV (1950), 21–27; reprinted in *Islam: Essays in the Nature and Growth of a Cultural Tradition* (Menasha, Wis., and London, 1955), pp. 159–67. The Gnostic motif—discussed on p. 26 and p. 26, n. 1 (*Islam*, p. 164 and p. 166, n. 16)—of the soul's investment with the qualities specific to the planetary spheres traversed is resumed in some detail by Ghazzâlî, *Mishkât al-anwâr*, trans. W. H. T. Gairdner (London, 1924), pp. 54, 64–65. Ghazzâlî's own reaction to the motif appears to have been rather reserved; cf. A. J. Wensinck, *Semietische Studiën uit de Nalatenschap* (Leiden, 1941), pp. 210–11. On pp. 203–5, Wensinck retranslates the passages from the Leiden MS of the *Mishkât* and arrives at a somewhat clearer formulation of Ghazzâlî's thought than his predecessor. The correlation of unusual personal religious achievement and the grace of having miracles, *karâmât*, done through one is very clearly expressed by Sha'rânî (d. 1565), *Yawâqît wa-jawâhir; cf.* G. Flügel, *Zeitschrift der deutschen morgenländischen Gesellschaft*, XX (1866), 18. For the identification of the Perfect Man with Muḥammad, who is approximated to the Logos, cf. this writer's *Medieval Islam* (2nd ed.; Chicago, 1953), p. 141. The process is completed, except perhaps for the terminology, in Farîd ad-Dîn 'Aṭṭâr (1119–1230); cf. his *Manṭiq aṭ-ṭair*, ed. E. Hermelin (Stockholm, 1929), vss. 244 ff., esp. 255–61. His younger contemporary, Ibn al-'Arabî (1165–1240), developed a logos theory of much greater complexity giving consideration to the ontological and mystical aspects of the logos in addition to that of the logos as the Perfect Man, the only aspect which Jîlî's speculation seems to have taken up. Since the Perfect Man is the cause of creation and since therefore the dignity of man cannot, in Ibn al-'Arabî's view, be overrated, his philosophy, too, must be recognized as a symptom of the turn toward anthropocentrism in later medieval thought. The intellectual motif of the pre-existent Muḥammad-Logos had first been advanced by unorthodox circles. Ḥallâj (executed in 922) operates with it and Aḥmad b. al-Kayyâl (second half of eighth century; cf. Shahrastânî, *Kitâb al-milal wa'n-niḥal*, ed. W. Cureton [London, 1846], p. 138) describes the perfect *imâm* in terms that are suggestive of a universal activating principle; cf. A. E. Affifi, *The Mystical Philosophy of Muḥyid Dín Ibnul 'Arabí* (Cambridge, 1939), pp. 66–92. It deserves notice that Gregory Palamas (d. 1359) in his praise of the Theotokos (Homily XXXVI, in Migne, *Patrologia Graeca*, CLI, 460–73) now and then includes among her *manâqib* (or virtues) traits which would assimilate the "Mother of God" to the Logos (e.g., col. 473A: di' autês methéxousin hósoi dè methéxousi Theoû); my attention was called to the Homily by V. Lossky, *Essai sur la théologie mystique de l'église d'orient* (Paris, 1944), p. 191. (It should perhaps be noted expressly that the saint worship adopted by North African Islam has a different ideological foundation.)

14   *Khudâwand burhân-i nabawî-râ bâqî kardânîda ast;* cf. E. Blochet, *Journal asiatique*, 1902, 1, 529, n. 1.

15 *Khiṭaṭ* (Bûlâq, 1270/1854), II, 462 (referred to by Goldziher in a different context, *Revue de l'histoire des religions*, II [1880], 283–84, where "II, 436" is to be corrected to "II, 462"). Maqrîzî actually has 474/1081–82 as the year of the building and the request. Unless we are to assume that Niẓâm al-Mulk approached Badr al-Jamâlî only after the *madrasa* had been in operation for some time, Maqrîzî's dating must be considered erroneous. A. Talas, *L'enseignement chez les Arabes; la madrasa Niẓâmiyya et son histoire* (Paris, 1939), does not refer to the episode.

16 Greek-speaking Ṣûfîs are evidenced by the *sufische Sentenzen* (K. Krumbacher, *Geschichte der byzantinischen Literatur* [2nd ed.; Munich, 1897], p. 819) in twenty-two couplets found in some manuscripts of Sulṭân Walad's (d. 1312) *Rabâb-Nâmah;* the poem (composed *ca.* A.D. 1300) has been preserved in Arabic script; it was published by G. Meyer, *Byzantinische Zeitschrift*, IV (1895), 401–11.

17 In this context belongs the protection accorded the Ṣûfîs by the Mamlûk government against the attacks of Ibn Taimiyya (d. 1328). It should be recalled that already a century earlier the leading Ḥanbalite jurist of his time, Muwaffaq ad-Dîn Ibn Qudâma (d. 1223), showed himself rather lenient toward the popular cult of the saints; cf. H. Laoust, *Essai sur les doctrines sociales et politiques de Taḳî-d-Dîn Aḥmed b. Taimîya* (Cairo, 1939), p. 79.

18 Cf. the information gathered by A. Malvezzi, *L'Islamismo e la cultura europea* (Florence, 1956), pp. 93, 97–98.

19 Usâma's memoirs, the *Kitâb al-iʿtibâr*, were translated into English by P. K. Hitti under the title *An Arab-Syrian Gentleman and Warrior in the Period of the Crusades* (New York, 1929); his observations on character and mores of the Franks are on pp. 161–70 (those on Frankish medical techniques on pp. 162–63 and 166–67). The impression left by the Crusades on Muslim historians can now be fairly accurately followed by means of F. Gabrieli's selection (in Italian) of relevant passages from *Storici Arabi delle Crociate* (Turin?, 1957 [*Scrittori di storia. Collezione diretta da F. Chabod.*, Vol. 6]).

INDEX

INDEX

For the greater part, medieval persons are listed under their given names, for instance, Peter Lombard. Books, when listed, are entered under the author's name. Books of the Bible are entered under *Bible*.

TWELFTH-CENTURY EUROPE AND THE FOUNDATIONS OF MODERN SOCIETY

Edited by Marshall Clagett, Gaines Post, and Robert Reynolds

PART I   THOUGHT IN EUROPEAN SOCIETY

PART II   TRANSITIONS IN ECONOMY AND SOCIETY

PART III   EASTERN INFLUENCES ON EUROPEAN CULTUI

THE UNIVERSITY OF WISCONSIN PRESS
P.O. Box 1379   Madison, Wisconsin   53701